CW01637942

Bosnian, C
Montenegrin and Serbian

Bosnian, Croatian, Montenegrin and Serbian: An Essential Grammar is intended for beginners and intermediate students who need a reference that explains grammar in straightforward terms. It covers all the main areas of the modern single BCMS grammatical system in an accessible way, and free from jargon. When linguistic terminology is used, it is explained in layman's terms, the logic of a rule is presented simply and near parallels are drawn with English. This book covers all the grammar necessary for everyday communication (reaching B1 and B2 of the CEFR, ACTFL Intermediate–Intermediate-Mid).

The book comprises of extensive chapters on all parts of speech, the creation of different word forms (endings for cases in nouns and adjectives, case forms for pronouns, tenses, verbal modes, verbal aspect etc.) and their uses in sentences. Each rule is illustrated with numerous examples from everyday living language used in Bosnia-Herzegovina, Croatia, Montenegro and Serbia.

It is a unique reference book in English aimed at this level of language study that treats BCMS as a single grammar system, explaining and highlighting all the small differences between the four variants of this polycentric language.

Željko Vrabec has professional translation experience gained at the BBC and the UN. He is a multilingual specialist with over 25 years of BBC editorial experience in different roles – from copy-editing breaking European stories and writing in-depth political analytical reports to media landscape surveys. Recently he has worked as a dialogue coach and cultural approximation consultant to Oscar-winning actors. In the past few years he has been teaching BCMS at a language school in London.

Routledge Essential Grammars

Essential Grammars describe clearly and succinctly the core rules of each language and are up-to-date and practical reference guides to the most important aspects of languages used by contemporary native speakers. They are designed for elementary to intermediate learners and present an accessible description of the language, focusing on the real patterns of use today.

Essential Grammars are a reference source for the learner and user of the language, irrespective of level, setting out the complexities of the language in short, readable sections that are clear and free from jargon.

Essential Grammars are ideal either for independent study or for students in schools, colleges, universities and adult classes of all types.

Essential Grammars are available for languages including:

Bosnian, Croatian, Montenegrin and Serbian
Catalan
Chinese
Czech
Danish
Dutch
English
Finnish
German
Greek
Hindi
Hungarian
Korean
Latvian
Modern Hebrew
North Sámi
Norwegian
Polish
Portuguese
Romanian
Serbian
Spanish
Swedish
Thai
Turkish
Urdu
Vietnamese
West Greenlandic

For a full list of available languages and more information about this series, please visit: www.routledge.com/Routledge-Essential-Grammars/book-series/SE0549

Bosnian, Croatian, Montenegrin and Serbian

An Essential Grammar

Željko Vrabec

Routledge
Taylor & Francis Group
LONDON AND NEW YORK

First published 2022
by Routledge
2 Park Square, Milton Park, Abingdon, Oxon OX14 4RN

and by Routledge
605 Third Avenue, New York, NY 10158

Routledge is an imprint of the Taylor & Francis Group, an informa business

© 2022 Željko Vrabec

The right of Željko Vrabec to be identified as author of this work has been asserted by him in accordance with sections 77 and 78 of the Copyright, Designs and Patents Act 1988.

All rights reserved. No part of this book may be reprinted or reproduced or utilised in any form or by any electronic, mechanical, or other means, now known or hereafter invented, including photocopying and recording, or in any information storage or retrieval system, without permission in writing from the publishers.

Trademark notice: Product or corporate names may be trademarks or registered trademarks, and are used only for identification and explanation without intent to infringe.

British Library Cataloguing-in-Publication Data
A catalogue record for this book is available from the British Library

Library of Congress Cataloging-in-Publication Data
Names: Vrabec, Zeljko, author.
Title: Bosnian, Croatian, Montenegrin and Serbian : an essential grammar / Zeljko Vrabec.
Description: London ; New York : Routledge, 2021. | Series: Routledge essential grammars | Includes bibliographical references and index.
Identifiers: LCCN 2021010130 (print) | LCCN 2021010131 (ebook)
Subjects: LCSH: Serbo-Croatian language—Grammar. | Serbian language—Montenegro—Grammar.
Classification: LCC PG1229 .V73 2021 (print) | LCC PG1229 (ebook) | DDC 491.8/282421—dc23
LC record available at https://lccn.loc.gov/2021010130
LC ebook record available at https://lccn.loc.gov/2021010131

ISBN: 978-0-367-72364-4 (hbk)
ISBN: 978-0-367-72363-7 (pbk)
ISBN: 978-1-003-15452-5 (ebk)

DOI: 10.4324/9781003154525

Typeset in Times New Roman
by Apex CoVantage, LLC

I dedicate this book to the memory of my mother and father, who taught me two variants of this rich and beautiful language.

Contents

Chapter 13 Croatian-Serbian glossary 264

Chapter 14 Verb conjugation tables 273

Introduction

This grammar book is intended for beginners and intermediate students, those who need a compact reference book that explains grammar in simple terms, a gentle introduction into serious language study.

While I call it an introduction, it does cover all the main areas of the modern single BCMS grammatical system, but it does so in an accessible way, free from heavy linguistic terminology, unnecessary exceptions and useless examples. When linguistic terminology is used, it is explained in layman's terms, the logic of a rule is presented simply and near parallels are drawn with English – even for concepts that do not exist in English.

The guiding principle is to be pragmatic. Before explaining any rule the author asked himself if a learner will encounter it in everyday communication. The book illustrates those rules with numerous examples from everyday communication in BCMS.

It is a unique reference book in English for this level that treats Bosnian/Croatian/Montenegrin/Serbian as a single grammar system, explaining and highlighting all the small differences between the four variants of this polycentric language.

Those studying BCMS from English language textbooks will have snippets of grammar explained in different lessons, scattered across the textbook. When looking for an answer to a particular grammatical issue, a learner may have difficulty finding the previous lesson that explained it. This book presents explanations in a logical, systematic way, where learners will easily find answers to their dilemmas.

This book only focuses on the parts of grammar necessary for understanding the structures of modern spoken BCMS at beginner and intermediate levels – it covers all the grammar necessary for easy everyday communication (reaching up to between B1 and B2 of the CEFR).

The main body of the book comprises extensive chapters on all parts of speech, where both morphology and syntax are intertwined. They tackle in the same chapter both the creation of different word forms (inflectional morphology – endings for cases in nouns, adjectives, some pronouns; tenses, verbal aspect, verbal mood etc) and their usage in sentences. Each rule is illustrated with examples from everyday living language used in Bosnia-Herzegovina, Croatia, Montenegro and Serbia.

A separate chapter deals with pronunciation and the alphabets (Latin and Cyrillic); however, no explanations of word accentuation are given at this level, as they would add nothing to an understanding of the language. Unlike English, where moving the accent to a different syllable may signal the difference between a noun and a verb (e.g. a record and to record), in BCMS there are negligibly few instances where accent alters meaning.

The guiding principle for this book was not to overwhelm the English-speaking student at beginner to intermediate level. For example, native English speakers have a set of five forms of some irregular verbs in their tool kit to articulate all their verbal meanings (e.g. to speak – speak, speaks, spoke, spoken, speaking). In contrast, BCMS has over two dozen corresponding forms, and that excludes passive participles – equivalents to "spoken" which can have 16 different forms as they follow adjectival declensions in three genders. This is already sufficiently daunting without adding information on moving accents in various verb forms which do not change the meaning and are not always observed by native speakers.

Neither is there any extensive syntactic analysis of various clauses – something more appropriate to the advanced academic level. There is, however, a chapter called "Sentence Structure" (Chapter 11) which outlines the basics of free word order and the all-important order of enclitics, as well as predicate-only sentences (called either impersonal or subjectless in other grammar books) and negative sentences, the formation of which is somewhat different from English.

There is also a chapter called "Word Creation" (derivational morphology; Chapter 12), but it only contains the most productive suffixes and prefixes – these are presented as tools for learning many new words quickly from roots already encountered at this level of language study. There is also a "Croatian-Serbian Glossary" (Chapter 13) highlighting the most frequent examples where Croatian and Serbian use different words in everyday speech – some 200 of them. This glossary also marks Bosnian and Montenegrin word variations, with Bosnian oscillating between the Serbian and Croatian versions, and Montenegrin almost always preferring the Serbian versions.

The final part is "Verb Conjugation Tables" (Chapter 14), where the learner will find conjugation tables for all regular, irregular and pattern verbs.

How to use this book

This is how the differences between the four variants are marked:

Where the most frequent difference is only *-ije-*, *-je-* (Iyekavian) as opposed to *-e-* (Ekavian), both forms of the word are given connected by the equal sign = (e.g. *Dijete = dete čita knjigu*). This book adheres strictly to the order of placing the Iyekavian pronunciation to the left of the equal sign and the Ekavian to the right.

Please note that **Iyekavian pronunciation is used in Croatia, Bosnia and Montenegro; in Serbia, mostly Ekavian** is used, with small pockets of Iyekavian (in the Bosniak-populated Sandžak area and western Serbia along the Bosnian border). Therefore, those learning Croatian, Bosnian or Montenegrin variants should use Iyekavian pronunciation versions; those learning Serbian, the Ekavian versions. For a quick visual guide – see Map 1.

The reader is reminded of the previously mentioned most frequent difference when it is encountered for the first time in each chapter. Throughout the rest of the chapter only the equal sign is used if the distribution of the difference is (Iyekavian) = (Ekavian).

In some instances, where other differences exist, they are marked according to the variant to which they belong, as **bh** for Bosnian, **hr** for Croatian, **mont** for Montenegrin and **srb** for Serbian, e.g.:

> *Ovog tjedna idem u kazalište* (hr).
> *Ove sedmice idem u pozorište* (bh-mont).
> *Ove nedelje idem u pozorište* (srb).

Sometimes Bosnian, Montenegrin and Serbian are identical and Croatian differs. In those instances the marking (hr) is written next to the word that is the Croatian version. The two versions are not connected with the equal sign but with either "or" or a dash (–).

Where there are real contrasts between the four variants, they are explained with the asterisk and the word ***contrast** in bold given before the explanation.

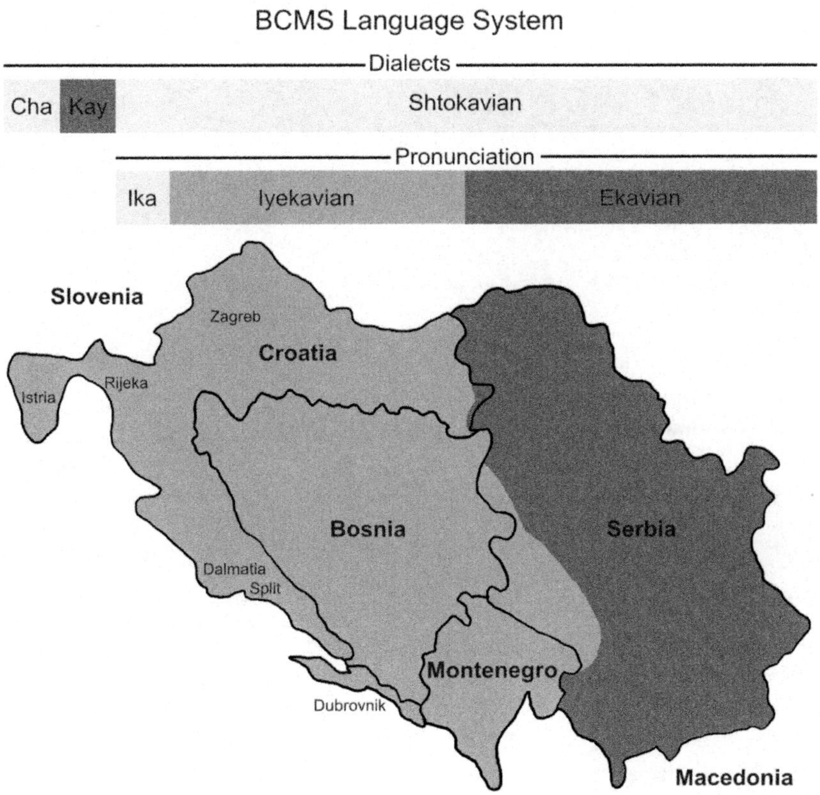

Map 1 The map shows only the standard Shtokavian dialect and the two standard pronunciations

Cha – Chakavian dialect – spoken in parts of Istria, Rijeka, Split, Dalmatia and most Croatian Adriatic islands (not Dubrovnik area and the southernmost islands)

Kay – Kaykavian dialect – spoken in Zagreb and northwest Croatia, along the Slovene border

Ika – Ikavian pronunciation (of Shtokavian dialect) – spoken in coastal Croatia (apart from Dubrovnik area), Dalmatian islands and parts of Bosnia bordering on Dalmatia

Abbreviations

acc	accusative
anim	animate
bh	Bosnia-Herzegovina
colloq	colloquial
gen	genitive
hr	Croatia
dat	dative
fem	feminine
imperf	imperfective verb
inanim	inanimate
instr	instrumental
loc	locative
masc	masculine
mont	Montenegro
neut	neuter
nom	nominative
perf	perfective verb
pl	plural
reflex	reflexive verb
srb	Serbia
sing	singular
trans	transitive verb
voc	Vocative
1p sing	1st person singular (verbs)
2p sing	2nd person singular (verbs)
3p sing	3rd person singular (verbs)
1p pl	1st person plural (verbs)
2p pl	2nd person plural (verbs)
3p pl	3rd person plural (verbs)

Chapter 1

The story of "four languages"

The Bosnian/Croatian/Montenegrin/Serbian language system (also known as BCMS) belongs to the South-Slavonic group of languages, which includes Slovene, Macedonian and Bulgarian. These languages are also closely related to the wider Slavonic language family: eastern Slavonic – Russian, Ukrainian and Belarusian; and western Slavonic – Polish, Czech and Slovak. This language system was previously known as Serbo-Croatian; it is spoken in Bosnia-Herzegovina, Croatia, Montenegro and Serbia.

Modern Serbo-Croatian was born in the mid-19th century with the signing of the Vienna Literary Agreement by Serbian and Croatian language scholars, led by Serbian linguist and folklorist Vuk Karadžic, and the Croatian Illyrian movement in Zagreb, led by Ljudevit Gaj. The movement's aim was to achieve cultural and linguistic unity of the south Slavs. The Shtokavian dialect spoken in Eastern Herzegovina, western Montenegro and the Dubrovnik area was chosen as the basis for this unified language. It entered into official usage in the Kingdom of the Serbs, Croats and Slovenes in 1918 (later renamed the Kingdom of Yugoslavia) and continued as one of the main state languages of the Socialist Federal Republic of Yugoslavia from 1945 to 1991. In the wake of Yugoslavia's disintegration it has been renamed according to the newly created states as Bosnian, Croatian, Montenegrin and Serbian "languages", which are essentially variants of the same system and display minimal variance in structure.

BCMS is a polycentric language like English, German, French, Portuguese or Spanish, all of which have several interacting codified standards. BCMS has two distinct codified standards: its western variant – Croatian – codified in Zagreb, and its eastern variant – Serbian – codified in Belgrade. Another two standards, recently codified in Sarajevo as Bosnian and in Podgorica as Montenegrin, may be seen as a mixture of these two standards, although they have a few of their own distinguishing features.

The basis of the BCMS language system is the Shtokavian dialect (*štokavski*), named after the interrogative pronoun *što* (what). BCMS has another two dialects, Chakavian (*čakavski*, in which this pronoun is *ča*) and Kaykavian (*kajkavski*, in

DOI: 10.4324/9781003154525-1

which this pronoun is *kaj*). The latter two dialects are spoken in parts of Croatia (*čakavski* on Adriatic islands, in Istria, Dalmatia and the Croatian littoral; *kajkavski* in northwestern Croatia, around Zagreb and along the Slovene border) but are not recognised as standard. Croatian literary works were written in Kaykavian until mid-19th century. Many works of the Dalmatian Renaissance literature, poetry in particular, were written in Chakavian.

1.1 Ekavian and Iyekavian pronunciations

The main difference between the eastern and western variants of the Shtokavian dialect is to do with the reflexes of the old long Slavonic vowel *yat*. In most of Serbia, it is pronounced as a long *E /e:/* and spelt as *E* (*mleko* – milk, or *deca* – children) – the pronunciation is therefore called Ekavian. In the west (Croatia, Bosnia, Montenegro and parts of western Serbia along the Bosnian border), this long vowel is pronounced either as *IJE* or *JE /ije/* (*mlijeko* – milk, *djeca* – children) and the pronunciation is called Iyekavian. There is a third pronunciation in which the letter is pronounced as a long i /i:/ (as in m*ee*t) – *mliko* and *dica*. This pronunciation is called Ikavian and is not recognised as standard pronunciation in any of the four countries but is seen as a localism (mainly spoken in coastal Croatia and the islands) (see Map 1).

Bosnia is an interesting ethnic and linguistic patchwork where the western and eastern variants of BCMS intertwine. While inhabitants of the entire country speak Iyekavian, people living in parts of Bosnia closer to Serbia use more Serbian vocabulary variations and some sentence structure patterns, while those bordering on Croatia opt for the Croatian variations. To complicate the issue further, speakers of what is essentially one and the same language, next-door neighbours living for years in the same building in Sarajevo, will call this language according to their nationality: a Serbian family will say they speak Serbian, a Bosniak family will call it Bosnian, while a Croatian family will call it Croatian. Serbs in northwest Bosnia's Banja Luka (the Bosnian Serb capital), a city only 180 kilometres from Zagreb, will say that they speak Serbian, even though they use Iyekavian and have a preference for vocabulary that is seen as Croatian. The fact that this essentially single language is called by three different names depending on national affiliation is best evidenced in the population census figures from Bosnia (see 1.2 "Number of Speakers, Official Language Names").

Montenegrin is a newcomer to this linguistic conundrum. Montenegrins speak Iyekavian and use Serbian – rather than Croatian – versions of the shared vocabulary (see Chapter 14) and grammatical patterns (see 1.3 "Brief Outline of Main Grammatical Differences"). Together with Serbia, Montenegro was a member of the rump Yugoslavia between 1992 and 2006, when Montenegro gained independence. The official language of the rump federation was Serbian, with both Ekavian and Iyekavian pronunciations in official use. Efforts to codify a separate standard gained momentum after the country became independent. With that aim in mind, a couple of prominent linguists from Croatia were engaged to help a local Montenegrin linguist to write a Montenegrin grammar, which was published in 2010, introducing two new (superfluous) letters to the alphabet (replacing the letters sj and zj – a cluster of sounds that appears in only a few words, such as *sjutra* – tomorrow, *sjekira* – axe or *zjenica* – pupil of the eye – with single letters). At the time of writing this book (2020), no Montenegrin newspaper or web-based news platform has adopted the new letters, so Montenegrin is presented here as sharing its alphabet and pronunciation with Bosnian, Croatian and Serbian. In 2017, the Montenegrin language was granted an international ISO code by the International Organization for Standardization, the global standard-setting body.

It would be worth mentioning the following fact to illustrate the linguistic confusion surrounding the name of the language: Montenegrin primary school language classes are officially called neither Serbian nor Montenegrin but rather "*Crnogorski-srpski, bosanski, hrvatski jezik i književnost*" (Montenegrin-Serbian, Bosnian, Croatian language and literature).

As far as accent is concerned, all four variants have their distinct accent, and all native BCMS speakers recognise the provenance of their fellow BCMS speakers – that is, it is easy to tell a speaker of the Montenegrin variant in Belgrade, someone from Herzegovina in Zagreb, or a speaker of the Croatian variant in Montenegro by their accent. There are also easily recognisable regional accents in each of the four countries. They are more impacted by geography than national affiliation. For example, Croatian speakers in Vukovar (a town in easternmost Croatia) have more in common with Serbian speakers just across the border in Vojvodina (northern Serbia) than with their compatriots in Dubrovnik (southern Croatia), whose dialect and accent is closer to the Montenegrin variant spoken in Herceg-Novi (a Montenegrin coastal town near the Croatian border).

1.2 Number of speakers, official language names

Bosnia-Herzegovina

Census: According to the 2013 census, Bosnia has just over 3.5 million people; 50 per cent of the population say they are Bosniaks, 30 per cent Serbs and 15 per cent Croats. In the census, 52 per cent of the population declared that they speak

Bosnian, 30 per cent Serbian and 14 per cent Croatian, almost exactly mirroring the ethnic composition of the country.

Constitution: The official languages are Bosnian, Croatian and Serbian. Both Latin and Cyrillic alphabets are in official use.

Pronunciation standard: Iyekavian.

Croatia

Census: According to the 2011 census, Croatia has just under 4.3 million people, 90 per cent of whom say they are Croats, and just under 5 per cent that they are Serbs – the largest national minority. Some 4 million people declared that they speak Croatian.

Constitution: The official language is Croatian, and the Latin alphabet is in official use.

Pronunciation standard: Iyekavian.

Montenegro

Census: According to the 2011 census, Montenegro has a population of some 620,000 people, 45 per cent of whom say they are Montenegrin; some 30 per cent say they are Serbian, and about 9 per cent that they are Bosniak.

About 43 per cent of the population declared as speaking Serbian, 37 per cent Montenegrin and five per cent Bosnian.

Constitution: Under the Montenegrin Constitution (2007), the official language is Montenegrin and the Cyrillic and Latin alphabets enjoy equal status. However, Serbian, Bosnian, Albanian and Croatian are all in official use (sequence of languages as cited in the Constitution).

Pronunciation standard: Iyekavian.

Serbia

Census: According to the 2011 census, Serbia has a population of just over 7 million people, 83 per cent of whom are Serbs; the largest national minority is formed by Hungarians, who account for 3.5 per cent; the next largest minority are Bosniaks – about 2 per cent; 88 per cent of the population say they speak Serbian; the second language is Hungarian, at 3.5 per cent, and the third is Bosnian at ca. 2 per cent.

Constitution: Serbian and Cyrillic are the official language and alphabet.

Pronunciation standard: Mostly Ekavian with pockets of Iyekavian (in the Bosniak-populated Sandžak area and western Serbia along the Bosnian border).

1.3 Brief outline of main grammatical differences

Here it may be worthwhile to extract a sentence from a Wikipedia entry citing a leading Croatian linguist (found in Wikipedia in Croatian, March 2017):

> *Hrvatski i srpski (moglo bi se dodati – i bošnjački) ne razlikuju se ovoliko ili onoliko, puno ili malo. Kao standardni jezici razlikuju se potpuno.*

Now let us see the same statement in Serbian:

> *Hrvatski i srpski (moglo bi se dodati – i bošnjački) ne razlikuju se ovoliko ili onoliko, puno ili malo. Kao standardni jezici razlikuju se potpuno.*
>
> (Croatian and Serbian/one might add – Bosniak too/do not differ this much or that much, a lot or a little. As standard languages they are completely different).

It is obvious even to someone who has never seen anything written in either of these two "languages" that the statement arguing that they are "completely different" does not differ by a single letter in either version. This is not helpful and would appear to be fuelled by emotion or political interference in linguistic matters.

Differences do exist and should not be papered over, but they are minimal and do not affect understanding of even the most complex communication, including poetry, humour, wordplay, double entendres or political negotiations. For example, after a few drinks and a hearty exchange of jokes with their fellow BCMS speakers from a neighbouring country, even the most rabid nationalists and language pedants will laughingly agree that the jokes they have just heard were in one and the same language – with no translator needed even for the most subtle nuances.

In the more elevated register of diplomacy or governance, language differences are certainly more noticeable but still not significant enough to make the variant incomprehensible to speakers in other BCMS-speaking countries. The same may be said of most other languages, where the everyday spoken idiom is quite different from the legal, bureaucratic or academic language. This book focuses only on the former, free from the constraints of political and nationalistic pressures.

Iyekavian/Ekavian pronunciations

The most significant and most frequent difference is the Iyekavian and Ekavian pronunciations. Whenever a word that has two different spellings is mentioned in this book, both are given: first the Iyekavian (used in Bosnia, Croatia, Montenegro and small areas of western Serbia along the Bosnian border) followed by the equal sign and then the Ekavian (used by the largest majority in Serbia) (for example *mlijeko* = *mleko*). This is treated as an identical word because it is indeed the same word with a minute difference in pronunciation, almost inaudible to the foreign speaker.

Vocabulary

There are important and noticeable differences in the vocabulary used in everyday communication (see Chapter 13), mostly in Croatia on the one hand and Bosnia, Montenegro and Serbia on the other. This is similar to British and American English, which uses different words for the same thing, for example, lift – elevator, pavement – sidewalk. Somewhat coincidentally, Serbian and Croatian use different words to denote the very same ideas: *lift* (srb) – *dizalo* (hr) and *trotoar* (srb) – *pločnik* (hr). These differences are noted throughout the book.

Future tense

In Croatia and parts of Bosnia, the auxiliary verb *ću* is written separately from the modified infinitive of the main verb, for example, *pisat ću* (I will write); in Serbia, Montenegro and most of Bosnia, the auxiliary verb *ću* is written together with the modified infinitive – *pisaću*. (see 7.4.3. "Future Tense").

Irregular masculine L-participle

In Iyekavian, the masculine singular form of the L-participle of *-jeti* infinitives (e.g. *voljeti, živjeti, željeti, razumjeti, donijeti*) is irregular – *volio, živio, želio, razumio, donio* (other forms are regular *voljela, voljelo, voljeli* etc). In Ekavian, all forms are regular (*voleti – voleo, volela; živeti – živeo, živela; želeti – želeo, želela; razumeo – razumela; doneo – donela*) (see 7.6.1 "L-Participle").

Modal verb trebati

The use of the modal verb *trebati* (should, need, ought to) is markedly different in Croatian and Serbian – *Trebam ići na posao* (hr), or *Treba da idem na posao* (srb) – I should go to work. (see 7.3.6 *trebati*).

Verbs created from internationalism

There is a difference in how some internationalisms are transformed into verbs in Croatian on the one hand and in Bosnian, Montenegrin and Serbian on the other, for example: "to control" – *kontrolirati* (hr) – *kontrolisati* (bh-mont-srb); "to organize" – *organizirati* – *organizovati* etc. (see 12.4.1 "Suffixes that Change Foreign Words into Verbs").

Interrogative and indefinite pronouns

Some interrogative and indefinite pronouns are different in Croatian from the forms used in Bosnian, Montenegrin and Serbian – the difference is only one letter: *tko* (hr) – *ko* (who), *što* (hr) – *šta* (what), *netko* (hr) – *neko* (somebody), *nitko* (hr) – *niko* (nobody) and *svatko* (hr) – *svako* (everybody); this difference only applies to the nominative case of these pronouns – in all other cases they are identical in all four variants (see 5.4 and 5.6.).

One possessive pronoun

One possessive pronoun is different – in Croatian, *njezin* (hers) is considered standard; in Bosnian, Montenegrin and Serbian *njen* is used. This is not to say that *njen* is not used in Croatia or *njezin* in Bosnia, Montenegro and Serbia.

Question words

Croatian distinguishes between the question words for location *gdje* (where) and for direction *kamo* (where to), as in: *Gdje stanuješ?* (Where do you live?) as opposed to *Kamo ideš?* (Where are you going (to)?). Instead of *kamo* Bosnian, Montenegrin and Serbian use *kuda* (as in *Kuda ideš?*), or colloquially *gdje* = *gde* in both contexts.

The **interrogative phrase *da li*** is considered ungrammatical in Croatia, where the standard way of asking questions is to insert the interrogative particle *li* after the verb. In Serbia the former is the most common way of asking questions.

Modal verbs with infinitive or da plus present tense

In terms of sentence structure, there is one noticeable contrast between Croatian and Bosnian on the one hand and Serbian and Montenegrin on the other. It is to do with using either the infinitive after a modal verb or *da* plus present tense: "I want to read" in Croatian and Bosnian is rendered as a finite verb form (in this case present tense) plus infinitive – *Želim čitati* (identical to English); in Serbian and Montenegrin, it is mostly rendered as a finite verb form plus *da* plus the present tense – *Želim da čitam* (literally: I want that I read). Note that this difference in usage is not absolute; it varies regionally and in many instances depends on the speaker's personal preferences.

* * *

The reader can see that differences are few and far between and mainly have to do with spelling and pronunciation, with just a few instances of structural contrasts.

Furthermore, when two widely used international linguistic tools to determine the interrelatedness of languages are applied, the four variants do not qualify as separate languages.

US linguist Morris Swadesh drew up a list of 100 basic words consisting of personal and demonstrative pronouns (e.g. I, you, we, this, that), numbers (e.g. one, two), names for animals (e.g. fish, dog), body parts (e.g. heart, head), colours (e.g. yellow, green) and basic verbs (e.g. to sleep, to eat) to test the interrelatedness of dialects/languages. If two idioms share over 81 words from the list, Swadesh argues that they are the same language. Not surprisingly, Bosnian, Croatian, Montenegrin and Serbian share all 100 words.

Another internationally recognized linguistic criterion is mutual intelligibility. As described earlier, speakers of the four variants have absolutely no problem understanding each other, even in the most nuanced use of the language, with mutual intelligibility being close to 100 per cent.

It is therefore linguistically sound to treat the BCMS system as one. Those who take offence at this are guided by politics and nationalism, not by linguistic considerations. The fact that translation and second language teaching of these languages is either impossible or absurd proves the point.

For further reading on this fascinating topic see Ronelle Alexander's excellent *Bosnian, Croatian, Serbian – A Grammar with Sociolinguistic Commentary* – Chapter 26 "One Language or More Than One?".

Chapter 2

Alphabet, pronunciation, spelling

BCMS is a unique European language in that it uses two alphabets – Latin (*latinica*) and Cyrillic (*ćirilica*). In Croatia, only the Latin alphabet is used. In Serbia, Montenegro and parts of Bosnia-Hercegovina both Latin and Cyrillic are used. This book focuses only on the Latin alphabet, the script used by all BCMS speakers, easy for English speakers to learn. Those wishing to learn Cyrillic may use Table 2.1 as a starting point.

Modern BCMS was born when its alphabet and grammar were standardised in mid-19th century by Serbian and Croatian linguists and writers, led by Vuk Karadžić and his Croatian counterpart Ljudevit Gaj of the Illyrian movement. Prior to that, Serbian had been written in the Church Slavonic Cyrillic, a form which had many letters with no corresponding sounds in the spoken language. Along the Dalmatian coast and in the islands, Croatian had been written according to Italian orthography, while continental Croatia followed the Hungarian standard.

Vuk Karadžić's basic idea was: "write as you speak and read as it is written". This produced an alphabet that is easy to learn – there are 30 letters for 30 corresponding sounds. Once the pronunciation of each letter is mastered it is possible to read any word in BCMS – with none of the spelling difficulties that one encounters in English or in French. Just one lesson is usually enough to master (almost all) spelling and pronunciation.

The set of Latin letters is called *Abeceda* and the set of Cyrillic letters is called *Azbuka* (*Азбука*).

The most basic and wonderfully helpful rule for newcomers to BCMS is that each of these letters is pronounced the same in each and every word that contains it. Furthermore, all the letters are pronounced in every word; that is, there are no silent letters.

DOI: 10.4324/9781003154525-2

2.1 Vowels

There are five vowels – **A, E, I, O, U**.

The vowels are single sounds, or monophthongs, just like in Italian; there are no diphthongs, where two vowels glide into each other, almost fusing into one sound, as when pronouncing "hair" or "lower", and of which there are many in English.

A – is pronounced as in *f**a**ther*
E – is pronounced as in *m**e**t*
I – is pronounced as in *s**i**t*
O – is pronounced as in *p**o**t*
U – is as in *p**u**t*.

2.2 Consonants

There are 25 consonants.

Consonants that exist in English, but are pronounced differently:

J – is always pronounces as **y in yes** (never as *j* in *Jim*)
yes, yet, yo-yo
C – is always pronounced as **ts in puts** (never as *c* in *cat*)
puts, tsar
G – is always pronounced as **g in get** (never as *g* in *gin*)
get, goggles, garden
S – is always pronounced as **s in sun** (never as *s* in *measure*)
bliss, sun, son

Letters that do not exist in English are mostly a fusion of two sounds:

Č – stands for the fused sounds **t + ch** as in *chips, chair*
Ć – stands for the fused sounds **t + chj** (very similar to the *č* sound) as in
chunky, choo-choo train
(notice the slight *j* sound after *tch*)
(the difference in sound between *č* and *ć* is minimal)
Dž – stands for the fused sounds **d + zh** as in *magic, James, jeans*
Đ – stands for the fused sounds **d + y** (very similar to the *dž* sound) as in *during, duration*

Lj – stands for the fused sounds **l + y** (a soft version of the *L* sound) as in
million, colliery

Nj – stands for the fused sounds **n + y** (a soft version of the *n* sound) as in
new, manual, onion

Š – stands for the sound **sh** as in *shoes, show*

Ž – stands for the sound **zh** (very similar to the š sound) as in
pleasure, measure

All other consonants are pronounced in the same way or almost the same as in English (Table 2.1).

All vowels and all consonants are always pronounced in the same way.

Table 2.1

Latin	Cyrillic	Pronounced as in:	BCMS examples
A	А, а	f**a**ther	mama, tata
B	Б, б	**b**eer	bravo, banka, brat
C	Ц, ц	pu**ts**, **ts**ar	centar, car
Č	Ч, ч	**ch**ips, **ch**air	čips, čokolada
Ć	Ћ, ћ	**ch**unky, **ch**oo-**ch**oo	ćilim, ćevapčići
D	Д, д	**d**og	doktor, da, dobar
Dž	Џ, џ	**j**azz, ma**g**ic	džez, džemper, džudo
Đ	Ђ, ђ	**d**uring, **d**uration	mađioničar
E	Е, е	m**e**t, s**e**t	Engleska, ekonomija
F	Ф, ф	**f**actory	fabrika, fontana
G	Г, г	**g**et, **g**o**gg**les	galerija, generacija
H	Х, х	**h**otel, **H**olland	Holandija, hvala, humor
I	И, и	s**i**t, p**i**ty	industrija, informacija
J	J, j	**y**es, **y**o-**y**o	Japan, jupi, jo-jo
K	К, к	**k**ilo	kilogram, kikiriki
L	Л, л	**l**ove	limun, lokal, lift
Lj	Љ, љ	mi**ll**ion	ljiljan, Ljubljana
M	М, м	**m**other	mobilni, medicina, moda
N	Н, н	**n**ot	nos, ne, nervozan

Latin	Cyrillic	Pronounced as in:	BCMS examples
Nj	Њ, њ	ma**n**ual, o**n**ion	svinja
O	О, о	p**o**t	orkestar, objekt
P	П, п	**p**en	politika, parking, park
R	Р, р	**r**abbit, ba**rr**el	restoran, religija, rakija
S	С, с	**s**it	sestra, stil, student, sport
Š	Ш, ш	**sh**oes, **sh**ow	šampanj(ac), šampion, šok
T	Т, т	**t**op	telefon, taksi, televizor
U	У, у	p**u**t	univerzitet
V	В, в	**v**ictim	vino, voda, vikend
Z	З, з	**z**ebra	zebra, zona
Ž	Ж, ж	plea**su**re	žirafa

For further learning it is also useful to mention that consonants can be divided according to two classifications:

1 according to whether the vocal cords vibrate when they are pronounced – into voiced (vocal cords vibrate) and unvoiced, and
2 according to whether they are pronounced using the palate – into palatal (soft) and non-palatal (hard).

2.2.1 *Voiced/unvoiced consonants*

It is important to know if consonants are voiced or unvoiced to be able to understand some spelling and pronunciation rules outlined in section 2.3.

	voiced – unvoiced pairs							
Voiced	**B**	**D**	**G**	**Z**	**Ž**	**Đ**	**Dž**	
Unvoiced	**P**	**T**	**K**	**S**	**Š**	**Ć**	**Č**	**F C H**
plus	**J L Lj M N Nj R are voiced, with no pair**							

2.2.2 *Soft/hard consonants*

As for the soft and hard consonants, it is important to know this distinction when choosing what endings are added in some instances (e.g. the *-ovi* or *-evi* ending for the extended plural of single-syllable masculine nouns, the choice of masculine vocative endings, the *-om* or *-em* ending for the masculine instrumental singular, the choice of masculine and neuter adjective case endings, the choice of case endings for many pronouns ending in a soft consonant etc).

Very helpfully, all soft consonants are those that are spelt with little wiggly bits (diacritical marks) characteristic of BCMS, plus C and J:

C ČĆ Dž, Đ, Lj, Nj, Š, Ž, J

2.3 Consonant and vowel alternations

The consonant and vowel alternations listed here need not be memorised at this stage of language learning. It is good to have them explained briefly in one place, in case it is sometimes not clear why some words are spelt differently when certain suffixes or prefixes are added.

2.3.1 *Consonant softening before -E (palatalisation)*

This change takes place when consonants **K, G** or **H** change to **Č, Ž** or **Š** (and **C** changes to **Č**) mostly before **E** (in very few instances before **I**).

This change occurs in:

- The vocative of masculine nouns:

čovjek – čovječe (Iyekavian) = *čovek – čoveče* (Ekavian)*
putnik – putniče
bog – bože
stric – striče
otac – oče

* This difference (Iyekavian = Ekavian) will be marked by = in the rest of the chapter (see "How to Use This Book").

- Two irregular plurals:

oko – oči
uho – uši

- The formation of possessive adjectives with the suffixes *-ov* or *-ev* and *-in* from nouns for kinship:

stric – stričev
otac – očev

majka – majčin
djevoka – djevojčin = devojka – devojčin

- The present tense of some verbs that end in *-ći:*

moći – oni mogu – možeš, može, možemo, možete
peći – oni peku – pečeš, peče, pečemo, pečete

2.3.2 Consonant softening before -I (sibilarisation)

This change takes place when consonants **K, G** or **H** change to **C, Z** or **S** before **I**.

This change occurs in:

- The nominative plural of some masculine nouns:

putnik – putnici
rođak – rođaci
izlog – izlozi
prijedlog – prijedlozi = predlog – predlozi
orah – orasi

- The dative/locative/instrumental plural (these three forms are identical) of some masculine nouns:

putnik – putnicima
rođak – rođacima
izlog – izlozima
prijedlog – prijedlozima = predlog – predlozima
orah – orasima

- The dative/locative singular (these two forms are identical) of some feminine nouns:

knjiga – knjizi
noga – nozi
ruka – ruci
slika – slici
rijeka – rijeci = reka – reci

2.3.3 J-changes (yotation)

This change takes place when the final consonant of a word is blended with the initial *-J* of an ending, which results in a new fused consonant.

This change occurs in:

- Neuter collective nouns formed by adding -*JE* to the singular (see 3.2.4):

T + J = Ć

cvijet + *je* = *cvijeće*	flower – flowers
= *cvet* + *je* = *cveće*	
list + *je* = *lisće*	
(+ further adjustment) = *lišće*	leaf – leaves

N + J = NJ

kamen + *je* = *kamenje*	rock – rocks

D + J = Đ

grozd + *je* = *grozđe*	
(+ further adjustment) = *grožđe*	grape – grapes

- Comparatives formed by adding -*JI* to some adjectives:

D + J = Đ

tvrd + *ji* = *tvrđi*	firm, firmer

K + J = Č

jak + *ji* = *jači*	strong, stronger

G + J = Ž

drag + *ji* = *draži*	dear, dearer
strog + *ji* = *stroži*	strict, stricter

- Passive participles formed by adding the ending -*JEN* and verbal nouns formed by adding -*JENJE* to verb roots:

uraditi	*urađen*	to do – done
izgraditi	*izgrađen*	to build – built
posjetiti	*posjećen*	to visit – visited
= *posetiti*	*posećen*	
koristiti	*korišćen*	to use – used
iznenaditi	*iznenađen*	to surprise – surprised
izlaziti	*izlaženje*	to go out – going out
ulaziti	*ulaženje*	to go in – going in
prevoditi	*prevođenje*	to translate – translating
buditi	*buđenje*	to awake – awakening
koristiti	*korišćenje*	to use – usage

misliti	*mišljenje*	to think – thinking, opinion
graditi	*građenje*	to build – building
sniziti	*sniženje*	to reduce – reducing, sales

- In the present tense of some *-ATI -EM* pattern verbs:

pisati-pišem, lagati-lažem, kazati-kažem, disati-dišem, funkcionisati-funkcionišem (bh-mont-srb), *jahati-jašem, plakati-plačem, pomagati-pomažem, kretati-krećem, vezati-vežem, stizati-stižem* etc.

2.3.4 *Voicing assimilation*

This change takes place when voiced and unvoiced consonants are placed next to each other – one of them has to change, as they both have to be either voiced or unvoiced. In this instance the second impacts the first.

Voiced	**B**	**D**	**G**	**Z**	**Ž**	**Đ**	**Dž**			
Unvoiced	**P**	**T**	**K**	**S**	**Š**	**Ć**	**Č**	**F**	**C**	**H**
plus	**J L Lj M N Nj R are voiced with no pair**									

This change usually occurs when prefixes or suffixes are added to words:

poD + Pisati = potpisati
Here the voiced D – before the unvoiced P – turns into its unvoiced pair T.
beZ + Platno = besplatno
Here the voiced Z – before the unvoiced P – turns into its unvoiced pair S.
SrB + Kinja = Srpkinja
Here the voiced B – before the unvoiced K – turns into its unvoiced pair P.

This change also occurs after fleeting *-a-* disappears from the masculine nominative form of adjectives when case endings are added, leaving two consonants next to each other. It occurs in all feminine and neuter forms.

teŽak – teŽK – teška, teško
teškog, teškom, teškim, teški, teških, teške
sladak – slaDK – slatka, slatko
slatkog, slatkom, slatkim, slatki, slatkih, slatke

2.3.5 L/O changes

This alternation takes place mostly in words where the final *-O* currently stands instead of an earlier *-L*.

This change occurs in:

- At the end of the L-participle – masculine singular form:

  bio (used to be *bil*) – *bila* – *bilo* – *bili*
  gledao (used to be *gledal*) – *gledala* – *gledalo*

It is useful to look at this example to illustrate how this alternation works: historically, the masculine ending for the L-participle was *-L*. Added to the infinitive root, e.g. *bi-ti, gleda-ti* – it had the forms *biL*, *gledaL*. As *-L* occurred at the end of the word, it changed to *-O* = *bio, gledao*. In other L-participle endings, *-L* is not in the final position and it did not change to -O.

- Masculine form of adjectives ending in *-o:*

  topao – *topla* – *toplo*
  beo – *bela* – *belo* (Ekavian)
  debeo – *debela* – *debelo*
  cio – *cijela* – *cijelo* = *ceo* – *cela* – *celo*

Historically, the masculine forms of adjectives were *topal, debel*. As the *-L* consonant was at the end of the word it changed to *-O*. It reappears when case endings are added, or when feminine and neuter endings are added, as it no longer occupies the final position:

topao, toplog, toplom, toplim, topli etc.

- Masculine nouns ending in *-O* in the nominative case (and the feminine noun *misao*); final *-O* regresses to *-L* when other case endings are added:

  posao – *posla, poslu, poslom, poslovi* etc.
  ugao – *ugla*
  dio – *dijela* = *deo* – *dela*
  pepeo – *pepela*
  misao – *misli* (fem)

N.B. In masculine nouns that end in *-ao*, the final *-a-* is fleeting *-a-* that disappears when case endings are added:

posao – *o* changes back to *-L*: *posaL;* fleeting *-a-* disappears when case endings are added: *posla* (gen), *poslu* (dat/loc), *poslom* (inst), *poslovi* (nom pl) etc (see Table 3.5)

- In masculine nouns ending in *-lac* in the nominative case; when other case endings are added (apart from the genitive plural) *-lac* changes to *-oca, -ocu, -ocem* etc (see Table 3.12):

gledalac – gledaoca, gledaocu, gledaocem, gledaoci, gledaocima
čitalac – čitaoca, čitaocu, čitaocem, čitaoci, čitaocima

2.3.6 Fleeting -a-

This vocal alternation takes place in the final syllable of a word:

- Masculine nouns ending in *-ac* or *-ak* have fleeing *-a-* only in the nominative singular and the genitive plural. In all other cases they lose this *-a-*:

nom sing	gen sing	nom pl	gen pl
stranac	*stranca*	*stranci*	*stranAca*
muškarac	*muškarca*	*muškarci*	*muškarAca*
dolazak	*dolaska*	*dolasci*	*dolazAka*
početak	*početka*	*počeci*	*početAka*

- Some masculine nouns whose nominative plural form ends in *-ovi* or *-evi* (*stupanj – stupnjevi* (bh-hr), *ritam – ritmovi*) have fleeting *-a-* only in the nominative singular. Fleeting *-a-* disappears in all other cases:

ritam	*ritma* (gen sing)	*ritmovi* (nom pl)	*ritmova* (gen pl)
stupanj	*stupnja* (gen sing)	*stupnjevi* (nom pl)	*stupnjeva* (gen pl) (hr)

- Masculine nouns of foreign origin and some feminine and neuter nouns which have consonant clusters in the final syllable have fleeting *-a-* only in the genitive plural which breaks up that consonant cluster:

nom sing	gen sing	nom pl	gen pl
student	*studenta*	*studenti*	*studenAta*
pacijent	*pacijenta*	*pacijenti*	*pacijenAta*
sestra	*sestre*	*sestre*	*sestAra*

djevojka	*djevojke*	*djevojke*	*djevojAka*
= devojka	*= devojke*	*= devojke*	*= devojAka*
pismo	*pisma*	*pisma*	*pisAma*

- Masculine adjectives (short form) ending in *-ar*, *-an* and *-ak* have fleeting *-a-* only in the nominative singular form. In all other cases and in all feminine and neuter forms fleeting *-a-* disappears:

  dobar, dobra, dobro
  gladan, gladna, gladno
  težak, teška, teško

N.B. This rule also applies to number "one" (as it has the form and is used as an adjective ending in *-an*):

jedan, jedna, jedno
jednog, jednom, jednim

- Masculine pronouns ending in *-av* have fleeting *-a-* only in the nominative singular form. In all other cases and in all feminine and neuter forms fleeting *-a-* disappears:

  sav, sva, sve; sveg, svem, svim
  kakav, kakva, kakvo
  ovakav, ovakva, ovakvo; takav, takva, takvo; onakav, onakva, onakvo
  nikakav, nikakva, nikakvo; nekakav, nekakva, nekakvo; ikakav, ikakva, ikakvo

- The L-participles of the verbs whose infinitives end in *-ći* (see 7.6.1) have fleeting *-a-* in the masculine singular; in all other forms (masculine plural, feminine and neuter sing and plural) fleeting *-a-* disappears in combination with the *L/O* changes:

išao (from *išal*)	*išla – išlo – išli*
došao (from *došal*)	*došla – došlo – došli*
mogao (from *mogal*)	*mogla – moglo – mogli*
rekao (from *rekal*)	*rekla – reklo -rekli*

- The cardinal numbers *sedam* and *osam* lose this *-a-* when ordinal number endings are added:

  sedam – sedmi, sedma, sedmo
  osam – osmi, osma, osmo.

2.3.7 *Removal of a duplicated consonant*

In BCMS, two identical consonants placed next to each other are not tolerated. If two identical consonants find themselves next to each other one will disappear.

This happens when prefixes or suffixes are added to a word:

Rus + ski – russki = ruski
bez + zub – bezzub = bezub
pod + držati – poddržati = podržati

Explanation:

When the suffix for relational adjectives *-ski* is added to the noun *Rus* (Russian man) the resulting adjective should be *russki*, but one of the duplicated consonants is dropped, resulting in *ruski* (Russian).

The same goes for the words *bez* (without) plus *zub* (tooth) which forms the adjective *bezub* (toothless); or *pod* (under) plus *držati* (hold) forming the verb *podržati* (to support).

Voicing assimilation (see 2.3.4) occurs in many instances before the removal of a duplicated consonant:

pet + deset = ped + deset = pedeset	five + ten = fifty
Francuz + ski = francusski = francuski	Frenchman + adjective suffix = French
Englez + ski = englesski = engleski	Englishman + adjective suffix = English
iz + seliti = isseliti = iseliti	out + to move = to move out

In some instances it is not immediately obvious that this process happens – like in the declension of the noun *otac* (father). This is because the sound *c* is a fusion of the sounds *t* and *s*; fleeting *-a-* is first dropped before two letters *t* find themselves next to each other:

otac – otca (this stands for *ottsa*) = *oca.*

An exception to this rule is when the superlative prefix *naj-* is added to an adjective that starts with a *j* – both consonants are kept and pronounced:

najjeftiniji	the cheapest
najjužniji	the southernmost
najjači	the strongest

2.3.8 *Multiple alternations*

Many words undergo multiple consonant and vowel alternations when some grammatical endings are added. Here are a couple of examples to illustrate this complex process:

dolazak – dolasci arrival – arrivals

The first thing that one may notice upon arriving by air in a country where BCMS is spoken is a sign at the airport saying *DOLASCI* – arrivals. This is the plural form of the noun *dolazak*. How do we get from *dolazak* to *dolasci*?

Phase one:

The masculine plural ending *-i* is added to *dolazak* – the noun loses fleeting *-a-* = *dolazk* + *i*.

Phase two:

K in front of the plural ending *-i* turns into *c* (sibilarisation) = *dolazC* + *i*.

Phase three:

The voiced *z* is impacted by the voiceless *c*, turning it into its voiceless pair *s* (voicing assimilations), resulting in *dolasci*.

posao – poslovi job – jobs

How do we get from singular *posao* (job) to *poslovi* (jobs)?

Phase one:

The final *-o* regresses to *-l* as it will no longer occupy the final position when the plural ending is added = *posal*.

Phase two:

The noun loses fleeting *-a-* before the plural ending is added = *posl*.

Phase three:

The long masculine plural ending *-ovi* is added, as *posl* is a single syllable noun = *poslovi*.

Chapter 3

Nouns

Nouns are words that name objects, places, people, animals, concepts etc. Some nouns are proper nouns – like the names of people – John, Rebecca etc; some nouns are common nouns (they can be concrete – such as a table, a house, a city; or abstract – such as loneliness, happiness, beauty); some can be countable (ticket, tickets), some uncountable (sugar, water).

In English, nouns are grammatically marked by either being in the singular or plural and can be marked for one case – the Saxon Genitive (boy's – genitive singular; boys' – genitive plural).

In BCMS nouns have the markings of:

- one of three grammatical **genders**,
- they can be in the **singular** or the **plural**,
- they can have endings for different **cases** (seven in the singular and seven in the plural) (see 3.3) and
- masculine nouns can have endings for **animacy** (see accusative singular, 3.3.6).

3.1 Gender

Every noun in BCMS is marked by one of three grammatical genders – masculine, feminine or neuter.

Thus *grad* (town) is of masculine gender, because it ends in a consonant, as most nouns of masculine gender do.

By contrast, *stolica* (chair) is of feminine gender because it ends in *-a*, as most nouns of feminine gender do.

Pismo (letter) or *more* (sea) are of neuter gender, because they end in either *-o* or *-e*, as most nouns of neuter gender do.

DOI: 10.4324/9781003154525-3

3.1.1 Masculine nouns

A majority of masculine nouns end in a **consonant:**

prozor	window
grad	town
brod	ship
krevet	bed
prijatelj	male friend

There are a few exceptions to this rule:

Some nouns are masculine although they **end in *-a*** (they are mostly nouns whose biological gender is masculine):

tata	dad
kolega	colleague
sudija (bh-mont-srb)	judge
deda (srb)	grandfather
komšija (bh-mont-srb)	neighbour

Note that all words in a sentence that refer to these nouns are in the masculine gender, for example:

Moj tata je otišao na poslovni put.	My father has gone away on a business trip.

Just a few nouns that **end in *-o*** are masculine:

posao	work, job
ugao	corner
dio (Iyekavian) = *deo* (Ekavian)*	part

*This difference (Iyekavian = Ekavian) will be marked by = in the rest of the chapter (see "How to Use This Book").

Borrowed words, such as *metro, intervju, taksi, auto, radio* are also masculine, although they do not end in a consonant. All words in a sentence that refer to these nouns are in masculine gender:

Njegov novi auto je parkiran ispred zgrade.	His new car is parked in front of the building.

3.1.2 Feminine nouns

A majority of feminine nouns end in ***-a:***

prijateljica	female friend
škola	school
kuća	house
kava (hr)	coffee
– *kafa* (bh-mont-srb)	
– *kahva* (bh)	

There are a few feminine nouns that end in **a consonant**:

noć	night
večer (hr)	evening
stvar	thing
ljubav	love
smrt	death

and all abstract nouns ending in ***-ost;*** some in ***-est*** and ***-ast:***

radost	joy
stvarnost	reality
vijest = *vest*	news
čast	honour

For more examples see 3.3.13.

Note that all words in a sentence that refer to these nouns are in feminine gender, e.g.

To je bila moja velika ljubav. That was a great love affair of mine.

One feminine noun ends in ***-o:***

misao	thought

3.1.3 Neuter nouns

A majority of neuter nouns end in ***-o*** or ***-e***:

selo	village
pismo	letter
brdo	hill

more	sea
proljeće = *proleće*	spring
rješenje = *rešenje*	solution
pozorište (bh-mont-srb) – *kazalište* (hr)	theatre
dijete = *dete*	child
veče (bh-mont-srb)	evening

There is only one neuter noun that ends in ***-a***:

doba age, times (as in *Kameno doba* – The Stone Age)

A group of neuter nouns ends in ***-me***. They have specific case endings (see Table 3.4):

ime	name
prezime	surname
vrijeme = *vreme*	time, weather

3.2 Plural (nominative plural)

Masculine, feminine and neuter nouns have separate endings for nominative plural forms.

3.2.1 *Masculine nouns*

Plural of masculine nouns is created by adding:

-i:

hotel – hoteli	hotels
student – studenti	students
prijatelj – prijatelji	friends
doktor – doktori	doctors

-ovi when a noun is made of one syllable:

park – parkovi	parks
grad – gradovi	towns
brod – brodovi	ships
vrt – vrtovi	gardens
duh – duhovi	ghosts

-evi to single syllable nouns that end in a soft consonant (*c, č, ć, dž, đ, j, lj, nj, š, ž*):

muž – muževi	husbands
broj – brojevi	numbers
ključ – ključevi	keys

Exception – the plural of the following single syllable nouns is formed by adding ***-i:***

dan – dani	days
sat – sati	hours (plural *satovi* means clocks)
pas – psi	dogs
konj – konji	horses
zub – zubi	teeth

Irregular plurals:

čovjek – ljudi = čovek – ljudi	man, people
brat – braća	brothers
gospodin – gospoda	gentlemen

Nouns ending in *-a:* the final ***-a*** is replaced with ***-e***:

tata – tate	dads
deda – dede (srb)	grandfathers
kolega – kolege	colleagues

Nouns ending in *-in:* the final *-n* is dropped to form the plural:

građanin – građani	inhabitants
Srbin – Srbi	Serbs
Beograđanin – Beograđani	Belgrade inhabitants
Zagrepčanin – Zagrepčani	Zagreb inhabitants

Nouns ending in *-ista* (bh-mont-srb): the final ***-a*** is replaced with ***-i:***

taksista – taksisti	taxi drivers
sportista – sportisti	sportsmen
turista – turisti	tourists

Plurals of masculine nouns involving consonant and vowel changes

Masculine nouns **ending in *-ac*** and ***-at***: fleeting -a- is lost in the last syllable before -i (see 2.3.6. "Fleeting -a-"):

muškarac – muškarci	men
Nijemac – Nijemci = Nemac – Nemci	German men, Germans
starac – starci	old men
nokat – nokti	nails
profesionalac – profesionalci	professionals

Masculine nouns **ending in *-ak*** : fleeting *-a-* in the final syllable is lost, the final *-k* changes to *-c* and voicing assimilation occurs in some nouns (see 2.3.8 "Multiple Alternations"):

momak – momci	young men
dolazak – dolasci	arrivals
odlazak – odlasci	departures

Nouns ending in *-k, -g, -h* : these change to *c, z, s* before the plural ending *-i* (see 2.3.2 "Consonant Softening before *-i*"):

kiosk – kiosci	kiosks
stanovnik – stanovnici	inhabitants
psiholog – psiholozi	psychologists
biolog – biolozi	biologist
uspjeh – uspjesi	success
= uspeh – uspesi	

Single syllable **nouns ending in *-o*** historically used to end in *-l* (*anđel, posal, ugal, dijel = del*). The final *-l* shifted to *-o* a few centuries ago – *anđeo, posao, ugao, dio = deo*. When an *-i* or *-ovi* ending is added, the noun shifts back to its *-l* ending (see 2.3.5 "L/O Changes"):

anđeo – anđeli	angels
posao – poslovi	work, job
ugao – uglovi	corner
dio – dijelovi	parts
= deo – delovi	

Nouns ending in *-lac* : this ending changes to *-oci:*

mislilac – mislioci	thinkers
gledalac – gledaoci	viewers
prevodilac – prevodioci (bh-mont-srb)	translators

3.2.2 *Feminine nouns*

Plural of feminine nouns ending in *-a* is formed by replacing the final ***-a*** with ***-e:***

žena – žene	women
kuća – kuće	houses
ulica – ulice	streets

For feminine nouns ending in a consonant, ***-i*** is added:

stvar – stvari	things
noć – noći	nights
laž – laži	lies

For more examples, see 3.3.13.

3.2.3 *Neuter nouns*

Plural of neuter nouns is formed by replacing the final ***-o*** or ***-e*** with ***-a:***

selo – sela	villages
pismo – pisma	letters
more – mora	seas
rješenje – rješenja	solutions
= *rešenje – rešenja*	

For neuter nouns that end in ***-me***, plural is formed by adding ***-na***:

ime – imena	names
prezime – prezimena	surnames
vrijeme – vremena	times
= *vreme – vremena*	

Irregular plurals

oko – oči	eyes
uho – uši	ears
dijete – djeca	children
= dete – deca	
drvo – drveta or *drva*	trees
veče – večeri (bh-mont-srb)	evenings

3.2.4 Neuter collective nouns

Plural of some nouns is formed by adding *-je* to their singular form. Thus they become collective neuter nouns denoting something viewed as a single group consisting of many identical elements.

list – lišće	leaf, leaves
kamen – kamenje	rock, rocks
grozd – grožđe	bunch of grapes – grapes
drvo – drveće	tree – trees
cvijet – cvijeće	flowers
= cvet – cveće	

Note that *J*-changes take place here due to the addition of the *-je* suffix (see 2.3.3 "*J*-changes"). This is the most common way of forming the plural for these nouns.

There is an alternative way of forming their plural:

list – listovi	leaf, leaves
kamen – kamenovi	rock, rocks
cvijet – cvjetovi	flower, flowers
= cvet – cvetovi	
grozd – grozdovi	bunch of grapes, bunches of grapes
drvo – drveta or *drva*	tree, trees (irregular plural)

These nouns are treated as neuter singular grammatically. Therefore, the elements in a sentence (adjectives and pronouns) that describe a collective noun have neuter singular markings; in sentences where a collective noun acts as the subject, the verb is in the singular:

Ovo žuto lišće me podsjeća = podseća na jesen.	These yellow leaves remind me of autumn.

Ogromno kamenje je popadalo po plaži.	Huge rocks have fallen all over the beach.
Cvijeće = cveće u ovom parku je predivno.	The flowers in this park are beautiful.

3.3 Cases

A case is the form of a noun, pronoun, adjective and some numbers that shows its grammatical relationship to other words.

3.3.1 *Cases in English and BCMS*

Although the concept of cases may seem confusing and foreign to English speakers, cases are used in English too. Nouns do not have case forms in English (with one exception – the Saxon genitive – explained in the following examples), but some personal pronouns still have them. Consider the following two sentences in English:

Have you seen my glasses? John gave *them to me* at *Jordan's* party.

In the second sentence an English speaker uses three cases:

them – is the direct object case, called the accusative case. A direct object is an element in a clause or a sentence directly affected by the action of the verb; in this sentence, the subject of the sentence (John) gave the glasses – the object of the action (them). *Them* is the accusative case form of the personal pronoun "they".

to me – is the case of indirect object, called the dative case. It denotes to whom something is given. *To me* is the dative case of the personal pronoun "I".

Jordan's – is the Saxon genitive case replacing the phrase "of Jordan" (party of Jordan). The genitive case generally describes to whom something belongs.

How nouns change case endings in BCMS

London je grad.	London is a city.

London is the subject of the sentence and therefore is unmodified – when a noun is the subject of a sentence it is considered to be in the nominative case.

Big Ben je u Londonu. Big Ben is in London.

The noun *Londonu* is now modified by the addition of the *-u* ending, which describes the location of the subject of the sentence (Big Ben). With this modification *Londonu* is considered to be in the locative case.

Consider this passage:

***Bosna** je moja domovina. Glavni grad **Bosne** je Sarajevo. U **Bosni** ima puno rijeka i prekrasnih planina. Volim svoju zemlju **Bosnu** i zato sam **Bosni** dao obećanje da je nikada neću zaboraviti. S **Bosnom** u srcu pjevam: "**Bosno** moja!"*

(Bosnia is my home country. The capital of Bosnia is Sarajevo. In Bosnia, there are many rivers and beautiful mountains. I love my country Bosnia and that is why I have made a promise to Bosnia never to forget her. With Bosnia in my heart, I am singing "My dear Bosnia"!)

The use of the noun *Bosna* in this passage may help us understand how cases work in BCMS:

Bosna	nominative	used as the subject of the sentence;
Bosne	genitive	used to denote belonging – the capital of Bosnia;
u Bosni	locative	used to show that Bosnia is the location of rivers and mountains;
Bosnu	accusative	used as a direct object after the transitive verb "to love" – Bosnia is the object of my love;
Bosni	dative	used as an indirect object after the phrase "to make a promise to";
Bosnom	instrumental	used with the preposition *s* to denote company, togetherness;
Bosno	vocative	used to call somebody, here used poetically.

There are seven cases in BCMS in the singular and plural. The system of case endings for a group of nouns, adjectives, some pronouns and some numbers is called a declension.

Most grammars say that there are three noun declensions in BCMS:

The First Declension includes masculine and neuter nouns (as they share almost identical endings).

The Second Declension includes nouns ending in *-a* (most feminine nouns and some masculine nouns ending in *-a*, such as *tata, kolega*).

The Third Declension includes feminine nouns ending in a consonant.

3.3.2 The First and Second Declensions – singular

As most nouns decline according to the First and Second Declensions, explanations of how cases are used are given alongside the First and Second Declensions table (Table 3.1).

Table 3.1

	Masculine inanim & anim		Neuter	Feminine
N	hotel	Ivan	pismo	škola
Gen	hotel**A**	Ivan**A**	pism**A**	škol**E**
Dat	hotel**U**	Ivan**U**	pism**U**	škol**i**
Acc	hotel	Ivan**A**	pismo	škol**U**
Voc	hotel	Ivan**E**	pismo	škol**O**
Ins	hotel**OM**	Ivan**OM**	pism**OM**	škol**OM**
Loc	hotel**U**	Ivan**U**	pism**U**	škol**i**

3.3.3 Nominative

The nominative case is the unmodified form of a noun listed in a dictionary. This form also determines gender of a noun (see 3.1).

The nominative case serves as the subject of a sentence, as in:

1 *Marko parkira auto.* — Marko is parking the car.
Vesna voli crno vino. — Vesna loves red wine.

Marko and *Vesna* are subjects in these two sentences. The subject of a sentence is the person or thing performing the action or being described.

2 *Marko je gladan.* — Marko is hungry.
Zagreb je krasan grad. — Zagreb is a beautiful city.
Ova kuća je bila njegova prva radionica. — This house used to be his first workshop.

Marko, *Zagreb* and *ova kuća* are subjects of these three sentences, a topic described by the predicate (here the verb "to be" plus complements).

3 The nominative is also used when a noun, a pronoun, an adjective or a number act as the predicate of a sentence with the verb "to be". In these examples, *gladan*, *krasan grad* and *njegova prva radionica* are part of the predicate and are in the nominative case.

3.3.4 *Genitive*

The genitive case of nouns in the singular has the following endings (First and Second Declensions):

-a – masculine and neuter nouns	*grad – grada; more -mora*
-e – feminine nouns	*škola – škole*

N.B.1 Masculine nouns ending in *-ac, -ak* or *-at* have fleeting *-a-* (see 2.3.6 "Fleeting *-a-*"):

momak – momka
stranac – stranca
otac – oca (see Table 3.7)
nokat – nokta

N.B.2 Masculine nouns ending in *-ao* (*posao, ugao*) have fleeting *-a-* and undergo *L/O* changes (see Table 3.5):

posao – posla
ugao – ugla

* * *

In broad terms, the genitive case describes to whom something belongs; it describes a quantity or measure or where a person or an object is from. It has many functions in BCMS and responds to the questions *od koga* (of whom), *od čega* (of what) and *odakle* (from where). The genitive case also governs most prepositions.

The genitive case is used to express:

Belonging

In the most general terms, to translate the preposition "of":

part of town	*kraj grada*
centre of London	*centar Londona*
scent of a rose	*miris ruže*

To translate the *Saxon genitive:*

my husband's car	*automobil moga muža*
my sister's school	*škola moje sestre*
director's office	*kancelarija* or *ured* (hr) *direktora*

Quantity

With adverbs denoting quantity – *mnogo, puno* (a lot), *malo* (a little, a few), *koliko* (how much, how many), *više* (more), *manje* (less), *dosta* (enough):

a lot of work	*puno posla*
a bit of bread	*malo hljeba = malo hleba*
	or *malo kruha* (hr)
enough alcohol	*dosta alkohola*
a lot of students	*mnogo studenata*
a few letters	*malo pisama*

N.B. If adverbs denoting quantity are followed by an uncountable noun, the noun will be in the genitive singular. If they are followed by a countable noun, the noun will be in the genitive plural (as in the last two examples).

With units of measure – *kilogram* (or *kilo*), *litar* (bh-mont-srb) or *litra* (hr) etc:

a kilo of cheese	*kilogram sira*
a litre of wine	*litar vina* or *litra vina* (hr)

Ima/nema

With existentials *ima/nema* (there is/there are and there is no/there are no):

there is water	*ima vode*
there is no work	*nema posla*
there are no people	*nema ljudi*

(for more see "Existentials *ima/nema*" in 11.4.1)

Time

The temporal (time) genitive – when a time period is described by an adjective:

Idem u školu svakog dana.	I go to school every day.

Prošle subote smo bili na izletu u Novom Sadu.	Last Saturday we took a trip to Novi Sad.
Sljedećeg mjeseca = Sledećeg meseca idemo u Sloveniju.	We are going to Slovenia next month.

The temporal (time) genitive is also used in dates. To say that something is on a particular date, all elements of the date are in the genitive case. Note that there is no preposition (see: 6.8 "Numbers Used in Dates"):

Stigli smo u Sarajevo dvadeset prvog maja or *svibnja* (hr) *prošle godine.*	We arrived in Sarajevo on 21 May last year.

With numbers

The genitive case is used with all numbers apart from number one:

dva grada, pet gradova	two towns, five towns
dvije = dve žene, pet žena	two women, five women

(see 6.1.1 "Cardinal Numbers' Agreement with Nouns, Pronouns and Adjectives")

Direct object

The genitive can also act as a direct object when it means "some", "a bit of", "a lot of" (partitive genitive):

Želite li meda?	Do you want some honey?
Imate li šećera?	Have you got any sugar?

In these two sentences the speaker omits a quantifier (*malo*) and just uses the genitive with partitive meaning.

The genitive is also used with a negated verb as a direct object, with the same partitive meaning:

Nemam vremena.	I don't have (any) time.
Ona nema strpljenja za njegove priče.	She has no patience for his stories.

Evo, eto, eno

The genitive is also used after the demonstrative particles *evo, eto, eno:*

Evo me.	Here I am.
Eto dobrog prijedloga = predloga!	There is a good proposal!
Eno našeg tramvaja na kraju ulice.	There is our tram, at the end of the street.

With prepositions

The genitive case governs most prepositions:

For space

blizu	near
Blizu naše škole je veliki park.	A large park is near our school.
do	next to, up to, to
Put od Zagreba do Rijeke traje dva sata.	The trip from Zagreb to Rijeka lasts two hours.
duž	along
Duž cijele = cele obale se pruža divno šetalište.	A beautiful promenade stretches along the whole coast.
iz	from
Ona je iz Australije.	She is from Australia.
iza	behind
Iza kuće imamo mali voćnjak.	Behind the house we have a small orchard.
izvan	out of
Lijek = lek čuvajte izvan domašaja djece = dece.	Keep medicines out of reach of children.
između	between
Između vaše i naše kuće ima mali park.	There is a tiny park between your house and ours.
iznad	above
Iznad slike je zidna lampa.	A wall lamp is above the picture.
ispred	in front of
Ispred spomenika ima jedan veliki hrast.	There is a large oak tree in front of the monument.
ispod	under
Ispod stola leži preslatka mačka.	A very cute cat is lying under the table.
kod	at, near, at someone's place
Sutra uveče je zabava kod Jelene.	The party is at Jelena's tomorrow evening.
Jesi li kod kuće večeras?	Are you at home this evening?
kraj or *pokraj*	next to
Sjednite = sednite na klupu kraj mora i sačekajte me.	Sit on the bench next to the sea and wait for me.

mimo	past
Prošli smo mimo trga i izgubili se.	We went past the square and got lost.
nasred	in the middle of
Nasred sela je stara crkva.	In the middle the village is an old church.
nasuprot	opposite
Nasuprot crkve je nova kafana – kavana (hr).	Opposite the church is a new tavern.
od	from
Od Sarajeva do Mostara ima stara pruga.	There is an old railway line from Sarajevo to Mostar.
oko	around, about
Mnogo ljudi se okupilo oko fontane.	Many people have gathered around the fountain.
pored	next to
Veliki vinogradi se nalaze pored Skadarskog jezera.	Large vineyards are located next to Skadar Lake.
preko	across
Preko mosta je južni dio = deo grada.	Across the bridge is the southern part of the city.
s(a)	from
Moj učitelj je s otoka (hr-bh) or *ostrva* (mont-srb) *Krka.*	My teacher is from the island of Krk.
van	outside
Hajdemo na izlet van grada.	Let's go on an excursion outside the city.

For time

od	from
do	up to, till
Od jutra do večeri svira klavir.	She plays the piano from morning till night.
prije = pre	before
poslije = posle	after
Prije = pre koncerta idemo na piće, a poslije = posle koncerta na večeru.	We are going for a drink before the concert and for dinner after the concert.

nakon	after
Nakon filma su otišli u šetnju.	After the movie they went for a walk.
oko	around
Bura je počela oko ponoći.	A storm started around midnight.
uoči	on the eve of
Stigli su u Zagreb uoči praznika.	They arrived in Zagreb on the eve of the holiday.

Other

bez	without
Dajte mi jedan čaj bez šećera.	Give me a cup of tea without sugar, please.
zbog	due to
Zbog lošeg vremena je otkazan let za Podgoricu.	The flight to Podgorica has been cancelled due to bad weather.
mjesto = mesto	instead of
umjesto = umesto	
Pijte čaj i vodu umjesto = umesto alkoholnih pića.	Drink tea and water instead of alcoholic drinks.
osim or *sem*	apart from
Ničega se ne sjećam = sećam osim tog razgovora.	I do not remember anything else apart from that conversation.
protiv	against
Mnogo ljudi je bilo na demonstracijama protiv vlade.	Many people were at the demonstrations against the government.
radi	with the view to, in order to
Došli smo u Istru radi razgledanja Pulske Arene.	We came to Istria (in order) to see the Pula Arena.

With verbs

The genitive is used with the following reflexive verbs:

bojati se, *plašiti se* (to be afraid of), *čuvati se* (beware of), *paziti se* (to be careful, to watch out), *sjećati se* = *sećati se* (to remember), *stidjeti se* = *stideti se* (to be ashamed of)

Bojite li se mraka?	Are you afraid of the dark?
Čuvajte se falsifikata.	Beware of forgeries.
Možeš li se sjetiti = setiti našeg prvog razgovora?	Can you remember our first chat?

3.3.5 Dative

The dative case of nouns in the singular has the following endings (First and Second Declensions):

-u – masculine and neuter nouns *grad – gradu; more – moru*
-i – feminine nouns *škola – školi*

N.B.1 In some feminine nouns the last consonant of the root *k, g* or *h* changes to *c, z* or *s* before *-i* (see 2.3.2 "Consonant Softening before *-I*"):

noga – nozi
knjiga – knjizi
ruka – ruci
slika – slici
rijeka – rijeci = reka – reci

N.B.2 Masculine nouns ending in *-ac*, *-ak* or *-at* have fleeting *-a-* (see 2.3.6 "Fleeting *-a-*"):

momak – momku
stranac – strancu
otac – ocu (see Table 3.7)
nokat – noktu

N.B.3 Masculine nouns ending in *-ao* (*posao, ugao*) have fleeting *-a-* and undergo *L/O* changes (see Table 3.5):

posao – poslu
ugao – uglu

* * *

The dative case is used to describe to whom something is given or done. It responds to the questions *kome* (to whom) and *čemu* (to what).

In a sentence it plays the role of **indirect object**, without prepositions.

Moram pisati mami pismo.	I have to write a letter to Mum.
Želim poslati Marku poklon za rođendan.	I want to send a birthday gift to Marko.

In these examples direct objects are *pismo* (letter) and *poklon za rođendan* (birthday gift) and indirect objects are *mama* and *Marko*.

With prepositions

The dative case is used after the following prepositions:

prema	towards
Na putu prema moru proći ćete kroz Gorski Kotar.	On your journey towards the sea you will pass through Gorski Kotar.
k(a)	towards
Uzmite tramvaj koji vozi ka glavnom trgu.	Take the tram that goes towards the main square.
uprkos, usprkos or *unatoč* (hr)	despite
Uprkos kiši, idem u šetnju.	Despite the rain, I am going for a walk.
nasuprot	opposite
Nasuprot trgu je mala fontana.	Opposite the square is a small fountain.
zahvaljujući	thanks to
Pobijedili = pobedili smo zahvaljujući tebi.	We have won thanks to you.
pri	at, on, near to
Pri sebi nije imala novca.	She did not have any money on her.

With verbs

The following verbs are used with the dative case, as they can have both direct and indirect objects:

davati (to give), *pisati* (to write), *slati* (to send), *željeti* = *želeti* (to wish), *pomagati* (to help), *kazati* (to say), *govoriti* (to speak), *javljati* (to call, to inform), *zahvaliti se* (to thank), *objašnjavati* (to explain), *vjerovati* = *verovati* (to believe)

Majka je bebi dala mlijeka = mleka.	The mother gave some milk to her baby.
Želimo vam sve najbolje za Novu godinu.	We wish (to) you all the very best for the New Year.
Svoju riječ = reč vam dajem.	I am giving (to) you my word.
Roditelji su Ani obećali divan poklon za rođendan.	Her parents promised (to) Ana a lovely birthday present.
Javite nam čim saznate šta – što (hr) *se dogodilo.*	Inform us as soon as you learn what has happened.

Possession

The dative is used to denote possession, implying personal ties and closeness. Possession is expressed by the dative of the appropriate personal pronoun (see Table 5.1 and Table 5.2):

Mama mi je u banji.	My mum is at the spa.
Gdje = gde ti je sin?	Where is your son?
Gdje = gde su nam ključevi?	Where are our keys?

Idioms

The dative is used in the following useful idioms:

Drago mi je.	Pleased to meet you (literally – It is dear to me).
Hvala vam.	Thank you (literally – Thanks be to you).
Žao mi je.	I am sorry.
Sretan (bh-hr) or *srećan* (mont-srb) *ti put.*	Have a good trip (literally – Happy trip to you).
Želim vam sve najbolje.	I wish (to) you all the best.
Piši mi.	Write to me.
Javi mi se.	Get in touch.

The dative is also used in the following frequently used idioms:

Čini mi se.	It seems to me.
Sviđa mi se.	I like it (literally – It appeals to me).
Dopada mi se.	I like it (or literally – It appeals to me).
To mi smeta.	That bothers me.

N.B. These examples are given in the first person singular. For other persons, the relevant personal pronoun or a noun in the dative case is used instead of *mi*, for example:

Sviđa **nam** se.	We like it.
Je li **vam** se *sviđalo tamo?*	Did you like it over there?
Nije **im** se *sviđalo.*	They did not like it.
Marku se *ne sviđa novi posao.*	Marko does not like his new job.
Mački se *nije sviđala ta vrsta hrane.*	The cat did not like that type of food.
Čini ***joj*** se *da nisi u nju zaljubljen.*	It seems to her that you are not in love with her.
Da li ***ti*** se *dopada moja nova košulja?*	Do you like my new shirt?

Note the position of enclitics *mi, ti, mu, joj, nam, vam, im* – as they have to be placed as the second unit in a sentence, grouped with other enclitics (see 11.2 "Enclitics").

Predicate-only sentences

The dative is used in predicate-only sentences which describe how a state affects a human being and those expressing a subjective feeling (see 11.4.2. "Personalised Predicate-Only Sentences"):

Hladno mi je.	I am cold (literally – It is cold to me).
Vruće mi je.	I am hot (literally – It is hot to me).
Dosadno mi je.	I am bored (literally – It is boring to me).
Dobro mi je.	I feel well.
Nije mi dobro.	I do not feel well.
Teško mi je.	I find it difficult (literally – It is difficult to me).
Nije mi lako.	I don't find it easy (literally – It is not easy to me).

N.B. These examples are given in the first person singular. For other persons, the relevant personal pronoun or a noun in the dative case is used instead of *mi*, for example:

Hladno ***nam*** *je.*	We are cold.
Nije ***im*** *vruće.*	They are not hot.
Dobro ***joj*** *je.*	She is feeling fine.
Da li ***ti*** *je teško?*	Do you find it difficult?
Mladenu *je dosadno.*	Mladen is bored.

Note the position of enclitics *mi, ti, mu, joj, nam, vam, im* – as they have to be placed as the second unit in a sentence, grouped with other enclitics (see 11.2 "Enclitics").

Desire

There is specific idiomatic usage of personal pronouns or nouns in the dative case to express a desire to do something – the equivalent to the English phrase – "I feel like doing".

Spava mi se.	I feel like sleeping.

(For more, see 11.4.2 "Personalised Predicate-Only Sentences – Expressing a Desire").

3.3.6 *Accusative*

The accusative case of nouns in the singular has the following endings (First and Second Declensions):

masculine and neuter nouns	**as nominative**	*grad – grad; more – more*
feminine nouns	**-u**	*škola – školu*

Exception: masculine animate nouns

add **-*a***

Vuk je pojeo lava. (nom: *lav*).	The wolf has eaten the lion.
Vuka je pojeo lav.	The lion has eaten the wolf.

Masculine animate nouns do not include nouns denoting groups of human beings, such as:

tim	team
narod	people
Vidio = video sam ljutit narod na demonstracijama.	I saw angry people at the demonstrations.

N.B. Masculine animate nouns ending in *-ac* or *-ak* have fleeting *-a-* (see 2.3.6 "Fleeting *-a-*"):

momak – momka
stranac – stranca
otac – oca (see Table 3.7)

* * *

The accusative case responds to the questions – *šta – što* (hr) (what), *koga* (whom) and *kuda – kamo* (hr) (where to).

Accusative without prepositions

DIRECT OBJECT

The main function of the accusative case is to mark a direct object. A direct object is an element in a clause or a sentence directly affected by the action of the verb.

John has eaten sandwiches.	John has eaten them.
Tanja loves cakes.	She loves them.

In these sentences, John and Tanja are the subjects and the direct objects are the sandwiches and cakes (them).

In this usage the accusative does not require prepositions.

Jovan voli ovaj grad.	Jovan likes this city.
Maja voli svoju školu.	Maja likes her school.
Marko voli svoga sina.	Marko loves his son.

In these sentences *ovaj grad, svoju školu* and *svoga sina* are direct objects of the transitive verb *voljeti* = *voleti* (to love). Not all verbs require a direct object. Those that require it are called transitive verbs. Those that do not are called intransitive verbs (see 7.3.1 "Transitive/Intransitive verbs").

Accusative with prepositions

MOTION/DESTINATION

The accusative case is used with verbs of motion:

Vesna ide na izložbu.	Vesna is going to an exhibition.
Marko je otišao u školu.	Marko went to school.

Or with the idea of moving towards a location, even if there is no verb of motion in a sentence.

Sretan (hr-bh) or *srećan* (mont-srb) *vam put u Bosnu.*	Have a good trip to Bosnia.

When suggesting motion, it is used with the following prepositions:

u – Idemo u Bosnu.	We are going to Bosnia.
na – Hajdemo na pivo.	Let's go for a beer.

N.B.1 The prepositions *u* and *na* can also be used with the locative, when they mean "being at a location" (see 3.3.10 "Accusative vs Locative – Destination vs Location").

N.B.2 See 9.2.3 "Learning Tip: When to Use *U*, When *NA*"

Other prepositions

It is also used after the following prepositions:

za	for
Ovo je poklon za Vesnu.	This is a present for Vesna.
kroz	through
Šetamo kroz šumu.	We are walking through the woods.
uz	along, alongside
Uz obalu mora u Opatiji se nalaze prekrasne vile.	Beautiful villas are to be found along the sea coast in Opatija.
niz	alongside, down
Niz Savu je šetalište sve do mosta.	Along (the river) Sava is a promenade all the way to the bridge.
po	idiomatic usage – to fetch, to get
Idi na tržnicu (bh-hr) or *pijacu* (mont-srb) *po ribu i salatu.*	Go to the market to get some fish and salad.

The accusative also covers the **following areas of meaning** (with or without prepositions):

Time

WEEKDAYS

The accusative is used after the preposition *u* with the days of the week – for example "on Saturday":

u subotu	on Saturday
u petak	on Friday

"AGO"

The accusative is used with the preposition *prije* = *pre* (before) when it means "ago" – for example "a year ago".

To se desilo prije = pre godinu dana.	That happened a year ago.
Prije = pre tri godine smo bili na divnom putu po Bosni.	Three years ago we had a great trip in Bosnia.

DURATION

Without prepositions, the accusative is used to indicate that a certain action lasts a specified period of time. It replies to the question "how long?":

Put Zemlje oko Sunca traje godinu dana.	The Earth's revolution around the Sun lasts one year.
Ovaj tečaj traje mjesec = mesec dana.	This course lasts one month.
Zbog stresa na poslu neću spavati cijelu = celu noć.	Because of the stress at work, I will not sleep all night.

N.B. Note that the word *dana* (days) is added to the following nouns when they mean "one week", "one month" or "one year":

sedmicu dana (bh-mont) or *nedelju dana* (srb) or *tjedan dana* (hr)	one week
mjesec = mesec dana	one month
godinu dana	one year

To say that something lasts "one hour", the noun *vremena* is added to *sat* (hour).

Gledali smo TV sat vremena.	We watched TV one hour.

These added nouns have no specific meaning, nor do they emphasise anything; they are just part of idiomatic usage. They can be replaced by the number one:

jednu sedmicu (bh-mont) or *jednu nedelju* (srb) or *jedan tjedan (hr)*	one week
jedan mjesec = mesec	one month
jednu godinu	one year
jedan sat	one hour

***na* + acc in expressions of time** refers to an expected future duration of an action; it translates into English as "for one week" or similar:

Idemo na more na sedmicu dana (bh-mont) – *nedelju dana* (srb) – *tjedan dana* (hr).	We are going to the seaside for one week.

Idu na tečaj engleskog u Oksford na šest mjeseci = meseci.	They are going to Oxford for six months to do an English course.

***za* + acc in expressions of time** refers to a time lag before an expected action will take place; it translates into English as "in one week" or similar:

Poći ćemo u Alpe za sedmicu dana (bh-mont) – *nedelju dana* (srb) – *tjedan dana* (hr).	We shall go to the Alps in a week's time.
Za godinu dana ćete završiti studije.	You will complete your studies in a year's time.

Measure and value

In addition to expressing the duration of time (as in the previous section), the accusative is also used to express spatial measurements, weight and value. It replies to the questions "how long", "how tall" and "how much":

Šetalište od našeg hotela do plaže je dugo jednu milju.	The promenade from our hotel to the beach is one mile long.
Čaša vina u ovoj taverni košta samo jednu funtu.	A glass of wine in this tavern costs only one pound.
Ovaj kontejner teži jednu tonu.	This container weighs one ton.
Odmor u Opatiji vas može koštati cijelu mjesečnu platu or *plaću* (hr) = *celu mesečnu platu.*	A holiday in Opatija may cost you a whole month's salary.

Idiomatic usage – "to hurt"

To say that one has a headache, toothache or that one has pain in a specific body part, the person suffering the pain is in the accusative case (mostly the enclitic form of the personal pronoun – *me, te, ga, je, nas, vas, ih*). The part of the body that hurts is the subject. Literally translated, the BCMS idiom is: "The head hurts me".

Boli me glava.	I have a headache.
Često te boli zub.	You frequently have a toothache.
Jesu li ih boljele = bolele noge sinoć?	Did their legs hurt last night?
Da li Marka još bole leđa?	Does Marko still have a backache?

3.3.7 *Vocative*

The vocative case has a few different endings and many exceptions. The most important ones to remember are:

-e – masculine nouns	*gospodin – gospodine; sin – sine*
-u – masculine nouns ending in a soft consonant (*c, č, ć, dž, đ, j, lj, nj, š, ž*)	*prijatelj – prijatelju; učitelj – učitelju*
-o – feminine nouns ending in *-a*	*žena – ženo, sestra – sestro, majka – majko, baka – bako*
-e – feminine nouns ending in *-ica*	*profesorica – profesorice* (bh-hr); *prijateljica – prijateljice.*

no change – neuter nouns and masculine nouns ending in *-o*

N.B. In some masculine nouns the last consonant *k, g* or *h* changes to *č, ž* or *š* (and *c* to *č*) before *-e* (see 2.3.1 "Consonant Softening before -*E*").

bog – bože
stric – striče
otac – oče (see Table 3.7)
čovjek – čovječe = čovek – čoveče

There are many exceptions for vocative endings, and it is best to use this case sparingly – it is slowly disappearing in the spoken language in Croatia. Only nouns can have separate vocative case endings.

* * *

The vocative is used for calling or addressing people.

Gospodine Jovane, jeste li dobro? (nom: *Gospodin Jovan*)	Mr Jovan, are you OK?
Draga gospođo Simić, kako ste? (nom: *Draga gospođa Simić*)	Dear Mrs Simić, how are you?

N.B. It is normal to address somebody as *Mr Jovan* even though *Jovan* is the person's Christian name, not a family name.

It is mostly used with personal names but also with nouns for human beings and professions (as in *čovječe = čoveče, doktore, profesore, predsjedniče = predsedniče*).

It is very frequently used in exclamations of incredulity or surprise:

Bože! (nom: *bog*)	Oh God!
Gospode bože!	Dear Lord!
Majko Isusova!	Mother of God!
Isuse Hriste!	Jesus Christ!

It is sometimes used with inanimate nouns in a poetic style, or in terms of endearment:

Zemljo moja!	My dear country!
Oh živote!	Oh my days!
Dušo moja.	My sweetheart!
Ljubavi moja	My love!
Lijepa naša domovino, oj junačka zemljo mila ...	(the Croatian national anthem)
Oj svijetla majska zoro, majko naša Crna Goro ...	(the Montenegrin national anthem)

It is also used to throw insults at people, mostly using names of animals plus – *jedan, jedna* or *jedno:*

Svinjo jedna!	You swine!
Konju jedan!	You are horse-shit!
Kravo jedna!	You are such a cow!
Idiote jedan!	What an idiot!

3.3.8 Instrumental

The instrumental case of nouns in the singular has the following endings (First and Second Declensions):

-om – all nouns *voz – vozom* (bh-mont-srb) or *vlak – vlakom* (hr)
mama – mamom
vino – vinom

N.B.1 After soft consonants *(c, č, ć, dž, đ, j, lj, nj, š, ž)* the instrumental marking for masculine nouns is ***-em:***

muž – mužem

The same applies to neuter nouns ending in *-e*:

> *pozorište – pozorištem* (bh-mont-srb)
> or *kazalište – kazalištem* (hr)
> *more – morem*

N.B.2 Masculine nouns ending in *-ac, -ak* or *-at* have fleeting *-a-* (see 2.3.6 "Fleeting *-a-*"):

> *momak – momkom*
> *stranac – strancem*
> *otac – ocem* (see Table 3.7)

N.B.3 Masculine nouns ending in *-ao* (*posao, ugao*) have fleeting *-a-* and undergo *L/O* changes (see Table 3.5):

> *posao – poslom*
> *ugao – uglom*

* * *

The instrumental case responds to the questions *s kim* (with whom) and *čime* (by what). It covers the following areas of meaning:

Instrument/means

The instrumental case is used to describe the instrument/means with which something is done – hence its name. When indicating means or an instrument, it is used **without prepositions**:

Idemo na posao vozom or *vlakom* (hr).	We are going to work by train.
Pišemo pismo olovkom.	We are writing a letter with a pencil.

Many native BCMS speakers use the preposition *s(a)* here. That is grammatically incorrect.

Company

It follows the **preposition *s(a)*** (with) when indicating company or describing that two things are together:

Želimo putovati s mamom.	We would like to travel with Mum.
Najviše volim burek sa sirom.	I like burek with cheese best.

Location

The instrumental case is also used **with the following prepositions** to denote a location:

nad	above
Nad oblacima je sunce.	The sun is above the clouds.
Nad rijekom = rekom leti jato ptica.	A flock of birds is flying above the river.
pod	under
Tvoj mobilni je pod jastukom.	Your mobile phone is under the pillow.
Ona je pod velikim stresom.	She is very stressed out (under a lot of stress).
pred	in front of
Videli su ga pred autobusom.	They saw him in front of the bus.
Pred vratima leži mačka.	A cat is lying in front of the door.
među	among
Našao sam tvoju sliku među starim pismima.	I found your photo among old letters.
za	at
Sjede = sede za stolom i piju domaću rakiju.	They are sitting at the table drinking home-brewed brandy.
Cijeli dan sjedimo = celi dan sedimo za kompjuterom.	We are sitting at the computer all day.
Za barom stoji lijepa djevojka = lepa devojka.	A beautiful girl is standing at the bar.

N.B. The main meaning of the preposition *za* is "for" or "behind"; it is also used in the idiomatic expressions "at the table" or "at the computer".

The instrumental can also be used **without prepositions** to indicate a location meaning "across" or "around":

Prošetali su centrom grada.	They took a walk around the city centre.
Brod plovi morem.	The boat is sailing on the sea.

Time

The instrumental can also be used to denote time in the following instances:

1 With the days of the week to express that something happens repeatedly or regularly on a particular week day:

Naš tečaj jezika je utorkom.	Our language course is on Tuesdays.
Banka je zatvorena subotom i nedjeljom = nedeljom.	The bank is closed on Saturdays and Sundays.

2 With the following nouns in the plural denoting long periods of time: *satima* (for hours), *danima* (days), *tjednima* (hr) or *nedjeljama = nedeljama* (weeks), *mjesecima = mesecima* (months), *godinama* (years):

Čekao sam te satima, ali se nisi pojavio.	I waited for you for hours but you did not turn up.
Godinama je učila francuski, ali ga nije naučila.	She has been studying French for years, but she has not mastered it.

3 With the nouns *početak* (start), *sredina* (bh-hr-mont-srb) or *polovica* (hr) (middle, mid-) and *kraj* (bh-hr-mont-srb) or *konac* (hr) (end) to locate an action at a particular time within a longer period:

To se desilo početkom ove godine.	That happened at the start of this year.
Sredinom jula idemo na odmor (bh-mont-srb), or	
Polovicom sedmog mjeseca idemo na odmor (hr).	We are going on holiday in mid-July.
Selimo se krajem or *koncem* (hr) *ove godine.*	We are moving at the end of this year.

With adjectives

Some adjectives require the instrumental case (good dictionaries mention this):

zadovoljan	satisfied with, pleased with
Zadovoljni samo rezultatima koje smo postigli na ispitu.	We are satisfied with the results that we achieved in the exam.
oduševljen	thrilled, enthused, amazed, impressed
Oduševljena sam njihovom novom kućom.	I am impressed by their new house.
fasciniran	fascinated
Bili su fascinirani ljepotom = lepotom Plitvičkih jezera.	They were fascinated by the beauty of Plitvice Lakes.

With verbs

The instrumental is used with the following verbs:

baviti se (to be occupied with, to play a sport), *ženiti se* (to marry – for a man):

Kojim sportom se bavite?	Which sport do you play?
Oženio se Bosankom u Sarajevu prošle godine.	He married a Bosnian woman in Sarajevo last year.

3.3.9 Locative

The locative case is formed in the same way as the dative case.

* * *

The locative is the only case that **cannot be used without prepositions**. It is used to denote a location – hence its name – with the following prepositions:

u, na	in, on, at
o	about
po	all over, according to

It responds to the questions *gdje* = *gde* (where), *o kome* (about whom), *o čemu* (about what).

Marko je u gradu.	Marko is in town.
Vesna je provela odmor na otoku (bh-hr) - *ostrvu* (mont-srb) *Braču.*	Vesna spent her holiday on the island of Brač.
Sada smo u školi.	We are at school now.
Sinoć smo bili na koncertu.	We were at a concert last night.
Razgovarali su o Londonu.	They spoke about London.

N.B. Prepositions *u* and *na* can denote a physical location (*u gradu*) or an abstract location (*na koncertu*) (see 9.2.3 "Learning: when to use *U*, when *NA*").

The locative is also used with the preposition ***po***, which means "across", "all over" or "according to":

Razgledali su spomenike po Parizu.	They toured monuments all over Paris.
Po mom mišljenju, Pariz je divan.	In (according to) my opinion, Paris is beautiful.

The locative is also used with months and years after the preposition *u*:

Rođen sam u hiljadu or *tisuću* (hr) *devetsto šezdeset petoj godini.*	I was born in 1965.
U julu idemo u Dalmaciju na deset dana. (bh-mont-srb)	
U srpnju (or *sedmom mjesecu* (colloq)) *idemo u Dalmaciju na deset dana.* (hr)	In July we are going to Dalmatia for ten days.

Locative of country names

Some country names are ordinary nouns taking predictable locative endings after the prepositions *u* or *na*:

u Bosni, u Italiji, u Srbiji, u Rusiji, na Islandu	in Bosnia, in Italy, in Serbia, in Russia, in Iceland

Many country names are feminine adjectives by their grammatical form (ending in *-ska /Hrvatska/*, *-ška /Norveška/* or *-čka /Grčka/*); that is why they decline as feminine adjectives (see 4.4 "Case Endings"):

u Hrvatskoj, u Engleskoj, u Francuskoj, u Grčkoj	in Croatia, in England, in France, in Greece

If a country name is made of an adjective and a noun, as in *Crna Gora*, *Novi Zeland* or *Velika Britanija*, the elements decline according to adjectival and noun declensions:

u Crnoj Gori, na Novom Zelandu, u Velikoj Britaniji	in Montenegro, in New Zealand, in Great Britain

3.3.10 Accusative vs locative (destination vs location)

Note the difference in the usage of *u* and *na* followed by the accusative or the locative case; the accusative denotes movement towards a location or destination and the locative denotes being at a location:

Marko ide u restoran. (acc)	Marko is going to the restaurant.
Marko je u restoranu. (loc)	Marko is in the restaurant.
Vesna ide u Bosnu. (acc)	Vesna is going to Bosnia.
Vesna je u Bosni. (loc)	Vesna is in Bosnia.
Idemo na plažu. (acc)	Let's go to the beach.
Mi smo na plaži. (loc)	We are on the beach.

Table 3.2

	Masculine	Neuter	Feminine
N	hoteli	pism**A**	škol**E**
Gen	hotel**A**	pis**A**m**A**	škol**A**
Dat	hotel**IMA**	pism**IMA**	škol**AMA**
Acc	hotel**E**	pism**A**	škol**E**
Voc	hoteli	pism**A**	škol**E**
Ins	hotel**IMA**	pism**IMA**	škol**AMA**
Loc	hotel**IMA**	pism**IMA**	škol**AMA**

3.3.11 The First and Second Declensions plural

Case endings for the **Nominative plural** are explained in 3.2 "Plural (Nominative Plural").

Dative, accusative, vocative, instrumental and locative case endings in the plural are regular – see Table 3.2.

N.B.1 In some masculine nouns, the last consonant *k, g* or *h* changes to *c, z* or *s* before *-ima* in the dat/loc/instr (these three forms are identical) (see 2.3.2 "Consonant Softening before -I"):

putnik – putnicima
rođak – rođacima
izlog – izlozima
prijedlog – prijedlozima = predlog – predlozima
orah – orasima

N.B.2 Masculine nouns ending in *-ac, -ak* or *-at* have fleeting *-a-* in all cases apart from the genitive plural (see 2.3.6 "Fleeting *-a-*"):

momak – momci, momcima, momke
stranac – stranci, strancima, strance
nokat – nokti, noktima, nokte

N.B.3 Masculine nouns ending in *-ao* (*posao, ugao*) have fleeting *-a-* and undergo *L/O* changes in all cases in the plural (see Table 3.5):

posao – poslovi, poslova, poslovima, poslove
ugao – uglovi, uglova, uglovima, uglove

The only case in the plural that needs further explanation is the genitive plural.

3.3.12 Genitive plural

-*a* ending

Regular genitive plural ending for all nouns (First and Second Declension) is ***-a***.

učenik	*mnogo učenika*	many students
učitelj	*nekoliko učitelja*	a few male teachers
žena	*mnogo žena*	a lot of women
učiteljica	*puno učiteljica*	a lot of female teachers
selo	*puno sela*	a lot of villages

(Most feminine nouns ending in *-a* in the nominative singular remain unchanged – in pronunciation this final *-a* is long.)

If a noun ends in a sequence of consonants, an **extra *-a-*** is inserted between the last two consonants:

student	*šest studenata*	six students
marka	*pet maraka*	five stamps
pismo	*nekoliko pisama*	several letters

For single syllable masculine nouns whose plural is formed by extending the noun with the infix *-ov-* or *-ev-*, that infix is kept in all plural forms:

grad (nom sing)	city
gradovi (nom pl)	
gradova (gen pl)	
gradovima (dat/inst/loc pl)	

For the neuter nouns *ime, prezime, vrijeme*, whose plural is formed by extending the noun by inserting the consonant *-n-*, that infix is kept in all plural forms:

ime	*mnogo imena*	a lot of names

-*i* ending

For feminine nouns ending in a consonant (Third Declension – *stvar, ljubav, opasnost, bolest*) the genitive plural is formed by adding *-i*:

stvar	*puno stvari*	a lot of things

Exceptions

The following **feminine nouns** ending in *-a* also take the *-i* ending in the genitive plural. These are mostly words of foreign origin, such as:

torta	*torti*	gateau
milijarda	*milijardi*	billion
konzerva	*konzervi*	tin
uniforma	*uniformi*	uniform
jakna	*jakni*	jacket
funta	*funti*	pound
šansa	*šansi*	chance
bomba	*bombi*	bombs

This also applies to a few nouns which are not of foreign origin, such as:

majka	*majki*	mother
tajna	*tajni*	secret

The following **masculine nouns** (mostly units of time) also take the *-i* ending in the genitive plural:

sat	*sati*	hour
stepen	*stepeni* (bh-mont-srb)	degree
mjesec = *mesec*	*mjeseci* = *meseci*	month
sekund	*sekundi*	second
čovjek = *čovek*	*ljudi*	man, people

Irregular genitive plural

The following nouns have irregular endings in the genitive plural:

-iju ending

Mostly nouns denoting parts of body:

prst	finger, toe
oko	eye
uho	ear
kost	bone
nokat	nail

mnogo prstiju, očiju, ušiju, kostiju

and the noun

gost guest

nekoliko gostiju

-*u* ending

noga	leg, foot
ruka	hand, arm

mnogo nogu, mnogo ruku

3.3.13 *The Third Declension (feminine nouns ending in a consonant)*

This declension (Table 3.3) includes:

1 A small group of feminine nouns that end in a consonant, such as:

stvar	thing
večer (hr)	evening
noć	night
ljubav	love
smrt	death
riječ = reč	word
laž	lie
obitelj (bh-hr)	family

2 Nouns ending in ***-ST:***

a) A large group of abstract nouns that end in ***-ost***:

mladost	youth
starost	old age
slabost	weakness
hrabrost	bravery
vjernost = vernost	loyalty
stvarnost	reality
normalnost	normality
realnost	reality
profesionalnost	professionalism

b) A group of nouns that end in ***-est***:

bolest	illness
vijest = vest	news
savjest = savest	conscience
svijest = svest	awareness

N.B. Nouns of foreign origin ending in *-est* like *protest*, *test* are masculine.

c) A group of nouns that end in ***-ast:***

čast	honour
vlast	rule

mast	lard
strast	passion

3 One feminine noun that ends in ***-o*** – *misao* (thought).

These nouns have a simple declension.

Table 3.3

	Singular	Plural
Nom	ljubav	ljubavi
Gen	ljubavi	ljubavi
Dat	ljubavi	ljubavima
Acc	ljubav	ljubavi
Voc	ljubavi	ljubavi
Inst	ljubavi (also: ljubavlju)	ljubavima
Loc	ljubavi	ljubavima

3.3.14 *Frequently used nouns with irregularities in declension*

vrijeme = vreme, ime

There is a very small group of neuter nouns in which the root is extended by the consonant ***-n-*** before a case ending:

ime	name
prezime	surname
vrijeme = vreme	time, weather
rame	shoulder

Table 3.4

	Singular	Plural
Nom	vrijeme = vreme	vremena
Gen	vremena	vremena
Dat	vremenu	vremenima
Acc	vrijeme = vreme	vremena
Voc	vrijeme = vreme	vremena
Inst	vremenom	vremenima
Loc	vremenu	vremenima

posao, ugao

When case endings are added to the masculine nouns *posao* (work, job) and *ugao* (corner), fleeting *-a-* is lost and the final *-o-* regresses to *-l-*.

N.B. As they are single syllable masculine nouns, *-ov-* is inserted before the standard plural endings.

Table 3.5

	Singular	Plural
N	posao	poslovi
Gen	posla	poslova
Dat	poslu	poslovima
Acc	posao	poslove
Voc	posao	poslovi
Inst	poslom	poslovima
Loc	poslu	poslovima

dio = deo (part)

In Ekavian, the final *-o-* changes to *-l-* before the standard masculine case endings are added.

In Iyekavian, *-je-* is inserted before the final *-o-* changes to *-l-*, and then the standard masculine case endings are added.

N.B. As it is a single syllable masculine noun, the infix *-ov-* is added in the plural before the standard plural endings (Table 3.6).

Table 3.6

	Singular	Plural
N	dio = deo	dijelovi = delovi
Gen	dijela = dela	dijelova = delova
Dat	dijelu = delu	dijelovima = delovima
Acc	dio = deo	dijelove = delove

Voc	-	-
Inst	dijelom = delom	dijelovima = delovima
Loc	dijelu = delu	dijelovima = delovima

Family members

otac

For the noun *otac* (father), fleeting *-a-* is lost and the consonant *-t-* is dropped when case endings are added. In the singular vocative case and in all plural forms it undergoes consonant softening before *-e* (*c* changes to *č*):

Table 3.7

	Singular	Plural
N	otac	očevi
Gen	oca	očeva
Dat	ocu	očevima
Acc	oca	očeve
Voc	oče	očevi
Inst	ocem	očevima
Loc	ocu	očevima

kći, kćerka, ćerka

Each of these three nouns means "daughter". In Croatian, only *kći* is the standard form, although all three forms are used in spoken language. In Bosnian, Montenegrin and Serbian all three forms are used, with *kći* sounding bookish, *kćerka* neutral and *ćerka* having a colloquial touch.

Kći is part of the Third Declension for feminine nouns ending in a consonant (see Table 3.8); the only irregularity is the nominative case *kći*. Many native speakers use the accusative form *kćer* as the nominative case, which is grammatically wrong.

Kćerka and *ćerka* follow the standard Second Declension for feminine nouns ending in *-a* (see Table 3.1).

Table 3.8

	Singular	Plural
N	kći	kćeri
Gen	kćeri	kćeri
Dat	kćeri	kćerima
Acc	kćer	kćeri
Voc	kćeri	kćeri
Inst	kćeri	kćerima
Loc	kćeri	kćerima

dijete = dete

For the neuter noun *dijete* = *dete* (child) and a group of neuter nouns for the offspring of animals – *mače* (kitten), *kuče* (puppy), *prase* (piglet), *pile* (chick), *tele* (calf) etc – the root is extended by the consonant ***-t-*** before regular neuter case endings in the singular are added (see Table 3.9).

Table 3.9

	Singular	Plural
N	dijete = dete	djeca = deca
Gen	djeteta = deteta	djece = dece
Dat	djetetu = detetu	djeci = deci
Acc	dijete = dete	djecu = decu
Voc	dijete = dete	djeco = deco
Inst	djetetom = detetom	djecom = decom
Loc	djetetu = detetu	djeci = deci

The plural of ***dijete*** = ***dete*** is irregular – ***djeca*** = ***deca***; it declines as a standard feminine singular noun.

Vidio = video sam malu djecu = decu kako se igraju u parku.	I saw little children playing in the park.

When acting as the subject of a sentence, *djeca* = *deca* requires the verb to be in the plural form and all elements that describe it (adjectives and pronouns) to end in *-a*, agreeing with the final *-a* in *djeca* = *deca*.

Naša dobra djeca = deca idu u školu svaki dan.	Our good children go to school every day.

In compound tenses, the auxiliary verb is in the plural, the ending of the L-participle is *-a*, agreeing with the final *-a* in *djeca* = *deca*.

Dobra djeca = deca su išla u školu svaki dan.	Good children went to school every day.

mače

jaje

Before masculine plural case endings are added to nouns denoting the offspring of animals, the final *-e* is dropped and the infix ***-ić-*** is inserted (see Table 3.10):

mače	*mačići*	kittens
kuče	*kučići*	puppies
prase	*prasići*	piglets
pile	*pilići*	chicks
tele	*telići*	calves

Table 3.10

	Singular	Plural
N	mače	mačići
Gen	mačeta	mačića
Dat	mačetu	mačićima
Acc	mače	mačiće
Voc	mače	mačići
Inst	mačetom	mačićima
Loc	mačetu	mačićima

Somewhat logically, yet also weirdly, the **neuter noun *jaje*** (egg) belongs to this category in terms of the singular case endings (*-t-* is inserted: gen: *jajeta*, dat/loc: *jajetu*, instr: *jajetom*). In the plural, it remains neuter and is treated as a standard neuter noun (nom/gen/acc *jaja*, dat/inst/loc *jajima*)

Body parts

Nouns denoting body parts show irregularities in the formation of certain case forms. Some irregularities occur only in the genitive plural – *noga/nogu, ruka/ruku, prst/prstiju, nokat/noktiju, kost/kostiju* (see 3.3.12 "Genitive plural").

The nouns *leđa* (back), *usta* (mouth) and *grudi* (chest) only have plural forms (see 3.3.15).

In the singular, the nouns *oko* (eye) and *uho* = *uvo* (ear) are neuter and follow the standard neuter declension. In the plural, *oči* (eyes) and *uši* (ears) are feminine and irregular case endings are added (Table 3.11):

Table 3.11

	Plural OKO	Plural UHO
N	oči	uši
Gen	očiju	ušiju
Dat	očima	ušima
Acc	oči	uši
Voc	oči	uši
Inst	očima	ušima
Loc	očima	ušima

Nouns ending in *-lac*

Masculine nouns denoting human beings ending in *-lac* have this ending only in the nominative singular and *-laca* in the genitive plural.

mislilac – mislilaca	thinker
gledalac – gledalaca (bh-mont-srb)	viewer
prevodilac – prevodilaca (bh-mont-srb)	translator

In all other cases *-l-* changes to *-o-* and fleeting *-a-* is dropped:

Table 3.12

	Singular	Plural
N	gledalac	gledaoci
Gen	gledaoca	gledalaca
Dat	gledaocu	gledaocima
Acc	gledaoca	gledaoce
Voc	gledaoče	gledaoci
Inst	gledaocem	gledaocima
Loc	gledaocu	gledaocima

These nouns are mostly used in Bosnian, Montenegrin and Serbian. Croatian has a preference for using the *-telj* ending for these nouns:

gledatelj, prevoditelj

3.3.15 *Only plural nouns* (pluralia tantum)

Neuter

There are a few neuter nouns that only have the plural form (Table 3.13):

vrata	door
kola	car
leđa	back
usta	mouth

They are treated as neuter plural nouns:

Table 3.13

	Only plural		
N	vrata	usta	kola
Gen	vrata	usta	kola

	Only plural		
Dat	vratima	ustima	kolima
Acc	vrata	usta	kola
Voc	vrata	usta	kola
Inst	vratima	ustima	kolima
Loc	vratima	ustima	kolima

When acting as the subject of a sentence, these nouns require the verb and all elements that describe them to be in the plural form:

Naša vrata su vam uvek otvorena. — Our door is always open to you.
Vaša nova kola su stigla u garažu prošlog petka. — Your new car arrived at the garage last Friday.

Feminine

There are a few feminine nouns that have only the plural form. They are only plural nouns also in English:

pantalone (bh-mont-srb) or *hlače* (bh-hr)	trousers
farmerke (bh-mont-srb) or *traperice* (bh-hr) or *farmerice* (bh-hr)	jeans
naočale (bh-hr) or *naočare* (mont-srb)	glasses
makaze (bh-mont-srb) or *škare* (hr)	scissors

They have the standard plural forms of the Second Declension (see Table 3.2).

When acting as the subject of a sentence, these nouns require the verb and all elements that describe them to be in the plural form:

Jako mi se sviđaju tvoje nove sunčane naočale – naočare. Gdje = gde si ih kupila? — I like your new sunglasses a lot. Where did you buy them?

Chapter 4

Adjectives

Adjectives are words that describe nouns. In BCMS, they have to agree with the noun that they describe in gender, number and case. This means that an adjective that describes a masculine noun in the nominative singular must also be in the masculine form and nominative singular. For example:

veliki hotel and not *velikA hotel,* or *velikO hotel*	big hotel

If, for example, a feminine noun is in the accusative singular, then the adjective has to be in the feminine accusative singular:

hladna limunada (nom)	cold lemonade
Dajte mi jednU hladnU limunadU. (acc)	Please give me one cold lemonade.

Adjectives are listed in a dictionary in their masculine singular form, nominative case.

As in English, adjectives are placed directly before a noun that they describe, or with the verb *biti*, as part of a predicate:

velika kuća	a big house
Ova kuća je velika.	This house is big.

4.1 Descriptive and relational adjectives

By their meaning and form, adjectives can be divided into two large groups: descriptive and relational.

Descriptive adjectives, as their name suggests, describe a characteristic of a noun (*gladan* – hungry, *žut* – yellow, *hrabar* – brave). They can have both long and short forms (see 4.3).

DOI: 10.4324/9781003154525-4

Relational adjectives bear relation to another notion, like *planina – planinski* (mountain – mountainous), *inflacija – inflacioni* (inflation – inflationary), *godina – godišnji* (year – yearly). They only have long forms.

For suffixes and prefixes to form many adjectives, see 12.3 "Adjectives".

4.2 Gender

- Masculine forms of adjectives in the nominative singular end in a **consonant**, ***-o*** or ***-i***.
  star, mlad, nov, topao (or *stari, mladi, novi, topli* – for explanation see 4.3)
- Feminine forms of adjectives in the nominative singular always end in ***-a***.
- Neuter forms of adjectives in the nominative singular end either in ***-o*** or ***-e***.

masc	**fem**	**neut**	
velik	*velika*	*veliko*	big
nov	*nova*	*novo*	new
star	*stara*	*staro*	old
mlad	*mlada*	*mlado*	young
loš	*loša*	*loše*	bad

Adjectives whose masculine form ends in a soft consonant (*c, č, ć, đ, dž, j, lj, nj, š, ž*) have a neuter form that ends in *-e,* rather than *-o*:

loš	*loše*
svjež	*svježe* (Iyekavian)
= *svež*	*sveže* (Ekavian)*

*This difference (Iyekavian = Ekavian) will be marked by = in the rest of the chapter (see "How to Use This Book").

Many masculine forms adjectives end in ***-ar, -an*** or ***-ak***. The vowel ***-a*** in the final syllable is fleeting *-a-*, which disappears before the feminine ending *-a*, the neuter ending *-o*, or when case endings for all three genders are added (see 2.3.6):

dobar	*dobra*	*dobro*	good
gladan	*gladna*	*gladno*	hungry

N.B. Some of these adjectives undergo voicing assimilation after losing fleeting *-a-* (see 2.3.4 and 2.3.6):

težak	*teška*	*teško*	hard, difficult
nizak	*niska*	*nisko*	low
sladak	*slatka*	*slatko*	sweet

For adjectives that end in ***-ao*** or ***-eo***, the final *-o* regresses to *-l* and fleeting *-a-* is dropped before the feminine ending *-a*, the neuter ending *-o* or when case endings for all three genders are added (2.3.6 and 2.3.5):

topao	*topla*	*toplo*	warm
debeo	*debela*	*debelo*	fat
veseo	*vesela*	*veselo*	happy

There is a small group of adjectives that end in ***-stan***. They lose the *-ta-* segment when the feminine ending *-a*, the neuter ending *-o* or case endings for all three genders are added:

bolestan, bolesna, bolesno	ill, sick
mastan, masna, masno	greasy, fat
strastan, strasna, strasno	passionate
koristan, korisna, korisno	useful

4.3 Short–long forms

Descriptive masculine adjectives (in the nominative) have two forms – short and long forms (sometimes they are called indefinite and definite forms):

star or *stari*, *nov* or *novi*, *dobar* or *dobri*, *mlad* or *mladi*

This is a remnant of definite or indefinite markings of adjectives. In modern spoken language the distinction in the meaning between these two forms has almost disappeared.

The only rule that is still relevant is that the long (definite) forms can never be used predicatively (with the verb *biti*):

Ja sam mlad. correct
Ja sam mladi. incorrect
I am young.

On je umoran. correct
On je umorni. incorrect
He is tired.

4.4 Case endings

Adjectives have their separate declension. They do not have separate endings for the vocative case. To memorise adjectival case endings easily, see Table 4.2.

Case endings for feminine forms of adjectives in the singular (apart from the dat/loc) are identical to the case endings for feminine nouns ending in *-a* (Second Declension). Masculine and neuter singular case endings are different from the noun declension.

Table 4.1

	Masc sing	Fem sing	Neut sing	Mas pl	Fem pl	Neut pl
Nom	star**I**	star**A**	star**O**	star**I**	star**E**	star**A**
Gen	star**OG**	star**E**	star**OG**		star**IH**	
Dat	star**OM**	star**OJ**	star**OM**		star**IM**	
Acc	star star**OG** (animate)	star**U**	star**O**	star**E**		star**A**
Inst	star**IM**	star**OM**	star**IM**		star**IM**	
Loc	star**OM**	star**OJ**	star**OM**		star**IM**	

Notes on the table:

N.B.1 The masculine and neuter case endings *-og* and *-om* are ***-EG*** and ***-EM*** for masculine adjectives that end in a soft consonant (*c, č, ć, đ, dž, j, lj, nj, š, ž*) and neuter adjectives that end in *-e*.

N.B.2 In literary style, *-a* may be added to the genitive form *starog – staroga; -u* may be added to the dative form *starom – staromu* (hr) or *-e – starome* (bh-mont-srb); *-e* may be added to the locative form *starom – starome*. This does not change the meaning or usage, just lends a bookish touch and is very rarely used in the spoken language.

Learning tip

As this declension is also used for some pronouns, it is worthwhile condensing this long list of endings for the sake of committing it to memory easily:

Table 4.2

	Masc sing	Fem sing
Gen	**-G**	
Dat/Loc	**-M**	**-OJ**
Acc	**-G (anim)**	
Inst	**-IM**	

Notes on the table:

Where no ending is given in the feminine forms, adjectives decline as feminine nouns ending in *-a* (Second Declension). The choice of vowels (*-o-* or *-e-*) to connect an adjective root to the ending depends on whether the root ends in a soft consonant. (see N.B.1 after Table 4.1)

4.4.1 *Short form declension*

There is a different declension for short-form adjectives (descriptive, masculine and neuter singular). The case endings are identical to the masculine and neuter noun declension (First Declension).

Table 4.3

	Masc sing	Neut sing
N	star	staro
G	star**A**	star**A**
Dat	star**U**	star**U**
Acc	star star**A** (animate)	staro
Ins	star**IM**	star**IM**
Loc	star**U**	star**U**

This declension is very rarely used in Bosnia-Herzegovina, Montenegro and Serbia. The Croatian standard prescribes this declension, yet it is not used in the spoken language, as it sounds archaic and excessively bookish, as illustrated in these examples:

Vraćamo se sa stara trga (rather than *starog trga*).	We are on our way back from the old square.
Dao sam malo novca staru čovjeku na ulici (rather than *starome čovjeku*).	I have given a bit of money to an old man in the street.

4.5 Possessive adjectives (*Markov, Vesnin*)

Possessive adjectives describe belonging. They are derived from a personal name or a noun denoting a person. Being adjectives, they have to be in the same gender, number and case as the noun that they describe.

Ivanov brat	Ivan's brother
Ivanova mama	Ivan's mother
Vesnin brat	Vesna's brother
Vesnine sestre	Vesna's sisters

Possessive adjectives of masculine nouns are formed by adding ***-OV:***

Markov trg	Mark's square
predsjednikov auto = predsednikov auto	president's car

Masculine nouns that end in a soft consonant (*c, č, ć, đ, dž, j, lj, nj, š, ž*) and neuter nouns that end in *-e* add ***-EV:***

Miloševi roditelji	Miloš's parents
Sunčevi zraci	sun rays

Possessive adjectives of feminine nouns are formed by dropping *-a* and adding ***-IN:***

Vesna	*Vesnin*
Vesnin brat i Vesnina mama	Vesna's brother and Vesna's mother
prijateljica	*prijateljicin*
prijateljicin novi stan	(female) friend's new flat
Terezin koncert	Tereza's concert

N.B. This ending is also added to masculine nouns ending in *-a*, such as *tata, kolega, deda* (srb):

tatina sestra	dad's sister
kolegin sin	colleague's son

These endings can also be added to the nouns denoting animals, the names of celestial bodies or some inanimate nouns poetically:

oko sokolovo	eagle eye
Zemljina orbita	the Earth's orbit
Sunčevi zraci	Sun rays

As adjectives, they follow the adjectival declension (see Table 4.1).

To say "I was at Tereza's concert last night", the masculine ending for the locative of adjectives (*-om*) is added to the possessive adjective *Terezin*, to agree with *koncert*, a masculine noun which is in the locative case after the preposition *na:*

Bio sam na TerezINOM koncertU sinoć.

To say "I was in Tereza's house last night", the feminine ending for the locative of adjectives (*-oj*) is added to the possessive adjective *Terezin*, to agree with *kuća*, a feminine noun which is in the locative case after the preposition *u:*

Bio sam u TerezINOJ kući sinoć.

If the noun denoting a possessor needs to be qualified in some way, with a possessive pronoun or an adjective, then this construction cannot be used. In that case belonging is expressed by the genitive case:

"my brother's house" cannot be rendered as	*moj bratova kuća,*
but as	*kuća moga brata*
"my old friend's flat" cannot be rendered as	*moja stara prijateljicin stan*
but as	*stan moje stare prijateljice*

4.6 Comparison

To compare the properties of two or more concepts it is necessary to know how to form comparatives and superlatives of adjectives.

Comparatives and superlatives follow the adjectival declension (see Table 4.1).

Masculine and neuter forms add the ***-EG*** and ***-EM*** endings instead of *-og* and *-om* (e.g. nom – *stariji*, gen – *starijeg*, dat/loc – *starijem*, anim acc – *starijeg*, inst – *starijim*).

4.6.1 *Comparative*

Most comparatives are formed by adding the ***-IJI*** (masc), ***-IJA*** (fem) or ***-IJE*** (neut) endings to an adjective root. There are a few other endings and a few irregular comparatives – listed in this section.

An adjective root is derived from the female form of the adjective by dropping the *-a* ending:

gladn-a	*topl-a*	*strasn-a*
gladn+iji	*topl+iji*	*strasn+iji*

Comparatives can be formed in the following ways:

- by adding the ending ***-iji***, ***-ija***, ***-ije***
- for some adjectives ***-lji*** is added,
- for three adjectives ***-ši*** is added,
- in some adjectives *J*-changes are caused by adding ***-ji***
- **irregular** comparatives

- ***-IJI***

Most comparatives are formed by adding ***-iji, -ija*** or ***-ije*** to the adjective root:

nov	*noviji, novija, novije*	new – newer
star	*stariji, starija, starije*	old – older
bogat	*bogatiji . . .*	rich – richer
jeftin	*jeftiniji . . .*	cheap – cheaper
zanimljiv	*zanimljiviji . . .*	interesting – more interesting
svjež = svež	*svježiji = svežiji*	fresh – fresher

For adjectives that end in ***-an*** or ***-ar*** (those that have the so-called fleeting *-a-*), fleeting *-a-* disappears before the ending *-iji*:

gladan – gladniji	hungry – hungrier
modar – modriji	blue – bluer
vedar – vedriji	clear – clearer
umoran – umorniji	tired – more tired

For adjectives that end in ***-ao***, the final *-o* regresses to *-l* and fleeting *-a-* is dropped before the ending *-iji*:

topao – topliji	warm – warmer

For a small group of adjectives that end in ***-stan***, the *-ta-* segment is dropped before the ending *-iji* is added:

bolestan – bolesniji	sick – more sick
strastan – strasniji	passionate – more passionate
radostan – radosniji	happy – happier

- ***-LJI***

For adjectives that end in *-b, -p, -v, -h*, the ending ***-lji***, ***-lja***, ***-lje*** is added:

skup – skuplji	expensive – more expensive
grub – grublji	harsh – harsher, rough – rougher
suh – suvlji (bh-hr) or *suv – suvlji* (srb-mont)	dry – drier
glup – gluplji	stupid – more stupid

- ***-ŠI***

For three adjectives, the comparative is formed by adding ***-ši, -ša, -še*** :

lak – lakši, lakša, lakše	easy – easier
mek – mekši, mekša, mekše	soft – softer
lijep – ljepši = lep – lepši	beautiful – more beautiful

- ***-JI***

This suffix is blended with the last consonant of the adjective (see 2.3.3 "*J*-changes"). These are mostly one-syllable adjectives:

d changes to đ

mlad – mlađi	young – younger
tvrd – tvrđi	hard – harder
lud – luđi	crazy – crazier

g changes to ž

blag – blaži	mild – milder
drag – draži	dear – dearer
strog – stroži	strict – stricter
dug – duži	long – longer

h changes to š

tih – tiši	quiet – quieter

k changes to *č*

jak – jači	strong – stronger

For many adjectives that end in ***-ak***, ***-ek*** or ***-ok***, that entire ending is dropped before *-ji* is added and blended with the preceding consonant where necessary:

blizak – bliz + ji = bliži, bliža, bliže	near – nearer
kratak – krat + ji = kraći	short – shorter
dalek – dal + ji = dalji	far – further
visok – vis + ji = viši	high – higher
težak – tež + ji = teži	difficult – more difficult

Irregular comparatives

The most frequently used comparatives are irregular, just like in English (bad – worse; good – better):

dobar	*bolji, bolja, bolje*	good – better
loš	*gori, gora, gore*	bad – worse
mali	*manji, manja, manje*	small – smaller
veliki	*veći, veća, veće*	big – bigger

4.6.2 *Superlative*

Forming superlatives is easy: the prefix ***NAJ-*** is added to the comparative form of the adjective:

dobar – bolji – najbolji
skup – skuplji – najskuplji
nov – noviji – najnoviji
loš – gori – najgori

4.6.3 *How to say "than"*

For the comparison of two elements in a sentence, the following words are used:

od or ***nego (or no)***

1 comparative + *od* + the genitive, or

2 comparative + *nego* (or *no*) + the nominative

Crna Gora je manja od Srbije or *Crna Gora je manja nego Srbija* or *Crna Gora je manja no Srbija.*	Montenegro is smaller than Serbia.
On je stariji od mene. *On je stariji nego ja.*	He is older than me.
Dalmatinski pršut je bolji od istarskog.	Dalmatian prosciutto is better than Istrian prosciutto.
Dalmatinski pršut je bolji nego istarski.	
Crna je modernija od crvene ove godine.	Black is more fashionable than red this year.
Crna je modernija nego crvena ove godine.	

If the second element of comparison starts with a preposition, only *nego* can be used:

Jadransko more u Hrvatskoj je ljepše = lepše nego u Italiji.	The Adriatic Sea in Croatia is more beautiful than in Italy.

For the comparison of two verbs or phrases – see *nego što* and *no što* in "Compound Conjunctions", 10.2.

Chapter 5

Pronouns

Pronouns are predominantly short words that replace nouns and are used to make our speech or writing less repetitive. They act as a stand-in for nouns, as in:

Stipe je nov student. ***On*** *je iz Splita.*	Stipe is a new student. **He** is from Split.
Ana je dala Mariji pismo.	Ana has given a letter to Marija.
Ona joj ga *je dala.*	**She** has given **it** to **her**.

In BCMS there are seven categories of pronouns – personal, possessive, demonstrative, interrogative, relative, indefinite and reflexive.

Strictly speaking, the possessive, demonstrative, some interrogative and some indefinite pronouns are adjectives, as they stand in front of nouns and provide more information on them. However, these very same words can also stand on their own – replacing a noun – thus acting as pronouns.

Moreover, BCMS grammarians treat all of them as pronouns, subdividing them according to the function that they play in a sentence into adjective-like (adjectival) pronouns and noun-like (pronominal) pronouns. That is why they are all listed in this chapter.

5.1 Personal pronouns

	singular			plural	
1	***ja***	I	1	***mi***	we
2	***ti***	you	2	***vi***	you (pl and formal)
3	***on***	he	3	***oni***	they (masc)
	ona	she		***one***	they (fem)
	ono	it		***ona***	they (neut)

DOI: 10.4324/9781003154525-5

Both the third person singular and plural have forms for masculine, feminine and neuter gender.

The second person plural is used to address groups of people or a single individual politely and formally (like *vous* in French).

vi – plural	
Dragi prijatelji, vi ste uvijek (Iyekavian) = *uvek* (Ekavian)* *dobro došli u moju kuću.*	Dear friends, you are always welcome to my house.
vi – formal	
Gospodine, jeste li vi iz Engleske?	Sir, are you from England?

*This difference (Iyekavian = Ekavian) will be marked by = in the rest of the chapter (see "How to Use This Book").

When referring to nouns previously mentioned, the third person pronouns must have the gender and number of the noun that they replace. This is different from English, which uses the pronoun "it" to refer to things and "he" and "she" to refer to people. In BCMS a "house" is referred to as *ona* (she) because *kuća* is a feminine noun, a "child" is *ono* (it) because *dijete* = *dete* is a neuter noun, while a "bridge" is *on* (he) as the noun *most* is masculine.

Kupio sam novu kuću. Ona se nalazi u Kotoru.	I have bought a new house. It is located in Kotor.
Ana ima novi kaput. On je zelen.	Ana has a new coat. It is green.
Vidio sam = video sam vaše dijete = dete. Ono je trčalo po parku.	I saw your child. It was running in a park.

The third person plural *oni* refers to groups of masculine nouns or mixed groups; *one* refers to groups of feminine nouns only and *ona* to groups of neuter nouns only.

Tri mladića su na ulici. Oni su moji dobri prijatelji.	Three young men are in the street. They are my good friends.
Tri djevojke = devojke su u parku. One su moje koleginice – kolegice (hr).	Three young women are in the park. They are my colleagues.
Tri pisma su stigla iz Engleske. Ona te čekaju na stolu.	Three letters have arrived from England. They are waiting for you on the table.

It is not always necessary to use a personal pronoun when it acts as the subject of a sentence, as the verb itself has the forms of a person (see introduction to Chapter 7 – Verbs).

Personal pronouns decline and have unstressed (short) and stressed (long) forms – (see Tables 5.1 and 5.2). Short forms are enclitics, and as such have to be placed as the second unit in a sentence (see 11.2).

Short forms are used in most instances, apart from the following (in which the long forms must be used):

With prepositions:

Imam jedno pismo za ***njega.*** (*njega* – acc of *on*)	A have a letter for him.

With particles *a, i, ni* :

Dajte mu sok, a ***meni*** *dajte pivo.* (*mu* – short dat of *on; meni* – dat of *ja*)	One juice for him and one beer for me, please.
Ni ***njemu*** *ni* ***njoj*** *se ne sviđa film.* (*njemu* – dat of *on; njoj* – dat of *ona*)	Neither he nor she likes the movie.

Initial position in a sentence:

Njemu *sam dao pismo.* (*njemu* – dat of *on*)	I gave him the letter.

For emphasis:

Obratio se ***meni,*** *ne* ***tebi.*** (*meni* – dat of *ja; tebi* – dat of *ti*)	It is me, not you, that he spoke to.

Single word answer:

Koga si vidjela = videla? ***Nju.*** (*nju* – acc of *ona*)	Whom did you see? Her.

Declension singular

Table 5.1

	Nom.	Gen.	Dat.	Acc.	Inst.	Loc.
1 p	ja	mene, me	meni, mi	mene, me	mnom(e)	meni
2 p	ti	tebe, te	tebi, ti	tebe, te	tobom	tebi
3 p	on, ono	njega, ga	njemu, mu	njega, ga	njim(e)	njemu
	ona	nje, je	njoj, joj	nju, je, ju*	njom(e)	njoj

Notes on the table:

Instrumental forms can have an optional *-e* at the end; this does not change the meaning or usage. *On* and *ono* have the same forms in all cases apart from the nominative.

*The accusative of *ona* has three forms – the first is the longer form. The other two are shorter forms: *je* is used in most instances:

*Vidimo **je** u parku svaki dan.*	We see her in the park every day.
*Vidjeli = videli smo **je** u gradu u subotu.*	We saw her in the city on Saturday.

However, when placed next to the auxiliary verb *biti* to form the past tense in the third person singular (*je* or *nije*), the form *ju* must be used to avoid repetition:

*Ugledao **ju** je u parku.* He spotted her in the park.

(Otherwise, this sentence would incorrectly read: *Ugledao je je u parku*).

*Nije **ju** ugledao u parku.* He did not spot her in the park.

The locative does not have short forms because it cannot be used without prepositions.

Declension plural

Table 5.2

	Nom.	Gen.	Dat.	Acc.	Inst.	Loc.
1 p	mi	nas	nama, nam	nas	nama	nama
2 p	vi	vas	vama, vam	vas	vama	vama
3 p	oni, one, ona	njih, ih	njima, im	njih, ih	njima	njima

5.2 Possessive pronouns

As mentioned in the introduction, speaking in purely grammatical terms, possessive pronouns are adjectives, as they stand in front of nouns and describe them; they take their gender, number and case. They can also stand on their own, as English possessive pronouns do (mine, yours, his, hers, ours, yours, theirs) (Table 5.3.a and 5.3.b).

Table 5.3.a

	Singular			
	Masc	Fem	Neut	Engl.
1 p	*moj*	*moja*	*moje*	my, mine
2 p	*tvoj*	*tvoja*	*tvoje*	your, yours
3 p	*njegov*	*njegova*	*njegovo*	his, its
	njen - *njezin* (hr)	*njena* - *njezina* (hr)	*njeno* - *njezino* (hr)	her, hers or its

Table 5.3.b

	Plural			
	Masc	Fem	Neut	Engl.
1 p	*naš*	*naša*	*naše*	our, ours
2 p	*vaš*	*vaša*	*vaše*	your, yours
3 p	*njihov*	*njihova*	*njihovo*	their, theirs

Nominative singular forms of possessive pronouns in all three genders:

moj muž, moja žena, moje dijete = moje dete	my husband, my wife, my child
tvoj muž, tvoja žena, tvoje dijete = tvoje dete	your husband, your wife, your child

njegov muž, njegova žena, njegovo dijete = njegovo dete	his husband, his wife, his child
njen or *njezin* (hr) *muž, njena* (*njezina*) *žena, njeno* (*njezino*) *dijete = dete.*	her husband, her wife, her child

The third person singular of these pronouns has the forms of the possessor's gender (as in English) and the gender of the possessed noun (as in French) (this marking does not exist in English):

Mladen ima sestru i brata. ***Njegova*** *sestra je Ana,* ***njegov*** *brat je Ivan.*	Mladen has a sister and a brother. **His** sister is Ana, **his** brother is Ivan.
Vesna ima sestru i brata. ***Njena*** (or ***njezina***) *sestra je Milena,* ***njen*** (or ***njezin***) *brat je Marko.*	Vesna has a sister and a brother. **Her** sister is Milena, **her** brother is Marko.

Masculine and neuter forms marking the possessor in the third person singular are the same:

Ovo je moj otac (masc). ***Njegov*** *automobil je nov.*	This is my father. His car is new.
Ovo je moje predgrađe (neut). ***Njegov*** *položaj je divan.*	This is my suburb. Its location is wonderful.

There is only one form for the third person plural for all three genders:

Ovo su moji prijatelji. ***Njihova*** *kuća nije daleko.*	These are my male friends. Their house isn't far.
Ovo su moje prijateljice. ***Njihova*** *kuća je daleko.*	These are my female friends. Their house is far.
Ovo su moja djeca = deca. ***Njihova*** *kuća je blizu.*	These are my children. Their house is near.

The singular forms of feminine gender – *njen, njena, njeno* – have alternative forms – *njezin, njezina, njezino* – which are used in Croatian as the standard form. The pronoun *njen* is used in the spoken language in Croatia too.

Declension

Case endings of the standard adjectival declension are added to the possessive pronouns:

Table 5.4

	Masc sing	Fem sing	Neut sing	Masc Pl	Fem Pl	Neut Pl
N	no ending	**-A**	**-O** or **-E**	**-I**	**-E**	**-A**
G	**-OG**	**-E**	**-OG**		**-IH**	
Dat	**-OM**	**-OJ**	**-OM**		**-IM**	
Acc	no ending (inanm) **-OG** (anim)	**-U**	**-O**	**-E**	**-E**	**-A**
Ins	**-IM**	**-OM**	**-IM**		**-IM**	
Loc	**-OM**	**-OJ**	**-OM**		**-IM**	

Singular

Learning tips

To simplify the learning of these complicated declension tables, here are a few helpful tips (Tables 5.5 through 5.8). These endings are identical to the adjectival endings helpfully condensed in Table 4.2.

The ***-EG*** , ***-EM*** (rather than *-og, -om*) endings are added to masculine and neuter forms that end in a soft consonant (in this instance *-j* and *-š* – ***moj, tvoj, naš*** and ***vaš***).

Feminine forms always have the same endings as feminine adjectives. Therefore they are not separately listed in further text – for the endings see Table 5.4.

The standard endings for masculine and neuter adjectives ***-OG*** and ***-OM*** are added to ***njegov, njen (njezin)*** and ***njihov*** because they do not end in a soft consonant.

MOJ, MOJE my, mine
TVOJ, TVOJE your, yours

Table 5.5

	Masculine	Neuter	Masculine	Neuter
Nom	moj	moje	tvoj	tvoje
Gen	mojeg or MOG		tvojeg or TVOG	
Dat	mojem or MOM		tvojem or TVOM	
Acc	moj (inanim) mojeg or MOG (anim)	moje	tvoj (inanim) tvojeg – TVOG (anim)	tvoje
Inst	mojim		tvojim	
Loc	mojem or MOM		tvojem or TVOM	

Notes on the table:

N.B.1 Pronouns *moj, moje* and *tvoj, tvoje* have shortened forms *MOG* and *TVOG* (gen/anim acc) and *MOM* and *TVOM* (dat/loc). These forms are most frequently used in everyday language.

N.B.2 *Mojeg/mog* and *tvojeg/tvog* have optional forms *mojega/moga* and *tvojega/tvoga*; *mojem/mom* and *tvojem/tvom* have optional forms *mojemu/momu* (hr) or *mome* (bh-mont-srb) and *tvojemu/tvomu* (hr) or *tvome* (bh-mont-srb); these added vowels do not change the meaning or usage.

Ovo je novi automobil mojeg (or *mog*) *prijatelja.* (*mojeg* – masc gen sing)	This is my friend's new car.
Jesi li vidio = video moj novi kaput? (*moj* – inanimate masc acc sing)	Have you seen my new coat?
Da li ste upoznali mojeg (or mog) novog šefa? (*mojeg* – animate masc acc sing)	Have you met my new boss?

NAŠ, NAŠE our, ours
VAŠ, VAŠE your, yours

Table 5.6

	Masculine	Neuter	Masculine	Neuter
Nom	naš	naše	vaš	vaše
Gen	našEG		vašEG	
Dat	našEM		vašEM	
Acc	naš našEG (anim)	naše	vaš vašEG (anim)	vaše
Inst	našIM		vašIM	
Loc	našEM		vašEM	

Notes on the table:

N.B. *Našeg* and *vašeg* have optional forms *našega* and *vašega*; *našem* and *vašem* have optional forms *našemu* and *vašemu* (mostly in hr); these added vowels do not change the meaning or usage.

Dali smo poklon našem (or *našemu* in hr) *starom profesoru.* (*našem* – masc dat sing) — We have given a present to our old professor.

Jeste li putovali na more vašim novim autom? (*vašim* – masc inst sing) — Did you travel to the seaside by your new car?

NJEGOV, NJEGOVO — his
NJEN, NJENO (NJEZIN, NJEZINO) — her, hers

(Bosnian-Montenegrin-Serbian-colloquial Croatian)

Table 5.7

	Masculine	Neuter	Masculine	Neuter
Nom	njegov	njegovo	njen (njezin)	njeno (njezino)
Gen	njegovOG		njenOG (njezinog)	
Dat	njegovOM		njenOM (njezinom)	
Acc	njegov njegovOG (anim)	njegovo	njen (njezin) njenOG (njezinog) (anim)	njeno (njezino)
Inst	njegovIM		njenIM (njezinim)	
Loc	njegovOM		njenOM (njezinom)	

Notes on the table:

Njegovog, njenog and *njezinog* have optional forms *njegovoga, njenoga* and *njezinoga.*

Njegovom, njenom and *njezinom* have optional forms *njegovome, njenome* and *njezinome;* these forms do not change the meaning or usage.

Ovo je nova kuća njegovoga dobrog prijatelja. (*njegovoga* – masc gen sing) — This is a new house of his good friend.

Jesi li vidio = video njen (*njezin* in hr) *novi kaput?* (*njen* – inanim masc acc sing) — Have you seen her new coat?

Da li ste upoznali njegovoga novog šefa? (*njegovoga* – animate masc acc sing) — Have you met his new boss?

Njeno (*njezino* in hr) *dijete = dete je preslatko.* (*njeno* – nom neut sing) — Her child is very cute.

NJEGOV, NJEGOVO his
NJEZIN, NJEZINO her, hers

(educated Croatian)

Table 5.8

	Masculine	Neuter	Masculine	Neuter
Nom	njegov	njegovo	njezin	njezino
Gen	njegovA		njezinA	
Dat	njegovU		njezinU	
Acc	njegov njegovA (animate)	njegovo	njezin njezinA (animate)	njezino
Inst	njegovIM		njezinIM	
Loc	njegovU		njezinU	

There are two tables for *njegov, njegovo, njeno – njezino*; this is because a separate declension for these pronouns is now favoured in the Croatian standard – presented in the second table (this is short form adjectival declension – see Table 4.3). It is very rare to hear this usage in the spoken language; it sounds bookish and archaic:

Ovo je novi automobil njegova dobra prijatelja. (*njegova* – masc gen sing)	This is a new car of his good friend.
Jeste li upoznali njegova nova šefa? (*njegova* – animate masc acc sing)	Have you met his new boss?
Njezinu djetetu je dvije godine. (*njezinu* – dat neut sing)	Her child is 2 years old.

NJIHOV, NJIHOVO their, theirs

These pronouns follow the same declension as *njegov/njegovo* (see Table 5.7 and Table 5.8).

Plural

All possessive pronouns follow the standard adjectival declension for plural forms, and therefore they are not separately listed here (see Table 5.4).

5.2.1 Svoj – *possessive-reflexive pronoun for all persons*

The special possessive form *svoj, svoja, svoje* is used when a person or an object belongs to the subject of a sentence. It can be used for all persons singular and plural.

Marko i Jovan su prijatelji. Marko živi u svom stanu.	Marko and Jovan are friends. Marko lives in his flat.

This means that Marko lives in his own flat. If the same sentence was written:

Marko i Jovan su prijatelji. Marko živi u njegovom stanu.	(This would mean that Marko lives in Jovan's flat.)
***Ja** imam **svoju** knjigu, a **ona** ima **svoju**.*	I have my book, she has hers.

It would be incorrect to say (yet many native speakers do):

Ja** imam **moju** knjigu, a **ona** ima **njenu.

This possessive pronoun declines in the same way as *moj, tvoj* (as it ends in a *j*). It also has the contracted forms: *SVOG* (gen/anim acc) and *SVOM* (dat/loc) and the longer forms *svoga, svome, svomu* (hr) (see Table 5.5).

Tanja jako voli svojega (or *svoga*) *mlađeg brata.*	Tanja loves her younger brother a lot.
Zvonko ima djevojku = devojku i često ne spava u svojem (or *svom*) *stanu.*	Zvonko has a girlfriend and frequently does not sleep in his flat.

5.3 Demonstrative pronouns *ovaj – taj – onaj, ovakav, ovoliki*

These pronouns are used for pointing at something or someone. Unlike English, which has two sets of demonstrative pronouns – one set denoting objects or persons close to the speaker (this, these) and another set denoting objects or persons far from the speaker (that, those), BCMS has three sets:

1 ***Ovaj, ova, ovo*** – denoting objects or persons close to the speaker:

Ovaj telefon je moj.	This phone is mine.

2 ***Taj, ta, to*** – denoting objects or persons close to the listener:

Taj telefon koji držiš u ruci nije moj. That phone that you are holding in your hand isn't mine.

3 ***Onaj, ona, ono*** – denoting objects or persons far from both the speaker and the listener:

Onaj telefon u izlogu je isti kao tvoj. That phone in the shop window is the same as yours.

These pronouns can stand on their own:

Šta – *što* (hr) *je* ***ono*** *na putu?* What is that on the road?
O ***tome*** *možete pročitati u našim novinama.* You can read about that in our newspaper.

They can also act as adjectives, to describe a noun:

Ovaj *student je odličan,* ***onaj*** *je jako loš.* This student is excellent, that one is very bad.

Case endings of the standard adjectival declension are added to demonstrative pronouns (see Tables 4.1 and 4.2). The case endings are added to the roots: ***OV-*** , ***T-*** and ***ON-*** (all three sets follow the same pattern listed in Table 5.9):

Singular

Table 5.9

	Masculine	Neuter	Feminine
Nom	ov-AJ	ov-O	ov-A
Gen	ov-OG		ov-E
Dat	ov-OM		ov-OJ
Acc	ov-AJ ov-OG (anim)	ov-O	ov-U
Inst	ov-IM		ov-OM
Loc	ov-OM		ov-OJ

Notes on the table:

Ovog, tog, onog have optional forms *ovoga, toga, onoga* (gen/anim acc).

Ovom, tom, onom have optional forms *ovome, tome, onome* (dat/loc) or *ovomu, tomu, onomu* (dat hr); these added vowels do not change the meaning or usage (Table 5.10).

Plural

Table 5.10

	Masculine	Neuter	Feminine
Nom	ov-I	ov-A	ov-E
Gen		ov-IH	
Dat		ov-IM	
Acc	ov-E	ov-A	ov-E
Ins		ov-IM	
Loc		ov-IM	

Presentatives

Demonstrative pronouns can act as presentatives – they are used to present or introduce a person or thing or to bring them to the listener's attention.

The neuter singular forms (*ovo, to, ono*) are used as presentatives, irrespective of whether the noun phrase in the predicate is in the singular or the plural, which contrasts with English.

Ovo *je moj kaput.*	This is my coat.
Ovo *su moji kaputi.*	These are my coats.
To *je dobro sniženje.*	That is a good reduction.
To *su dobra sniženja.*	Those are good reductions.
Ono *je velika kuća.*	That is a large house.
Ono *su velike kuće.*	Those are large houses.

OVAKAV, TAKAV, ONAKAV
OVOLIKI, TOLIKI, ONOLIKI

There are another two sets of demonstrative pronouns based on the ***OV-***, ***T-*** and ***ON-*** roots; they follow the same logic of closeness and distance from the speaker or listener as described previously.

They reply to the questions *KAKAV* (what sort of) and *KOLIKI* (how big) and have the same case endings as *ovaj, taj, onaj* – (see Tables 5.9 and 5.10).

ovakav, ovakva, ovakvo	this kind (close to me), such
takav, takva, takvo	that kind (close to you), such
onakav, onakva, onakvo	that kind (over there), such

Ovakav stan nikad nisam vidio = video.	I have never seen such a flat (literally: this kind of flat).
Želite li ovakvu salatu (pointing at a salad in front of you) *ili onakvu?* (pointing at a salad served at another table).	Do you want this kind of salad or that one?
Takvo divno iznenađenje nisam očekivao.	I did not expect such a beautiful surprise.

ovoliki, ovolika, ovoliko	this big, of this size (close to me)
toliki, tolika, toliko	that big, of that size (close to you)
onoliki, onolika, onoliko	that big, of that size (over there)

Nikad nisam = nijesam (mont) *bio u ovolikom gradu.*	I have never been in such a big city as this one.
Vidjeli = videli smo tolikoga kita da nismo mogli očima vjerovati = verovati.	We saw such a big whale that we could not believe our eyes.

5.4 Interrogative pronouns *ko – tko, šta – što, koji, čiji, kakav, koliki*

As their name suggests, interrogative pronouns are used to ask questions:

ko (bh-mont-srb) – ***tko*** (hr) – who and ***šta*** (bh-mont-srb) – ***što*** (hr) – what

The pronoun for human beings *ko – tko* and the pronoun for things *šta – što* decline as follows (they do not have plural forms):

Table 5.11

	KO – TKO	ŠTA – ŠTO
Nom	ko – tko (hr)	šta – što (hr)
Gen	kog(a)	čega
Dat	kom(e) – kom(u) (hr)	čemu
Acc	kog(a)	šta – što (hr)
Inst	kim(e)	čim(e)
Loc	kom(e)	čemu

Notes on the table:

Kog and *kom* have optional forms *koga* and *kome* (*komu* dat – hr).

Kim and *čim* have optional forms *kime* and *čime*; these added vowels do not change the meaning or usage.

Ko – tko je ovo? (*ko* – animate nom)	Who is this?
Šta – što je to? (*šta* – inanimate nom)	What is that?
S kim želiš ići na odmor? (*kim* – animate inst)	With whom do you want to go on holiday?
O čemu mi hoćeš pričati? (bh-hr) (*čemu* – inanimate loc) – *O čemu hoćeš da mi pričaš?* (mont-srb)	What do you want to speak to me about?

In a compound tense:

ko – tko	requires the singular masculine L-participle:
Ko – tko je <u>bio</u> s vama na koncertu?	Who was at the concert with you?
šta – što	requires the singular neuter L-participle:
Šta – što se <u>desilo</u> juče(r)?	What happened yesterday?

Koji, koja, koje **which**

The interrogative pronoun *koji* (masc), *koja* (fem), *koje* (neut) agrees with the noun that it refers to in gender, number and case.

It declines in the same way as the possessive pronoun *moj* – for masculine and neuter singular forms.

All other forms – the feminine singular and all plural forms – follow the standard adjectival declension (see Table 5.4).

As in English, these pronouns can also be relative pronouns (5.5).

Table 5.12

<table>
<tr><th></th><th>KOJI (masc)</th><th>KOJE (neut)</th></tr>
<tr><td>Nom</td><td>koji</td><td>koje</td></tr>
<tr><td>Gen</td><td colspan="2">kojeg (kog)</td></tr>
<tr><td>Dat</td><td colspan="2">kojem (kom)</td></tr>
<tr><td>Acc</td><td>koji
kojeg (kog) (anim)</td><td>koje</td></tr>
<tr><td>Inst</td><td colspan="2">kojim</td></tr>
<tr><td>Loc</td><td colspan="2">kojem (kom)</td></tr>
</table>

Notes on the table:

N.B.1 In Montenegrin and Serbian, *kojeg* has the contracted form *kog; kojem* has the contracted form *kom.*

N.B.2 *Kojeg/kog* have optional forms *kojega, koga*; *kojem/kom* have optional forms *kojemu, kome*; these added vowels do not change the meaning or usage.

Koja ti prijateljica živi u Mostaru? (*koja* – nom fem sing)	Which (female) friend of yours lives in Mostar?
Koji prijatelj te danas zove na piće? (*koji* – nom masc sing)	Which (male) friend is inviting you out for drinks today?
O kojim knjigama govoriš? (*kojim* – loc fem pl)	Which books are you talking about?
Na kojem katu stanuješ? (hr-bh) (*kojem* – loc masc sing) – *Na kom spratu stanuješ?* (mont-srb)	On which floor do you live?

čiji, čija, čije **whose**

This interrogative pronoun agrees with the noun that it refers to in gender, number and case.

Its masculine and neuter singular forms decline in the same way as the interrogative pronoun *koji, koje* (see Table 5.12).

All other forms – the feminine singular and all plural forms – follow the standard adjectival declension (see Table 5.4).

As in English, these pronouns can also be relative pronouns (see 5.5).

Čiji je ovo kaput? (*čiji* – nom masc sing)	Whose coat is this?
O čijoj kući si juče(r) pričao? (*čijoj* – loc fem sing)	Whose house did you talk about yesterday?
Čijeg sina si upoznala? (*čijeg* – anim acc masc sing)	Whose son did you meet?
Čiju kćer ste upoznali? (*čiju* – fem acc sing)	Whose daughter did you meet?
Na čije koncerte najviše volite ići (bh-hr) – *volite da idete?* (mont-srb) (*čije* – acc masc pl)	Whose concerts do you like best to go to?

kakav, kakva, kakvo **what kind of**

This interrogative pronoun declines as a standard adjective (see Table 5.4), agreeing with the noun that it refers to in gender, number and case. It means "what kind of", "what sort of". In a majority of instances it is synonymous with *koji, koja, koje*.

Kakav stan planirate kupiti? (*kakav* – inanim masc acc sing)	What kind of flat are you planning to buy?
Kakvu limunadu želite popiti? (*kakvu* – fem acc sing)	What kind of lemonade would you like to drink?
O kakvom trošku se radi? (*kakvom* – masc loc sing)	What kind of expenditure is this about?
Kakve filmove najviše volite? (*kakve* – masc acc pl)	What kind of movies do you like best?

It can also be used in exclamations:

Kakvo predivno iznenađenje! (*kakvo* – neut nom sing)	What a great surprise!
Kakav užas! (*kakav* – masc nom sing)	Shock horror! (How terrible!)

koliki, kolika, koliko **how big**

This interrogative pronoun follows the standard adjectival declension (see Table 5.4). It agrees with the noun that it refers to in gender, number and case. It is used to ask questions about the size and quantity – "how large", "how big", "how much", "how many".

Kolika je tvoja kuća na moru? (*kolika* – fem nom sing)	How large is your house by the sea?
Koliki je park u centru grada? (*koliki* – masc nom sing)	How big is the park in the centre of the city?
Koliku ribu je upecao? (*koliku* – fem acc sing)	How big is the fish that he caught?

To ask questions about quantity BCMS uses the neuter form of this pronoun – *koliko:*

Koliko košta karta za Pulu?	How much does a ticket to Pula cost?

(In this usage *koliko* no longer functions as a pronoun, but as an adverb.)

5.5 Relative pronouns – *koji, što, čiji, kakav, ko*

Relative pronouns introduce an additional statement that provides more information about a noun, a pronoun or a noun phrase from the main sentence (or as grammarians put it – they introduce a relative clause which describes a noun, a pronoun or a noun phrase from the main sentence):

The thick green book which I mentioned yesterday is very good.
The English people about whom I told you yesterday are my friends.

koji, koja, koje

Pronouns *koji, koja, koje* are used to introduce most relative clauses.

They have the same form and follow the same declension as the interrogative pronouns *koji, koja, koje* (Table 5.12); they agree with the noun from the main sentence which they describe in gender and number. The case ending depends on the role that the relative pronoun plays in the clause that it introduces:

Žena koju ste upoznali u Rovinju je moja najbolja prijateljica. (*koju* – fem acc sing)	The woman (whom) you met in Rovinj is my best friend.

Taj mladi čovjek = čovek kojeg(a) ste upoznali je moj brat. (*kojeg* – anim masc acc sing)	The young man (whom) you met is my brother.
Kaput koji ste kupili je moderan. (*koji* – inanim masc acc sing)	The coat (which) you bought is fashionable.
Taj mladi kardiolog koji te je pregledao je iz Niša. (*koji* – masc nom sing)	The young cardiologist who examined you is from Niš.
Knjige o kojima ste govorili su sjajne. (*kojima* – fem loc pl)	The books (that) you spoke about are brilliant.

N.B. In English, a relative pronoun can be omitted (noted in the above examples with the relative pronoun in English in brackets); **it cannot be omitted in BCMS.**

što

The relative pronoun *što* **is used to refer to the entire statement** from the preceding sentence:

Let za Beograd je kasnio dva sata, što nam je pokvarilo planove.	The flight to Belgrade was delayed two hours, which ruined our plans.

Acting as a relative pronoun, *što* is always **used after pronouns *ovo, to, ono, sve, nešto*:**

Ono što znaš o meni nije tačno – točno (hr).	What you know about me is not true.
Kod nas kupite sve što vam treba za kuću.	Everything that you need for the home you can buy in our shop.
To što si mi ispričao o njima je zaista čudno.	What you have told me about them is really strange.
Brine me nešto što si mi rekao jutros.	I am worried about something that you told me this morning.

In this usage *što* may be in a case form other than the nominative and is declined in the same way as the interrogative pronoun *šta – što* (see Table 5.11):

Voda je nešto bez čega se ne može živjeti = živeti.	Water is something one cannot live without. (literally – Water is something without which one cannot live.)

N.B. In this example the preposition *bez* requires *što* to be in the genitive case – *čega*.

The relative pronoun *što* can also be used to introduce a relative clause instead of the relative pronoun *koji, koja, koje*. It has this one form for all three genders, singular and plural:

Žene koje šetaju glavnim trgom su iz Engleske, or *Žene što šetaju glavnim trgom su iz Engleske.*	The women (who are) walking in the main square are from England.

čiji, čija, čije

This relative pronoun is identical to the interrogative pronoun *čiji, čija, čije*. Its gender, number and case endings depend on the role that the relative pronoun plays in the clause that it introduces:

Ovo je žena čiju majku ste upoznali juče(r). (*čiju* – fem acc sing)	This is the woman whose mother you met yesterday.
Ovo je gospodin čiju ste ženu upoznali juče(r). (*čiju* – fem acc sing)	This is the gentleman whose mother you met yesterday.
Ovo je dečko čijeg brata ste upoznali u Ulcinju. (*čijeg* – anim masc acc sing)	This is the young man whose brother you met in Ulcinj.
Ovo je dečko čije ste roditelje upoznali u Ulcinju. (*čije* – masc acc pl)	This is the young man whose parents you met in Ulcinj.

kakav, kakva, kakvo

This relative pronoun is identical to the interrogative pronoun *kakav, kakva, kakvo*. It agrees with the noun in the main sentence which it describes in gender and number. The case ending depends on the role that the relative pronoun plays in the clause that it introduces:

On je kolega kakvog svi žele. (*kakvog* – anim masc acc sing)	Everyone wants that kind of colleague (male). (literally: He is the colleague whose sort everybody wants).
Ona je koleginica – kolegica (hr) *kakvu svi žele.* (*kakvu* – fem acc sing)	Everyone wants that kind of colleague (female).
To je dijete = dete o kakvom se samo sanja. (*kakvom* – neut loc sing)	That is a child you can only dream about (literally: That is a child about whose sort one dreams about).

ko – tko

This relative pronoun is used to refer to a masculine singular pronoun from the main clause. It declines in the same way as the interrogative pronoun *ko – tko* (hr).

Ovo vam govori <u>*neko ko*</u> or *netko tko* (hr) *vam je pravi prijatelj* (*ko - tko* nom).	Someone who is your real friend is telling you this.
To se može dobiti samo od <u>*nekoga koga*</u> *dobro poznajete* (*koga* - acc).	One can get this only from somebody whom you know very well.

5.6 Indefinite pronouns

Indefinite pronouns (Table 5.13) are created from interrogative pronouns *ko – tko* (hr)*; šta – što* (hr)*; koji; čiji* and *kakav* by adding the following prefixes:

- the prefix ***NE-*** has the meaning of "some" (someone, something, some, somebody's and some kind of);
- the prefix ***NI-*** has the meaning of "no" (no one, nothing, not a single one, nobody's and no kind of);
- the prefix ***SVA-*** has the meaning of "every" (everyone, everything, every single one, everybody's and every kind of);
- the prefix ***I-*** has the meaning of "any at all" (anyone at all, anything at all, any single one, anybody's and any kind of).

N.B. The *I*-prefixed pronouns are used mostly in interrogative sentences and are not used with another negation, as would be the case with English pronouns "any", "anything", "anybody's". In English, they are used to avoid multiple negatives, which in contrast are mandatory in BCMS (see 11.5).

Table 5.13

ko – tko (hr) (anim) who	**šta – što** (hr) (inanim) what	**koji, koja, koje** which	**čiji, čija, čije** whose	**kakav, kakva, kakvo** what kind of
neko - netko (hr) someone	**nešto** something	**neki, neka, neko** some	**nečiji, nečija, nečije** someone's	**nekakav, nekakva, nekakvo** some kind of

niko - nitko (hr) no one	**ništa** nothing	**nijedan, nijedna, nijedno** not a single one	**ničiji, ničija, ničije** no one's	**nikakav, nikakva, nikakvo** no kind of
svako – svatko (hr) everyone	**svašta** everything	**svaki, svaka, svako** every single one	**svačiji, svačija, svačije** everyone's	**svakakav, svakakva, svakakvo** all kinds of
iko - itko (hr) anyone at all	**išta** anything at all	**ijedan, ijedna, ijedno** any single one	**ičiji, ičija, ičije** anyone's	**ikakav, ikakva, ikakvo** any kind of

The pronouns derived from *ko – tko* are declined in the same way as *ko – tko* (see Table 5.11). Note that the Croatian version – *netko, nitko, svatko and itko* – has the middle letter *-t-* only in the nominative case. In other cases it disappears:

neTko – nekoga, nekom, nekim
niTko – nikoga, nikom
svaTko – svakoga, svakom, svakim
iTko – ikoga, ikom, ikim

Bosnian, Montenegrin and Serbian use the version without the middle *-t-* in all case forms.

The pronouns derived from *šta – što* (hr) are declined in the same way as *šta – što* (see Table 5.11).

The pronouns *neki, nijedan, svaki* and *ijedan* are declined as adjectives and agree with the noun to which they refer in gender, number and case (see Table 5.4).

The pronouns derived from *čiji – nečiji, ničiji, svačiji* and *ičiji* – are declined as adjectives ending in a soft consonant (see Table 5.4) and agree with the noun to which they refer in gender, number and case.

The pronouns derived from *kakav* are declined in the same way as *kakav, kakva, kakvo* (see Table 5.4) and agree with the noun to which they refer in gender, number and case.

Pronouns *niko – nitko* (hr), *ništa, nijedan, ničiji, nikakav* are negative and are always used with a negated verb, to follow the multiple negation rule (see 11.5):

Jeste li sreli nekoga na odmoru? (*nekoga* – acc of *neko – netko*)	Did you meet someone on holiday?
Ne, nismo sreli nikoga. (*nikoga* – acc of *niko – nitko*)	No, we met no one.
Niko – nitko (hr) *nije govorio naš jezik.* (*niko – nitko* – nom)	No one spoke our language.
Ništa nismo mogli razumjeti = *razumeti.* (*ništa* – acc)	We understood nothing.
Nije to ničija greška. (*ničija* – fem nom sing)	That is no one's fault.
Svako voli da govori svoj jezik. (bh-mont-srb) (*svako* – nom) *Svatko voli govoriti svoj jezik.* (hr)	Everyone likes to speak one's own language.
Znaš li ijednu riječ = *reč na engleskom?* (*ijednu* – fem acc sing)	Do you know a single word in English?
Znam svakakve izraze na francuskom, (*svakakve* – masc acc pl)	I know all kinds of expressions in French,
ali nikakve na engleskom. (*nikakve* – masc acc pl)	. . . but nothing (literally: no kind) in English.
Neki ljudi teško uče strane jezike. (*neki* – masc nom pl)	Some people learn foreign languages with difficulty.
Nikoga ne treba kriviti za to. (*nikoga* – acc of *niko – nitko*)	No one should be blamed for it.

5.6.1 Emphasised indefinite pronouns (whatever, whoever)

Emphasised indefinite pronouns are created from interrogative pronouns *ko – tko* (hr)*; šta – što* (hr)*; koji; čiji* and *kakav* in three ways, with:

the particle ***BILO*** before a pronoun,
the particle ***MA*** before a pronoun, or
the particle ***GOD*** after a pronoun

These particles are synonymous – they all mean:

bilo ko – tko	whoever
bilo šta – što	whatever
bilo koji	whichever
bilo čiji	no matter whose
bilo kakav	whatever sort of

They all decline as interrogative pronouns. *Ko – tko* refer to human beings, *šta – što* to things; *koji, čiji* and *kakav* agree with the noun to which they refer in gender, number and case ending.

Bilo and ***ma*** are placed in front of the interrogative pronouns:

bilo šta – bilo što
bilo ko – bilo tko
bilo koji, bilo koja, bilo koje
bilo čiji, bilo čija, bilo čije
bilo kakav, bilo kakva, bilo kakvo

ma šta – ma što
ma ko – ma tko
ma koji, ma koja, ma koje
ma čiji, ma čija, ma čije
ma kakav, ma kakva, ma kakvo

Bilo šta – bilo što (hr) *mi kažeš, ništa ti ne vjerujem = verujem.* (*bilo šta* – inanim acc)	Whatever you tell me I do not believe you anything.
Ma kakav poklon da joj kupimo, neće joj se dopasti. (*ma kakav* – masc inanim acc sing)	Whatever (kind of) present we buy her, she will not like it.
Roditelji će ti dati novac bilo koju kuću da kupiš. (*bilo koju* – fem acc sing)	Your parents will give you money whatever house you buy.
Ma kakvi da su, oni su ipak tvoji prijatelji. (*ma kakvi* – masc nom pl)	Whatever they are like, they are still your friends.
Njoj je dosadno o bilo čemu da joj pričaš. (*bilo čemu* – loc of *bilo šta*)	She is bored whatever you talk to her about.

God is placed after the interrogative pronouns:

šta god – što god
ko god – tko god
koji god, koja god, koje god
čiji god, čija god, čije god
kakav god, kakva god, kakvo god

N.B These same particles can be added to the adverbs *kada* (when), *gdje = gde* (where), *kuda – kamo* (hr) (where to), *kako* (how) and *koliko* (how much) to give the same spectrum of meanings – "wherever", "whenever", "however", "however much" (see Table 8.3).

5.7 Reflexive pronoun *sebe (se)*

The reflexive pronoun *sebe* is used with reflexive verbs (see 7.3.7) in its accusative enclitic form *se* – and translates into English as "oneself" (covers all English -self variations – myself, yourself, herself, himself, itself, ourselves, themselves):

Brijem **se** *svaki dan.*	I shave (myself) every day.
Povrijedila = povredila **se** *na poslu.*	She got hurt (hurt herself) at work.

Its long forms are used with prepositions, at the start of a sentence or a clause, or for emphasis in all cases (this pronoun does not have the nominative case form):

Gen: ***SEBE, SE***

Oko sebe je spazio mnogo ljudi.	He spotted a lot of people around himself.

Dat: ***SEBI, SI***

Sebi je kupio novi telefon.	He bought himself a new telephone, or
Kupio si je novi telefon.	

Acc: ***SEBE, SE***

Pogledao je sebe u ogledalu.	He looked at himself in the mirror, or
Pogledao se u ogledalu.	

Instr: ***SOBOM***

Sa sobom je poveo majku.	He took his mother with him.

Loc: ***SEBI***

O sebi je čula mnogo divnih stvari.	She has heard a lot of nice things about her(self).

Se is an enclitic, and as such it needs to follow strict word order (see 11.2 "Enclitics").

5.8 Pronoun *sav, sva, sve* (all, whole)

The pronoun *sav, sva, sve* means "all" or "whole" and agrees with the noun that it refers to in gender, number and case. It declines in the same way as adjectives, with the masculine form *sav* and the neuter form *sve* declining as adjectives that end in a soft consonant (Tables 5.14 and 5.15):

Singular

Table 5.14

	Masculine	Feminine	Neuter
N	**sav**	**sva**	**sve**
Gen	sveg	sve	sveg
Dat	svem	svoj	svem
Acc	sav, sveg (anim)	svu	sve
Ins	svim	svom	svim
Loc	svem	svoj	svem

Sveg, svem and svim have optional forms *svega, svemu and svime*; these added vowels do not change the meaning or usage.

Plural

Table 5.15

	Masculine	Feminine	Neuter
N	**svi**	**sve**	**sva**
Gen		svih	
Dat		svim	
Acc	sve	sve	sva
Inst		svim	
Loc		svim	

The most frequently used forms are the nominative neuter singular ***SVE*** (everything) and the nominative masculine plural ***SVI*** (everyone, all). They can describe a noun or a pronoun or can stand on their own.

Examples:

Jeste li uradili svu domaću zadaću (bh-hr) – *sav domaći zadatak* (mont-srb)? (*svu* – fem acc sing; *sav* – masc acc sing)	Have you done all your homework?
Svi prijatelji koji me vole su došli na moj rođendan. (*svi* – masc nom pl)	All my friends who love me came to my birthday.
Svi su došli na moj rođendan.	Everyone came to my birthday.
Neki ljudi imaju sve, ali nisu sretni (bh-hr) – *srećni* (mont-srb). (*sve* - neut acc sing)	Some people have everything but are not happy.
Sve vrijeme = vreme na odmoru je padala kiša. (*sve* – neut nom sing)	It was raining all the time during our holiday.

N.B. In the spoken language *svo vrijeme* is sometimes used. This is wrong, as the neuter form *svo* does not exist in any of the BCMS standards.

5.9 Pronoun *sam, sama, samo*

Sam, sama, samo can function as a pronoun or as an adjective; it declines as an adjective (see Table 4.1) and agrees with the noun or pronoun to which is refers.

As a pronoun it can mean "alone, independently, without anybody's help":

Moj tata je sam popravio auto.	My father repaired the car by himself.
Sam svoj majstor	one's own handyman – the name of a popular DIY magazine and website
Jeste li sami uradili ovaj test, ili vam je neko – netko (hr) *pomogao?*	Did you do the test by yourself, or did someone help you?

It is also used to emphasise the reflexive pronoun ***SEBE*** :

Uplašio sam se samog sebe kad sam pogledao u ogledalo.	I got frightened of myself when I looked in the mirror.
Samoj sebi je dosadila pričama o razvodu.	She bored herself talking about her divorce.
Upoznaj sebe samoga.	*Nosce te ipsum* (Latin) – Know thyself.

It is also used to place a special emphasis on a noun where English would use one of the -self pronouns:

Sam Bog zna koliko te volim.	God himself knows how much I love you.
Na premijeri smo upoznali samu filmsku divu.	We met the movie star herself at the premiere.

This word also exists **as an adjective,** meaning "alone", "by oneself":

Svakog dana ona je sama kod kuće.	She is at home alone every day.
Marko i njegova žena su sami na odmoru.	Marko and his wife are on holiday on their own.

Chapter 6

Numerals

6.1 Cardinal numbers

Cardinal numbers from 1 to 10:

1 *jedan, jedna, jedno*
2 *dva, dvije* (Iyekavian) = *dve* (Ekavian)*
3 *tri*
4 *četiri*
5 *pet*
6 *šest*
7 *sedam*
8 *osam*
9 *devet*
10 *deset*

*This difference (Iyekavian = Ekavian) will be marked by = in the rest of the chapter (see "How to Use This Book").

Number one – *jedan, jedna, jedno*

Number one behaves as an adjective and takes the same gender, number and case as the noun which it describes.

jedan gospodin, jedna žena, jedno pismo	one gentleman, one woman, one letter
*Imam **jednog** brata.* (masc acc sing anim)	I have one brother.
*Upoznao sam **jednu** ženu u Varaždinu.* (fem acc sing)	I met a woman in Varaždin.
*Napisala je sve u **jednom** pismu.* (neut loc sing)	She wrote everything in one letter.

DOI: 10.4324/9781003154525-6

Number one is also used to describe a noun as indefinite, when the indefinite article (a, an) is used in English. Also, the indefinite pronoun *neki, neka, neko* (some) (see 5.6 "Indefinite Pronouns") may be used in BCMS as an equivalent to the indefinite article in English.

Jedan mladić te je tražio jutros.	A young man was looking for you this morning.
Neki mladić te je tražio jutros.	Some young man was looking for you this morning.

Number one also has plural forms, used with plural-only nouns (see 3.3.15):

Kada se jedna vrata zatvore, druga se otvore. (*jedna* – nom neut pl)	Once one door closes, another one opens.

Number two – *dva, dvije = dve*

Dva is used with nouns of masculine and neuter gender, *dvije = dve* with nouns of feminine gender (Table 6.1):

dva muškarca	two men
dvije žene = dve žene	two women
dva pisma	two letters

It declines in the following way, although in the modern spoken language this number is used mostly in the nominative case.

Table 6.1

	Masc/neut	Fem.
Nom	**dva**	**dvije = dve**
Gen	dvaju	dviju = dveju
Acc	dva	dvije = dve
Dat/Inst/Loc	dvama	dvjema = dvema

It is much more frequent to hear:

Dobio sam ove boce vina od dva vinara.	I received these bottles of wine from two wine merchants.

Otišao sam na piće sa dvije = dve prijateljice.	I went for a drink with two female friends.
Napisala je sve u dva pisma.	She wrote everything in two letters.

Than:

Dobio sam ove boce vina od dvaju vinara.
Otišao sam na piće sa dvjema = dvema prijateljicama.
Napisala je sve u dvama pismima.

(This is bookish and avoided in the spoken language.)

Both: ***oba, obje = obe***

(or colloquially ***obadva, obadvije = obadve)***

Oba refers to masculine and neuter nouns, ***obje = obe*** to feminine nouns.

Trenutno imam dva posla. Oba su mi važna.	I currently have two jobs. Both are important to me.
Imam dvije = dve prijateljice u Podgorici. Obje = obe su mi drage.	I have two (female) friends in Podgorica. Both are dear to me.

This form has its own declension (Table 6.2). The genitive forms are almost never used, but the dat/instr/loc forms are used in everyday communication, hence they are listed here:

Table 6.2

	Masc/neut	Fem.
Nom	**oba**	**obje = obe**
Gen	obaju	obiju = obeju
Acc	oba	obje = obe
Dat/Inst/Loc	oboma	objema = obema

Moja mama i sestra idu u Bosnu. Objema = obema sam rekao da se jave kad stignu.	My mother and sister are going to Bosnia. I told them both to call me when they arrive.
Tvoja dva brata su na Jahorini. Jesi li oboma rekao da sam i ja tamo?	Your two brothers are on Mt Jahorina. Have you told both of them that I am there too?

Numbers three and four – have the same form for all three genders and decline in the following way, although in the modern spoken language these numbers are almost always used only in the nominative case (Table 6.3).

Table 6.3

Nom	tri	četiri
Gen	triju	četiriju
Acc	tri	četiri
Dat/Inst/Loc	trima	četirima

tri or *četiri muškarca* three or four men
tri or *četiri žene* three or four women
tri or *četiri pisma* three or four letters

Numbers five and above are unchangeable, that is, they have only one form for all three genders and all cases.

Cardinal numbers 11–19:

These numbers are formed from the cardinal numbers 1–9 with the addition of ***-naest*** (note the slight spelling changes for 11, 14 and 16):

11 *jedanaest*
12 *dvanaest*
13 *trinaest*
14 *četrnaest*
15 *petnaest*
16 *šesnaest*
17 *sedamnaest*
18 *osamnaest*
19 *devetnaest*

Cardinal numbers 20, 30 . . . 90

These numbers are formed from the cardinal numbers 2–9 with the addition of ***deset*** (note the slight spelling changes for 40, 50, 60 and 90):

20 *dvadeset*
30 *trideset*
40 *četrdeset*

50 *pedeset*
60 *šezdeset*
70 *sedamdeset*
80 *osamdeset*
90 *devedeset*

To form numbers above 20, numerals are simply combined:

21 *dvadeset jedan, dvadeset jedna, dvadeset jedno*
32 *trideset dva, trideset dvije = dve*
44 *četrdeset četiri*
83 *osamdeset tri*
99 *devedeset devet*

Numbers above 100

100 *sto*
200 *dvjesto = dvesto*
300 *tristo*
400 *četiristo*
500 *petsto*
600 *šeststo*
700 *sedamsto*
800 *osamsto*
900 *devetsto*

Numbers 200 and 300 have alternative versions: *dvjesta = dvesta* and *trista*, which are seen as Montenegrin and Serbian, yet the Croatian national currency banknote for 200 kuna has *dvjesta kuna* printed on it.

There is another way of forming these numbers, using the feminine noun *stotina* – which also means a "hundred".

jedna stotina
dvije = dve stotine
tri stotine
četiri stotine
pet stotina
šest stotina
sedam stotina
osam stotina
devet stotina

To say "Hundreds of people", the word *stotina* in the plural is used: *Stotine ljudi.*

Thousand

hiljada (bh-mont-srb) or *tisuća* (hr)

Hiljada and *tisuća* meaning "one thousand" are used in their accusative forms – *hiljadu* or *tisuću:*

1.999 *hiljadu* or *tisuću* (hr) *devetsto devedeset devet*

To say "two, three, four, five or more thousand", *hiljada* and *tisuća* agree with numbers as feminine nouns (see 6.1.1 "Cardinal Numbers' Agreement with Nouns, Pronouns and Adjectives"):

2.019 *dvije hiljade devetnaest* = *dve hiljade devetnaest*

or *dvije tisuće devetnaest* (hr)

5.450 *pet hiljada* or *tisuća* (hr) *četiristo pedeset*

Million, billion, trillion

one million	*jedan milion* or *jedan milijun* (hr)
one billion	*jedna milijarda*
one trillion	*jedan trilion* or *jedan trilijun* (hr)

Milion or *milijun*, *trilion* or *trilijun* combine with numbers as masculine nouns; *milijarda* as a feminine noun (see 6.1.1 "Cardinal Numbers Agreement with Nouns, Pronouns and Adjectives").

N.B. A full stop, rather than a comma, is used to separate thousands from lower numbers in BCMS. Commas are used to separate the whole number from decimals – this is opposite to how numbers are written in English.

6.1.1 *Cardinal numbers' agreement with nouns, pronouns and adjectives*

In English, number one is followed by a noun in the singular; numbers two and above are followed by nouns in the plural:

one book, two books, a thousand books

In BCMS, using numbers with nouns, pronouns and adjectives is more complex.

Number one + nouns

The number *jedan, jedna, jedno* behaves as an adjective; it takes the same gender, number and case as the noun which it describes:

jedan grad
jedna škola
jedno pismo

Numbers two, three and four + nouns

Nouns that follow these three numbers have to be in a form identical to the genitive singular case:

dva gradA	(masc)
tri pismA	(neut)
četiri školE	(fem)
dvije tisućE (hr)	(fem)
tri hiljadE (bh-mont-srb)	(fem)

Adjectives and pronouns that refer to the noun have the same ending as the noun:

dva prijateljA – mojA dobrA dva prijateljA	my two good friends
četiri prijateljicE – ovE odanE četiri prijateljicE	these four loyal (female) friends

Numbers five to 20 are followed by the genitive plural:

pet gradova
trinaest žena
dvadeset pisama
deset hiljada or *tisuća* (hr)

Adjectives and pronouns that refer to the noun also have to be in the genitive plural:

mojih pet dobrih prijatelja	my five good friends
ovih odanih šest prijateljica	these six loyal female friends

Numbers above 20

A noun agrees with the last number of the numeral, following the same rule as described earlier for numbers one, two/three/four and above:

Nouns after *jedan, jedna, jedno* are always in the singular:

21 *dvadeset jedna žena*
51 *pedeset jedan film*

Nouns after *dva, tri* and *četiri* are always in the form identical to the genitive singular:

32 *trideset dva gradA*
52 *pedeset dvije = dve ženE*
44 *četrdeset četiri školE*
83 *osamdeset tri pismA*

Nouns after *pet, šest, sedam, osam* and *devet* are always in the genitive plural:

25 *dvadeset pet gradOVA*
37 *trideset sedam ženA*
99 *devedest devet pisAMA*

Numbers 30, 40, 50, 60, 70, 80 and 90 are followed by a noun in the genitive plural:

30 *gradOVA*
50 *školA*
70 *pisAMA*

Numbers *sto, hiljada* or *tisuća* (hr), *milion* or *milijun* (hr), *milijarda* and *trilion* or *trilijun* (hr) are followed by nouns in the genitive plural:

tisuću gradova
hiljadu škola
Dvadeset hiljada or *tisuća* (hr) *milja pod morem* (Jules Verne's *20,000 Leagues under the Sea*)
milion or *milijun* (hr) *pisama*

6.2 Ordinal numbers

Ordinal numbers are not used for counting but for placing things in a particular order. In BCMS, they are all adjectives and therefore agree with the noun that they describe in number, case and gender. As adjectives they follow the adjectival declension (see Table 4.1).

They are formed in the following way:

Ordinal numbers 1–4 have separate forms (they are not formed from cardinal numbers by the addition of simple endings):

first	*prvi, prva, prvo*
second	*drugi, druga, drugo*
third	*treći, treća, treće*
fourth	*četvrti, četvrta, četvrto*

Other ordinal numbers are formed by adding ***-i*** (masc), ***-a*** (fem) and ***-o*** (neut) to cardinal numbers:

fifth	*peti, peta, peto*
sixth	*šesti, šesta, šesto*
seventh	*sedmi, sedma, sedmo*
eighth	*osmi, osma, osmo*
ninth	*deveti, deveta, deveto*
tenth	*deseti, deseta, deseto*
twelfth	*dvanaesti . . .*

Note the spelling of *sedmi* and *osmi*.

Ordinal numbers for *sto, hiljada* or *tisuća* (hr), *milion* or *milijun* (hr) are formed in the following way:

sto	*stoti, stota, stoto*
hiljada	*hiljaditi, hiljadita, hiljadito*
tisuća	*tisućiti, tisućita, tisućito*
milion	*milioniti, milionita, milionito*
milijun	*milijuniti, milijunita, milijunito*

In a compound number, only the last numeral is ordinal:

1,814th	*hiljadu* or *tisuću* (hr) *osamsto četrnaesti*

6.3 Collective numbers *-oro* (two people, three people)

These numbers refer to groups consisting of both men and women or groups of children.

Collective numbers *-oro* (two people, three people)

Collective numbers are used less and less and cardinal numbers are used instead. However, there are instances in which it is impossible to replace them with cardinal numbers.

Želite li stol za dvoje?	Do you want a table for two?

This can also be said as:

Želite li stol za dvije = dve osobe?	Do you want a table for two persons?

For groups of two, three and four people there are separate forms:

dvoje	two people, a couple
oboje (from *oba*)	both people
troje	three people
četvoro – četvero (hr)	four people

For numbers above four they are formed by adding the following endings to the cardinal number:

-ORO (bh-mont-srb) or ***-ERO*** (hr)

pet	*petoro – petero*
šest	*šestoro – šestero*
sedam	*sedmoro – sedmero*
osam	*osmoro – osmero*
devet	*devetoro – devetero*
deset	*desetoro – desetero* etc.

Note the spelling of *sedmoro – sedmero* and *osmoro – osmero* .

In a compound numeral, only the last element is in the collective number form:

pedeset petoro	fifty-five people
trideset dvoje	thirty-two persons

They are followed by a noun in the genitive plural:

Nada ima dvoje djece = dece.	Nada has two children.
Ima devetoro – devetero (hr) *ljudi na trgu.*	There are nine people in the square.

They are preceded by a pronoun in the genitive case:

nas dvoje	the two of us (a man and a woman)
vas troje	three of you (a mixed group)
njih petoro	five of them (a mixed group)
vas oboje	both of you (a man and a woman)

These numbers are used for counting children:

dijete = *dete* (sing) and *djeca* = *deca* (pl)
jedno dijete = *dete*
dvoje djece = *dece*
troje djece = *dece*
četvoro or *četvero* (hr) *djece* = *četvoro dece*
petoro or *petero* (hr) *djece* = *petoro dece*

6.4 Numerical nouns *-orica* (two men, three men)

For groups consisting of men only, there is a special group of nouns called numerical nouns.

Numerical nouns for two, three and four men are created by adding ***-ICA*** to collective numbers (6.3):

dvojica (from *dvoje*)	two men, or two boys
obojica (from *oboje*)	both men, both boys
trojica (from *troje*)	three men, or three boys
četvorica (from *četvoro*)	four men, or four boys

Numerical nouns above four are created by adding ***-ORICA*** to cardinal numbers:

petorica
šestorica
sedmorica
osmorica etc.

Cardinal numbers (*dvije* = *dve, tri, četiri* etc) are used for groups consisting of women:

Od mojih deset prijatelja samo su trojica došla.	Of my ten (male) friends only three have turned up.
Od mojih deset prijateljica samo su tri došle.	Of my ten (female) friends only three have turned up.

Numerical nouns are followed by a masculine noun in the genitive plural or preceded by a personal pronoun in the genitive:

jedanaestorica fudbalera – nogometaša (hr)	11 footballers
nas dvojica	the two of us
vas četvorica	four of you
njih petorica	five of them
njih obojica	both of them

These nouns are feminine and decline according to the standard feminine declension (Second Declension):

Spazio sam petoricu zatvorenika.	I spotted (a group of) five prisoners.

6.5 Approximate numbers *-ak*

To create approximate numbers above ten, the suffix *-ak* is added to the relevant cardinal number (only teens and decade numbers are used with this suffix):

deset + ak – desetak	around ten, approximately ten, ten or so
dvadesetak	around 20
pedesetak	around 50
dvanaestak	a dozen or so

These numbers are not changeable (they have no forms for different genders and do not decline). They are always followed by nouns in the genitive plural:

U desetak gradova u Crnoj Gori su održani lokalni izbori.	Local elections were held in around 10 towns in Montenegro.
Imam desetak prijatelja u Zagrebu.	I have some ten friends in Zagreb.

To express approximate values with numbers between one and nine, two cardinal numbers are placed next to each other, connected by a hyphen:

pet-šest	five or six
dva-tri	two or three

The same rule applies to collective numbers and numerical nouns (these collocations are very frequently used in the spoken language):

dvoje-troje	two or three people
petorica-šestorica	five or six men

6.6 Fractions *-ina*

Fractions in BCMS are similar in form to their English equivalents. They are made up of two numerals – the first one is a cardinal number and the other is a special fractional numerical noun.

These are BCMS equivalents to English "half, third, quarter":

half	*polovina* or *polovica* (hr), *pola*
third	*trećina*
quarter	*četvrtina*
a half	*jedna polovina* or *polovica* (hr), *pola*
one-third	*jedna trećina*
two-thirds	*dvije = dve trećine*
three-quarters	*tri četvrtine*

Polovina – polovica (hr) has short forms *pol* and *po*. They are used to express "and a half"; for example, "two and a half" is *dva i pol*, or *dva i po*. *Pola* is used in the expressions of time (see 6.9)

For higher numbers, ordinal numbers are used in English; in BCMS, a special form is created by adding the suffix *-ina* to the cardinal number:

pet	*petina*
šest	*šestina*
sedam	*sedmina*
osam	*osmina*
devet	*devetina*
deset	*desetina* etc.

These words are feminine nouns. As such, they require numbers one and two to be in the feminine gender (*jedna petina, dvije = dve sedmine*).

As is the case with all nouns, when used with the number *jedna*, they have to be singular; with numbers *dvije = dve, tri* and *četiri*, they have to be in a form identical to the genitive singular (*-e* ending); with numbers five and above they have to be in the genitive plural (*-a* ending):

jedna polovina	a half
jedna trećina	one-third
dvije = dve trećine	two-thirds
jedna četvrtina	a quarter
tri četvrtine	three-quarters

četiri sedmine	four-sevenths
sedam desetina	seven-tenths

Za doručak sam pojeo polovinu – polovicu (hr) (or *pola*) *bureka koji si kupila.*	For breakfast I ate half of the burek that you had bought.
Uradili smo samo četvrtinu testa.	We completed only a quarter of the test.
Vidimo samo trećinu pozornice.	We can see only a third of the stage.

In these examples, *polovina, trećina* and *četvrtina* are in the accusative singular, as they act as direct objects.

6.7 Numerals acting as a subject

It is important to know how verbs agree with numerals when they act as the subject of a sentence.

Number one

With the number one, the verb is in the third person singular. In compound tenses formed with the L-participle, the L-participle is in the same gender as the subject of the sentence:

Jedna knjiga je na stolu.	One book is on the table.
Jedan mladić ide ulicom.	A young man is walking in the street.
Jedna knjiga je bila na stolu.	A book was on the table.
Jedan mladić je išao ulicom.	A young man was walking in the street.

Numbers two, three and four

The verb is in the third person plural. In compound tenses formed with the L-participle, the L-participle and the noun to which the number refers have identical final vowels:

Dvije = dve knjige su na stolu.	Two books are on the table.
Tri mladića idu ulicom.	Three young men are walking on the street.
Četiri knjigE su bilE na stolu.	Four books were on the table.
Dva mladićA su išlA ulicom.	Two young men were walking on the street.

Numbers five to 20

The verb is in the third person singular. In compound tenses that are formed with the L-participle, the L-participle is in the neuter singular:

Pet knjiga je na stolu.	Five books are on the table.
Šest mladića ide ulicom.	Six young men are walking along the street.
Sedam knjiga je bilo na stolu.	Seven books were on the table.
Osam mladića je išlo ulicom.	Eight young men were walking along the street.

Numbers above 20

For all compound numbers (**numbers above 20**) the last element of the number determines agreement with the verb.

Pedeset jedna knjiga je na stolu.	Fifty-one books are on the table.
Sedamdeset tri mladića su išla ulcom.	Seventy-three young men are walking on the street.
Devedeset devet knjiga je bilo na stolu.	Ninety-nine books were on the table.

With collective numbers – ***dvoje, troje, četvoro, petoro*** etc – the verb is in the third person singular. In compound tenses formed with the L-participle, the L-participle is in the neuter singular:

Vidim kako se troje djece = dece igra u parku.	I can see three children playing in the park.
Dvoje djece = dece je došlo u školu autobusom.	Two children came to the school by bus.
Trideset petoro – petero (hr) *studenata je protestovalo* (mont-srb) *– protestiralo* (bh-hr) *protiv novog dekana.*	Thirty-five students protested against the new dean.

With numerical nouns – ***dvojica, trojica, četvorica*** and other numerals ending in *-orica*, the verb is in the plural. In compound tenses formed with the L-participle, the L-participle is in the neuter plural:

Petorica zatvorenika ulaze u sudnicu.	Five prisoners are entering the courtroom.
Njih dvojica su došla na moj rođendan.	The two of them came to my birthday.

6.8 Numbers used in dates

Ordinal numbers are used to express dates. Ordinal numbers are adjectives that agree with the noun that they describe in gender, number and case:

Danas je drugi april or *travanj*. (hr)	Today is the second of April.

(*Drugi* is in masculine gender as it refers to *dan* (day), which is always omitted).

Note that the nominative case is used to say:

Danas je ...	Today is ...
Juče(r) je bio ...	Yesterday was ...
Jučer je bio drugi april or *travanj* (hr).	Yesterday was 2 April.

"What date is it today?" is asked as:

Koji je danas datum?

When expressing years, the last number is feminine as it agrees with the noun *godina* – year:

Sada je dvije = dve hiljade dvadeseta, or *Sada je dvije tisuće dvadeseta*. (hr)	Now is the year 2020.

N.B. In a compound number only the last numeral is ordinal, and it agrees with the noun in gender and case.

If the year is added to a particular date, the year will be in the genitive case (feminine):

Danas je drugi april dvije = dve hiljade dvadesete godine. or *Danas je drugi travanj dvije tisuće dvadeste godine*. (hr)	Today is 2 April 2020 (literally translated: Today is 2 April of the 2020th year).

To say that something is **on a particular date**, all elements of the date are in the genitive case. Note that there is no preposition:

Stigli smo u Sarajevo dvadeset prvog maja or *svibnja* (hr) *prošle godine*.	We arrived in Sarajevo on 21 May last year.
To se desilo šestog septembra hiljadu devetsto devedeset sedme. (bh-mont-srb) or *To se desilo šestog rujna tisuću devetsto devedeset sedme*. (hr)	That happened on 6 September 1997.

N.B. Ordinal numbers in dates are marked by a full-stop after the number:

Stigli smo u Sarajevo 21.5.2019. We arrived in Sarajevo on 21st May 2019.

To locate an event **in a particular year**, the genitive is used without a preposition, or the locative case with the preposition *u*:

Rođen sam hiljadu or *tisuću* (hr) *devetsto devedest pete godine*, or
Rođen sam u hiljadu or *tisuću* (hr) *devetsto devedest petoj godini.*
I was born in 1995.

The following question is used to ask on what date something will occur or has occurred:

Kojeg datuma ...?

6.8.1 Days of the week

Monday	*ponedjeljak = ponedeljak*
Tuesday	*utorak*
Wednesday	*srijeda = sreda*
Thursday	*četvrtak*
Friday	*petak*
Saturday	*subota*
Sunday	*nedjelja = nedelja*

Note that names of days of the week are not capitalised.

To say on a particular day in the week – for example, "on Friday" – the preposition ***u*** is used followed by the name of the day in the accusative case:

u petak	on Friday
u srijedu = u sredu	on Wednesday

If an adjective is added to the name of the day (e.g. this Saturday, last Wednesday, next Friday etc), the genitive case is used without any prepositions:

ove subote	this Saturday
prošle srijede = prošle srede	last Wednesday
sljedećeg petka = sledećeg petka	next Friday

To say "on Fridays" the name of the weekday has to be in the instrumental case:

petkom	on Fridays
subotom	on Saturdays

To say "every Friday" the adjective *svaki* (every) and the name of the day have to be in the genitive case:

svakog petka	every Friday
svake subote	every Saturday

6.8.2 *Months of the year*

Names of the months in Bosnian, Montenegrin and Serbian are derived from Latin:

januar, februar, mart, april, maj, jun(i), jul(i), avgust, septembar, oktobar, novembar and *decembar.*

Note that names of the months are not capitalised.

In literary Croatian, names of the months are derived from old Slavonic roots: they are descriptive, like *travanj* (April) – meaning "the month of the grass", *listopad* (October) – "the month of falling leaves", or *studeni* (November) "the chilly month" etc.

In the spoken language, very few people use these names but rather refer to months using ordinal numbers plus *mjesec* (month) – literally translated as "the first month" etc.

January	*siječanj*	*prvi mjesec*
February	*veljača*	*drugi mjesec*
March	*ožujak*	*treći mjesec*
April	*travanj*	*četvrti mjesec*
May	*svibanj*	*peti mjesec*
June	*lipanj*	*šesti mjesec*
July	*srpanj*	*sedmi mjesec*
August	*kolovoz*	*osmi mjesec*
September	*rujan*	*deveti mjesec*
October	*listopad*	*deseti mjesec*
November	*studeni*	*jedanaesti mjesec*
December	*prosinac*	*dvanaesti mjesec*

To say that something is in a particular month, the preposition ***u*** is followed by the name of the month in the locative case:

Naša svadba je u junu. (bh-mont-srb)
u lipnju. (hr formal)
u šestom mjesecu. (hr colloq) Our wedding is in June.

N.B. The formal Croatian word for November is an adjective and follows the adjectival declension, unlike other months which are nouns: to say "in November", the locative case form is *u studenom*.

As months are mostly used either in the genitive or locative cases, here is a list of all of them in the two cases:

Bosnian-Montenegrin-Serbian

Gen	Loc
januara	*u januaru*
februara	*u februaru*
marta	*u martu*
aprila	*u aprilu*
maja	*u maju*
juna	*u junu*
jula	*u julu*
augusta	*u augustu*
septembra	*u septembru*
oktobra	*u oktobru*
novembra	*u novembru*
decembra	*u decembru*

Croatian – standard

Gen	Loc
siječnja	*u siječnju*
veljače	*u veljači*
ožujka	*u ožujku*
travnja	*u travnju*
svibnja	*u svibnju*
lipnja	*u lipnju*
srpnja	*u srpnju*

kolovoza	*u kolovozu*
rujna	*u rujnu*
listopada	*u listopadu*
studenog	*u studenom*
prosinca	*u prosincu*

Croatian – colloquial

Gen	**Loc**
prvog mjeseca	*u prvom mjesecu*
drugog mjeseca	*u drugom mjesecu*
trećeg mjeseca	*u trećem mjesecu*
četvrtog mjeseca	*u četvrtom mjesecu*
petog mjeseca	*u petom mjesecu*
šestog mjeseca	*u šestom mjesecu*
sedmog mjeseca	*u sedmom mjesecu*
osmog mjeseca	*u osmom mjesecu*
devetog mjeseca	*u devetom mjesecu*
desetog mjeseca	*u desetom mjesecu*
jedanaestog mj.	*u jedanaestom mjesecu*
dvanaestog mj.	*u dvanaestom mjesecu*

6.9 How to tell the time

Expressing the time in BCMS is not difficult. Cardinal numbers are used.

To say **o'clock**, the masculine noun ***sat*** (hour) is used.

With number *jedan*	nom sing	*sat*
With numbers *dva/tri/četiri*	gen sing	*sata*
With numbers five and above	gen pl	*sati*

jedan sat	one o'clock
dva sata	two o'clock
tri sata	three o'clock
četiri sata	four o'clock
pet sati	five o'clock
šest sati	six o'clock etc.

Full hour

To say "It is one o'clock, two o'clock", predicate-only sentences are used; that is, there is no equivalent in BCMS to "it". (see 11.4.1 "Impersonal Predicate-Only Sentences"):

Šest je sati.	It is 6 o'clock.
Dvanaest je sati.	It is 12 o'clock.
Sada je jedan sat.	Now is 1 o'clock.
Bilo je dva sata.	It was 2 o'clock.
Već je šest sati.	It is already 6 o'clock.

N.B. Note the position of the enclitic *je*, which has to be placed as the second unit in a sentence.

Time past the hour

To express a **time past the hour**, the conjunction ***i*** (and) is used:

šest i deset	6:10
sedam i dvadeset	7:20
osam i dvadeset pet	8:25
devet i petnaest	9:15

(To say "quarter past nine" – "nine and fifteen" is used.)

The words *sat* (hour) and *minut* – *minuta* (hr) (minute) are usually omitted.

Time before the hour

A **time before the hour** is expressed by ***do*** – "until":

deset do šest	ten to six
dvadeset do sedam	twenty to seven
petnaest do osam	quarter to eight

Half past the hour

There are a few ways of saying **half past the hour**:

šest i trideset	6:30 (six and thirty)
šest i po(l)	6:30 (six and a half)

There is also the most frequently used colloquial way of saying the same by using *pola* (half):

pola sedam	6:30

N.B. *Pola* is followed by the number of the following hour. This is opposite to the colloquial "half six" in English, which stands for "half past six". In BCMS, this literally means "half of seven o'clock".

To say **at a certain hour**, the preposition *u* is used plus the number, which remains unchanged:

Vidimo se u jedan sat popodne.	See you at 1 p.m.
Stići ću danas na posao u osam i trideset.	I will arrive at work at 8:30 today.
Autobus kreće u šest sati ujutro.	The bus is leaving at 6 o'clock in the morning.

To locate an event **at a particular time of day,** the preposition *u* is used plus a noun in the accusative case:

Hidrogliser za Veneciju kreće u zoru.	The hydrofoil to Venice is leaving at dawn.
U podne se nalazim sa Sonjom, idemo na ručak.	I am meeting Sonja at noon, we are going to lunch.

In official announcements the 24-hour clock is used:

Večernji dnevnik se emituje (mont-srb) – *emitira* (bh-hr) *na našem kanalu u devetnaest i trideset.*	The evening news bulletin is broadcast on our channel at 19:30.

N.B. In official announcements in Serbia, the word *čas* (gen sing *časa*, gen pl *časova*) is used instead of *sat*.

What time is it? is asked as *Koliko je sati?* which is literally translated as "How many hours is it?"

N.B. The English question literally translated into BCMS reads: *Kakvo je vrijeme = vreme*? which means "What's the weather like", as *vrijeme = vreme* means both "time" and "weather".

6.10 Expressing age

The way that age is expressed in BCMS differs from how it is expressed in English. Translated literally, in BCMS it is expressed as "I have 25 years" (the same as in French or Italian).

Imam dvadeset pet godina.	I am 25 years old.
Moja mama ima pedeset jednu godinu.	My mother is 51 years old.

The noun *godina* is feminine; its case ending depends on to the number that precedes it (see 6.1.1):

jedna godina
dvije = dve godinE
tri godinE
četiri godinE
pet godinA

In compound numbers, it is the last number that determines the case ending in *godina*.

Moj brat ima dvadeset četiri godine.	My brother is 24 years old.
Moja sestra ima dvadeset sedam godina.	My sister is 27 years old.

If the last number is *jedna* – both *jedna* and *godina* have to be in the accusative case in this expression.

Imam trideset jednU godinU.	I am 31 years old.

This is because the transitive verb *imati* (to have) requires a direct object (accusative).

There is a more colloquial way of expressing age, using the dative. The person whose age is expressed is in the dative case (either a noun or personal pronoun – *meni/mi, tebi/ti, njemu/mu, njoj* or *njojzi* (hr)/*joj, nama/nam, vama/vam, njima/im* – for the use of long and short forms of personal pronouns see 5.1 "Personal Pronouns").

Dvadeset pet mi je godina, or *Meni je dvadeset pet godina.*	I am 25 years old.
Mojoj mami je pedeset jedna godina.	My mother is 51 years old.
Njoj je pedeset jedna godina, or *Pedeset jedna joj je godina.*	She is 51 years old.
Marku je bilo četrdeset godina kad je sreo Milenu.	Marko was 40 years old when he met Milena.
Njemu je bilo četrdeset godina kad je sreo Milenu, or *Četrdeset godina mu je bilo kad je sreo Milenu.*	He was 40 years old when he met Milena.

There are two ways of asking someone's age:

Koliko godina imate?	How old are you? (Literally: How many years do you have?)
Koliko godina ima tvoja mama?	How old is your mother?
Koliko godina ona ima?	How old is she?

or

Koliko vam je godina?
Koliko je godina tvojoj mami?
Koliko joj je godina?

Chapter 7

Verbs

Along with nouns, verbs are the most important part of a sentence. They are the engine of a sentence, as they describe an action or a state. They undergo many modifications to describe the time of an action, who performs the action, whether the action is completed or still in progress etc.

In BCMS it is not necessary to use personal pronouns with verbs, as their form already indicates which person or persons perform an action.

*Čita**mo** knjigu.*	We are reading a book.
*Ustaje**š** rano svaki dan.*	You get up early every day.

This is because the suffixes *-mo* and *-š* already denote that these are the *mi* and *ti* forms – the first person plural and the second person singular.

As is evident from these two examples, verbs can be grammatically marked for person and number (three persons singular and three persons plural).

They can also be marked for gender (the L-participle and the passive participle), aspect (perfective/imperfective), tense (present, past, future, future exact) and mood (imperative/potential). Verbs can also have participle forms (L-participle, passive participle), they can express reflexivity/reciprocity (reflexive verbs) and they can act as verbal adverbs (present and past).

In order to create these forms, it is necessary to start from the basic form of a verb (the infinitive) and to understand which family (conjugation) a verb belongs to.

7.1 Infinitives

An infinitive is the basic, neutral form of a verb listed in a dictionary. It does not indicate the person or persons performing the action, the tense or the mood in which the action is performed. In English all infinitives have the same form: "to" plus the verb – "to go", "to do", "to swim" etc.

DOI: 10.4324/9781003154525-7

In BCMS most infinitives end in ***-ti***

raditi, plivati, pisati, uzeti

A small number of infinitives end in ***-sti***

jesti, sresti, sjesti (Iyekavian) = *sesti* (Ekavian)*

A group of verbs, mainly denoting motion, derived from the verb *ići* end in ***-ći.***

ići, doći, stići

*This difference (Iyekavian = Ekavian) will be marked by = in the rest of the chapter (see "How to Use This Book").

7.2 Conjugations

A conjugation is the creation of different forms of a verb from its main form given in a dictionary (the infinitive and the present tense form). A conjugation is also the traditional name for a group of verbs that share an identical or similar pattern of creating particular forms.

While some grammars intimidatingly say that BCMS has six conjugations with 29 subcategories, the verbs most frequently used in modern language can be grouped into three conjugations.

7.2.1 Present tense stem

To determine which conjugation a verb belongs to, it is necessary to know its first person singular form in the present tense – the form that ends in *-m* (all good dictionaries list it alongside the infinitive form). The conjugation is determined by the vowel that occurs immediately before ***-m***. The present tense stem is the form of the verb that is arrived at by dropping this *-m* ending:

plivati	***pliva*** /m
raditi	***radi*** /m
trčati	***trči*** /m
uzeti	***uzme*** /m
jesti	***jede*** /m
ići	***ide*** /m

7.2.2 Three conjugations

The present tense stem can end in either *-a, -i* or *-e*; therefore, the three conjugations are named after these vowels:

A

imati – imam	to have
čitati – čitam	to read
gledati – gledam	to look at

I

raditi – radim	to work
voljeti – volim	to love
= voleti – volim	
trčati – trčim	to run

E

pisati – pišem	to write
jesti – jedem	to eat
ići – idem	to go

For more on the three conjugations, see 7.3.3 "Regular Verbs, Pattern Verbs, Irregular Verbs".

7.3 Types of verbs

7.3.1 Transitive/intransitive verbs

Verbs in both English and BCMS can be transitive or intransitive. Transitive verbs are those that take a direct object.

She is singing – what? – a song	– the verb is transitive.
We took – what? – a bag	– the verb is transitive.
We are sleeping – what?	– this cannot be asked – the verb is intransitive.

Transitive verbs in BCMS take a direct object – usually a noun or a pronoun in the accusative case:

Položila je <u>sve ispite.</u>	She has passed all exams.
Popili smo <u>rakiju.</u>	We drank brandy.

Intransitive verbs do not take a direct object:

Spavam do 8 svakog jutra.	I sleep till 8 every morning.
Došli smo autobusom.	We came by bus.

7.3.2 Auxiliary verbs – biti *and* htjeti = hteti

Biti (to be) is an irregular verb and is also used as an auxiliary verb to create compound tenses (see 7.4.2 "Past Tense" and 7.4.4 "Future Exact").

The verb ***htjeti*** = ***hteti*** is an irregular verb meaning "to want" or "to wish"; it is also used as an auxiliary verb to create the future tense (see 7.4.3).

a) BITI

In the present tense, *biti* has emphasised forms (long – here in bold) and enclitic (short) forms:

ja	***jesam***	*sam*	*mi*	***jesmo***	*smo*
ti	***jesi***	*si*	*vi*	***jeste***	*ste*
on	***jeste***	*je*	*oni*	***jesu***	*su*

The short forms are used in all instances, other than the following – where the long forms must be used:

1 Giving one-word answers

Da li ste u Londonu? Jesmo.	Are you in London? Yes, we are.

2 Emphasis

Ja nisam škrt, al ti stvarno jesi.	I am not stingy, but you really are.

3 Asking questions with *li*

Jesi li umoran?	Are you tired?

N.B. An exception in this instance is made in the third person singular. When used to ask questions in this way, the shorter form *je* is used rather than *jeste*:

Kako je tvoj brat? Je li bolestan?	How is your brother? Is he ill?

An affirmative answer to this question would be:

Jeste.	Yes, he is.

It is important to note that short forms are enclitics and as such cannot be used at the beginning of a sentence – they always occupy the second position in a sentence (see 11.2 "Enclitics").

Kako si? Ja sam dobro or *Dobro sam.*	How are you? I am fine.

Question forms of *biti* in the present tense are created:

1 By inserting ***LI*** immediately after the long form of *biti:*

Jesi li danas kod kuće?	Are you at home today?
Je li to tvoja sestra?	Is that your sister?

2 With the question phrase ***DA LI*** at the start of a sentence, followed by the short form of *biti. Da li* does not mean anything; it just signals that the statement being introduced is a question:

Danas si u Sohou.	You are in Soho today.
Da li si danas u Sohou?	Are you in Soho today?

N.B.1 The short forms are enclitics and as such are always placed as the second unit in a sentence, immediately after *da li*.

N.B.2 This form is not considered standard in literary Croatian, yet it is used in everyday communication.

3 In the spoken language – by just changing the intonation.

4 By starting a sentence with one of the following question words:

šta – što (hr), *ko – tko* (hr), *gdje = gde, kuda – kamo* (hr), *odakle, kad(a), kako, koliko, zašto*, immediately followed by the short form of *biti*:

Kada si na poslu danas?	When are you at work today?
Gdje = gde si danas?	Where are you today?
Odakle ste vi?	Where are you from?

Negative forms of *biti* in the present tense

There is only one set of forms, and they are not enclitics. This means that they can be placed at the beginning of a sentence. They mean: "I am not", "you are not", "he is not" etc.

ja nisam	*mi nismo*
ti nisi	*vi niste*
on nije	*oni nisu*

Jesi li danas u Zagrebu? Nisam danas u Zagrebu, u Puli sam.	Are you in Zagreb today? I am not in Zagreb today, I am in Pula.

Montenegrin has its own variation of the negative form:

ja nijesam	*mi nijesmo*
ti nijesi	*vi nijeste*
on nije	*oni nijesu*

For other tenses of *biti*, see conjugation tables 14.1.1 BITI.

b) HTJETI = HTETI

In the present tense *htjeti* = *hteti* has full and enclitic forms:

ja	***hoću***	*ću*	*mi*	***hoćemo***	*ćemo*
ti	***hoćeš***	*ćeš*	*vi*	***hoćete***	*ćete*
on	***hoće***	*će*	*oni*	***hoće***	*će*

The enclitic forms are used as an auxiliary verb to create the future tense – see 7.4.3.

The full forms are used with the meaning "to wish", "to want" or to form questions in the future tense.

The negative forms of the present tense are:

ja	***neću***	*mi*	***nećemo***
ti	***nećeš***	*vi*	***nećete***
on	***neće***	*oni*	***neće***

These forms are used for the negative future tense (see 7.4.3) and also to say: "I do not want to", "you do not want to" etc.

For other tenses of *htjeti* = *hteti*, see conjugation tables 14.1.3 HTJETI = HTETI

7.3.3 Regular verbs, pattern verbs, irregular verbs

To determine if a verb is regular or a pattern verb, it is necessary to compare the final vowel of the present tense stem (*-a, -i* or *-e*) to the vowel that directly precedes the *-ti* infinitive ending (*-a, -i* or *-e*).

Regular verbs: In all instances in the A conjugation and most instances in the I conjugation, these vowels are the same in the infinitive and the present tense stem (the *-a/-a* and *-i-/-i* combinations). These are regular verbs, and their conjugation is completely predictable.

Pattern verbs: When these two vowels are either different or the *-e/-e* combination (in the E conjugation), there are irregularities, and the infinitive and the present tense of a verb have to be memorised. All verbs whose infinitives end in *-ETI, -STI* and *-ĆI* are pattern verbs too.

Irregular verbs: There are only a few of these that need to be learnt at this level. Their conjugation cannot be predicted from the infinitive form and the present tense stem. Their present tense conjugation and some other forms have to be memorised.

A conjugation

This conjugation is home to regular verbs.

Some frequently used verbs of this conjugation are:

> *čekati-čekam, čitati-čitam, čuvati-čuvam (se), dati-dam, gledati-gledam (se), kupati-kupam (se), igrati-igram (se), imati-imam, morati-moram, nadati se-nadam se, navikavati-navikavam (se), nemati-nemam, objašnjavati-objašnjavam, otvarati-otvaram (se), pitati-pitam (se), plivati-plivam, pozdravljati-pozdravljam (se), sjećati se-sjećam se = sećati se-sećam se, shvaćati-shvaćam* (bh-hr) = *shvatati-shvatam* (bh-mont-srb), *slušati-slušam, spavati-spavam, sviđati se-sviđam se, šetati-šetam (se), trebati-trebam, umarati-umaram (se), upoznati-upoznam (se), uživati-uživam, vraćati-vraćam (se), zatvarati-zatvaram (se), završavati-završavam (se), znati-znam;*

and verbs created from foreign words (all in Croatian and many in Bosnian/Montenegrin/Serbian):

> *planirati-planiram, studirati-studiram, organizirati-organiziram* (hr), *reagirati-reagiram* (hr) etc.

(For the full conjugation table see 14.2)

N.B. The reflexive enclitic *se* in brackets means that the verb can be both transitive and reflexive, depending on the meaning; or that it can also be used to describe a reciprocal action with the addition of *se* (see "Reflexive Verbs", 7.3.7). Where *se* is not in brackets, the verb can only have the reflexive form.

I conjugation

This conjugation includes mostly regular verbs, with two irregularity patterns.

Some frequently used verbs of this conjugation are:

> *baviti se-bavim se, čuditi se-čudim se, dolaziti-dolazim* (and all other verbs of motion created from the *-laziti -lazim* root, like *odlaziti, ulaziti, izlaziti* etc), *družiti se-družim se, graditi-gradim, govoriti-govorim, izgubiti-izgubim (se), javiti-javim (se), kasniti-kasnim, koristiti-koristim (se), kupiti-kupim, ljubiti-ljubim (se), misliti-mislim (se), moliti-molim (se), nositi-nosim (se), objasniti-objasnim, otvoriti-otvorim (se), pobijediti-pobijedim = pobediti-pobedim, posjetiti-posjetim = posetiti-posetim, praviti-pravim (se), provoditi -provodim (se), raditi-radim, seliti se-selim se, sjediti-sjedim* (bh-hr), *trošiti-trošim (se), šaliti se-šalim se, učiti-učim, vratiti-vratim (se), voziti-vozim (se), zatvoriti-zatvorim (se), završiti-završim (se), žuriti-žurim (se).*

(For the full conjugation table, see 14.3)

Irregularity patterns

1 Some verbs with ***-ETI* infinitives** also conjugate in this way:

> *boljeti-bolim = boleti-bolim, letjeti-letim = leteti-letim* (plus prefixes *doletjeti, izletjeti, odletjeti, poletjeti, proletjeti, razletjeti, sletjeti*), *sjedjeti-sjedim* (mont) = *sedeti-sedim* (srb), *šutjeti-šutim* (bh-hr), *vidjeti-vidim (se)= videti-vidim (se), voljeti -volim (se) = voleti -volim (se), željeti-želim = želeti-želim, živjeti-živim = živeti-živim.*

(For the full conjugation table, see 14.3.1)

2 A few verbs with ***-ATI* infinitives** also conjugate in this way:

> *bježati-bježim = bežati-bežim, bojati se-bojim se, brojati-brojim, ćutati-ćutim* (mont-srb), *držati-držim, ležati-ležim, stajati-stojim, trčati-trčim, zaspati-zaspim.*

(For the full conjugation table, see 14.3.2)

E conjugation

This conjugation is home to irregularity pattern verbs.

The good news is that there is a pattern to their irregularities – hence their name (with a few exceptions, and those few verbs are called irregular verbs).

Therefore, the easiest way to learn them is to group them into patterns. This is not an exhaustive list of irregularity patterns but a dozen most-used ones:

1 **Pattern *-ATI -EM***

a) *stajati – stajem*

(and all verbs derived from ***stajati*** with prefixes)

izostajati-izostajem, nastajati-nastajem, nestajati-nestajem, ostajati-ostajem, prestajati-prestajem, pristajati-pristajem, postajati-postajem, rastajati se-rastajem se, sastajati se-sastajem se, ustajati-ustajem;

and verbs like

kašljati-kašljem, penjati se-penjem se, počinjati-počinjem, pominjati-pominjem, smijati se-smijem se = smejati se-smejem se, umirati-umirem.

(For the full conjugation table, see 14.4.1.a)

b) *pisati – pišem*

(verbs with changes in the final consonant of the root – *J*-changes)

disati-dišem, jahati-jašem, pisati-pišem, plesati-plešem;
funkcionisati-funkcionišem (bh-mont-srb)

and many loan words transformed into verbs in bh-mont-srb with the pattern – *isati -išem* (see 12.4.1);

kazati-kažem, plus prefixes – *dokazati-dokažem, otkazati-otkažem, pokazati-pokažem, prikazati-prikažem, zakazati-zakažem;*
kretati-krećem, plus prefixes – *okretati-okrećem (se), pokretati-pokrećem (se), skretati-skrećem;*
dolijetati-dolijećem = doletati-dolećem, polijetati-polijećem = poletati-polećem, prolijetati-prolijećem = proletati-prolećem, slijetati-slijećem = sletati-slećem;
lagati-lažem, predlagati-predlažem, plakati-plačem, pomagati-pomažem, sretati-srećem (se), vezati-vežem (se).

(For the full conjugation table, see 14.4.1.b)

c) *zvati – zovem*

(verbs with a significant vowel change in the present stem)
zvati-zovem (se), prati-perem, brati-berem.

(For the full conjugation table, see 14.4.1.c)

2 **Pattern *-ATI -ANEM***

stati – stanem

(all verbs derived from ***stati*** with prefixes – these are all perfective pairs of Group 1a verbs listed in 1) *izostati-izostanem, nastati-nastanem, nestati-nestanem, ostati-ostanem, postati-postanem, prestati-prestanem, pristati-pristanem, rastati se-rastanem se, sastati se-sastanem se, stati-stanem, ustati-ustanem.*

(For the full conjugation table, see 14.4.2)

3 **Pattern *-AVATI -AJEM***

davati – dajem
davati-dajem, plus prefixes – *dodavati-dodajem, izdavati-izdajem, predavati-predajem, prodavati-prodajem, udavati (se)-udajem (se);*

and verbs like

poznavati-poznajem, priznavati-priznajem, upoznavati-upoznajem (se).

(For the full conjugation table, see 14.4.3)

4 **Pattern *-OVATI -UJEM***

kupovati – kupujem
doručkovati-doručkujem, kupovati-kupujem, ljetovati-ljetujem = letovati-letujem, poštovati-poštujem;
putovati-putujem, plus prefixes *doputovati-doputujem, otputovati-otputujem;*
radovati se-radujem se, razlikovati-razlikujem (se), savjetovati-savjetujem (se) = savetovati-savetujem (se), stanovati-stanujem, vjerovati-vjerujem = verovati-verujem;

plus many verbs created from foreign words in Bosnian-Montenegrin-Serbian, such as:

diskutovati-diskutujem, organizovati-organizujem, pakovati-pakujem, reagovati-reagujem etc.

(For the full conjugation table, see 14.4.4)

5 **Pattern *-IVATI -UJEM***

dočekivati – dočekujem
dočekivati-dočekujem, iznajmljivati-iznajmljujem, naručivati-naručujem;
kazivati-kazujem, plus prefixes – *dokazivati, otkazivati, pokazivati,* *prikazivati, zakazivati;*
opisivati-opisujem, potpisivati-potpisujem, zapisivati-zapisujem;
ocjenjivati-ocjenjujem = ocenjivati-ocenjujem, objavljivati-objavljujem, pobjeđivati-pobjeđujem = pobeđivati-pobeđujem.

(For the full conjugation table, see 14.4.5)

6 **Pattern *-ETI -EM***

a) *umjeti-umijem = umeti-umem*

razumjeti-razumijem = razumeti-razumem (3p pl *razumiju = razumeju*), *smjeti-smijem = smeti-smem* (3p pl *smiju = smeju*), *umjeti-umijem =*

umeti-umem (3p pl – *umiju = umeju*), *uspjeti-uspijem = uspeti-uspem* (3p pl *uspiju = uspeju*)

and

umrijeti-umrem = umreti-umrem (3p pl *umru*).

(For the full conjugation table, see 14.4.6.a)

b) ***donijeti-donesem = doneti-donesem***

(change to the root – inserting *s*)
(and all verbs derived from the same root with prefixes)

iznijeti-iznesem = izneti-iznesem, odnijeti-odnesem = odneti-odnesem, podnijeti-podnesem = podneti-podnesem, prenijeti-prenesem = preneti-prenesem, unijeti-unesem = uneti-unesem.

(For the full conjugation table, see 14.4.6.a)

c) ***uzeti-uzmem***

(change to the root – inserting *m, n or nj*)

uzeti-uzmem, preuzeti-preuzmem, zauzeti-zauzmem;
početi-počnem, popeti se-popnem se, peti se-penjem se.

(For the full conjugation table, see 14.4.6.c)

7 **Pattern -*ITI -IJEM***

piti – pijem
piti-pijem, popiti-popijem, napiti se-napijem se;
kriti-krijem, otkriti-otkrijem, pokriti-pokrijem, sakriti-sakrijem (all verbs derived from *kriti* can also be reflexive);
biti-bijem (se), dobiti-dobijem, ubiti-ubijem (se);
umiti-umijem (se), šiti-šijem, sašiti-sašijem.

(For the full conjugation table, see 14.4.7)

8 **Pattern -*UTI -UJEM***

čuti – čujem
čuti-čujem (se), izuti-izujem (se), obuti-obujem (se).

(For the full conjugation table, see 14.4.8)

9 **Pattern -*NUTI -NEM***

krenuti-krenem
krenuti-krenem, plus prefixes – *okrenuti-okrenem (se), pokrenuti-pokrenem (se), skrenuti-skrenem;*
viknuti-viknem, plus prefixes *priviknuti-priviknem (se), naviknuti-naviknem (se);*

brinuti se-brinem se, pomenuti-pomenem, pritisnuti-pritisnem, skinuti-skinem (se), stisnuti-stisnem, šapnuti-šapnem.

(For the full conjugation table, see 14.4.9)

10 -*STI* infinitives

a) Pattern -*STI* -*DEM*

jesti-jedem
jesti-jedem; pojesti-pojedem;
dovesti-dovedem, izvesti-izvedem, odvesti-odvedem, povesti-povedem, prevesti-prevedem, provesti-provedem (se);
krasti-kradem, ukrasti-ukradem.

(For the full conjugation table, see 14.4.10.a)

b) Pattern -*STI* -*DNEM or* -*TNEM*

sresti-sretnem
pasti-padnem, sjesti-sjednem = sesti-sednem, sresti-sretnem (se).

(For the full conjugation table, see 14.4.10.b)

c) Pattern -*STI* -*ZEM*

dovesti-dovezem
dovesti-dovezem (se), izvesti-izvezem, odvesti-odvezem (se), prevesti-prevezem (se), uvesti-uvezem.

(For the full conjugation table, see 14.4.10.c)

d) Pattern -*STI* -*STEM*

rasti-rastem
rasti-rastem and prefixes: *izrasti, odrasti.*

(For the full conjugation table, see 14.4.10.d)

11 -*ĆI* infinitives

a) Pattern -*ĆI* -*DEM*

ići – idem
ići-idem, otići-odem.

(For the full conjugation table, see 14.4.11.a)

b) Pattern -*ĆI* -*ĐEM*

doći – dođem

Verbs of motion derived from the verb ***ići*** with prefixes:

doći-dođem, izići or *izaći – iziđem* or *izađem, prijeći-pređem = preći-pređem, proći-prođem, prići-priđem, poći-pođem, sići-siđem, ući-uđem.*

and verbs which are not verbs of motion but belong to this pattern –

naći-nađem, pronaći-pronađem.

(For the full conjugation table, see 14.4.11.b)

c) Pattern -*ĆI*, -*GNEM*, or -*KNEM*

stići – stignem
dići-dignem, podići-podignem; leći-legnem, pobjeći-pobjegnem = *pobeći-pobegnem, pomoći-pomognem, stići-stignem;*
taći-taknem, maći-maknem (se), navići-naviknem (se).

(For the full conjugation table, see 14.4.11.c)

d) Pattern -*ĆI*, -*ČEM*

peći – pečem
peći-pečem, ispeći-ispečem, reći-rečem;
sjeći-siječem = *seći-sečem, isjeći-isiječem* = *iseći-isečem, posjeći-posiječem* = *poseći-posečem* (all verbs derived from *sjeći* can also be reflexive);
teći-tečem, isteći-istečem, proteći-protečem;
tući-tučem (se), istući-istučem (se);
vući-vučem, dovući-dovučem, izvući-izvučem, provući-provučem, povući-povučem (all verbs derived from *vući* can also be reflexive);
obući-obučem (se).

(For the full conjugation table, see 14.4.11.d)

Irregular verbs

There are very few irregular verbs in BCMS. Their conjugation cannot be predicted from the infinitive form and the present tense stems. Their present tense conjugation and other forms have to be memorised.

biti (see "Auxiliary Verbs" 7.3.2),
htjeti = *hteti* (see "Auxiliary Verbs" 7.3.2),
moći and
slati

moći can, to be able to

ja mogu	*mi možemo*
ti možeš	*vi možete*
on može	*oni mogu*

For other tenses of *moći*, see conjugation tables 14.1.2 MOĆI

slati, to send

ja šaljem *mi šaljemo*
ti šalješ *vi šaljete*
on šalje *oni šalju*

For other tenses of *slati*, see conjugation tables 14.1.4 SLATI

N.B. A few other verbs are irregular, but they are either archaic or are to do with agricultural activities that a beginner or intermediate student will not need at this level of study (e.g. *strići-strižem* – to sheer sheep; *žeti-žanjem* or *žnjem* – to harvest; *zreti-zrijem* = *zreti-zrim* – to ripen).

7.3.4 Perfective/imperfective verbs

For almost every verbal meaning there are two separate verbs in BCMS. Most of these verbal pairs are closely related, built from the same root. In grammar, it is said that these two separate verbs are the perfective and imperfective aspects of the same verb. For example, the English verb "to read" can be translated into BCMS as either *čitati* or *pročitati*. *Čitati* is the imperfective verb, while *pročitati* is the perfective verb.

This is a particularly difficult notion for foreign learners, as their languages do not have this grammatical tool – unless they speak other Slavonic languages. However, almost all languages have a way of showing if an action is continuous/incomplete, repetitive, habitual, or sudden, brief and completed.

English uses tenses and phrasal verbs to describe this. Hence, five continuous tenses are used to speak of a continuing action in English – the present continuous (I am reading), past continuous (I was reading), future continuous (I will be reading), present perfect continuous (I have been reading) and the past perfect continuous (I had been reading).

Modern spoken BCMS uses only one present tense and mostly one past tense – so it needs a tool to express if an action is continuous, incomplete, repeated on the one hand or sudden or completed on the other. To do this, BCMS uses perfective and imperfective forms of verbs.

The imperfective aspect

It expresses an action in general, a continuing, habitual or repeated action – whether it is the present, past or future. Because of the nature of tenses, the present tense is expressed mostly by imperfective verbs, as the general meaning of the present tense is an action in progress, not yet completed.

action in general

Volim čitati bajke. (bh-hr) = *Volim da čitam bajke.* (mont-srb)	I like to read fairy tales.

frequent action

Čitam bajke svaki dan.	I read fairy tales every day.

continuous action

Već deset mjeseci = meseci učim francuski.	I have been learning French for 10 months.
Pjevali = pevali su cijelu = celu noć.	They sang all night long.

repeated action

Uzima lijek = lek tri puta na dan.	He is taking the medication three times a day.

The perfective aspect

It expresses a completed action, a single action, a sudden action or an action describing the beginning of a process. Perfective verbs occur more frequently in tenses other than the present tense.

completed action

Pročitala je svu stručnu literaturu pred ispit.	She had finished reading all expert literature before her exam.
Radila je na tom eseju deset sati juče(r), ali ga je tek danas uradila.	She worked on the essay for ten hours yesterday, but she finished it (finished working on it) only today.

single action

Obično pije čaj, ali sa mnom je danas popila sok.	She usually drinks tea, but she had a juice with me today.

sudden action

Upravo mi je pala na pamet jedna divna ideja.	I've just had a brilliant idea.

start of an action

Zapjevali = zapevali su glasno. They started singing loudly.

Consider this passage:

Nikad se nije ***osjećala*** *(= osećala) loše, ali je sinoć* ***osjetila*** *(= osetila) jaku bol u grudima. Obično po gradu* ***ne ide*** *taksijem, ali se* ***uplašila*** *i* ***otišla*** *taksijem u bolnicu. Kardiolog koji ju je* ***pregledao kazao*** *joj je da* ***uzme*** *jednu tabletu odmah, a onda da* ***uzima*** *po tri tablete na dan.* ***Posavjetovao*** *(= posavetovao) joj je da za tri dana* ***dođe*** *na kontrolu i* ***uradi*** *EKG.*

(She never used to feel unwell, but last night she felt a sharp pain in her chest. Normally, she does not travel around the city by taxi, but as she was frightened she went to the hospital in a cab. A cardiologist examined her and told her to take one tablet immediately, and then to take three tablets every day. He advised her to come back for a check-up in three days' time and do an ECG).

Let us analyse how imperfective and perfective verbs work in this passage:

osjećala se	imperfective form of the aspect pair *osjećati-osjetiti* – used here to describe a habitual action
osjetila	perfective form of the same verb – used here to describe a single sudden action
ide	bi-aspectual verb *ići* – used here in the imperfective sense for a frequent, habitual action
upašila se	perfective form of the aspect pair *plašiti se-uplašiti* se – used here to describe a single sudden action
otišla	perfective form of the aspect pair *odlaziti-otići* – used here to describe a completed single action
pregledao	perfective form of the aspect pair *pregledavati-pregledati* – used here to describe a completed single action
kazao	bi-aspectual verb *kazati* – used here in perfective sense for a completed single action
uzme	perfective form of the aspect pair *uzimati-uzeti* – used here to describe a single action that will be completed
uzima	imperfective form of the same verb – used here to describe a repeated action

posavjetovao	perfective form of the aspect pair *savjetovati-posavjetovati* – used here to describe a completed single action
dođe	perfective form of the aspect pair *dolaziti-doći* – used here to describe a single action that will be completed
uradi	perfective form of the aspect pair *raditi-uraditi* – used here to describe a single action that will be completed

How to know if a verb is perfective or imperfective?

Unfortunately, there are no obvious ways to work out if a verb is imperfective or perfective. It is necessary to learn both forms when learning a new verbal meaning. It is impossible to know the aspect of a verb just by its length or whether it is prefixed or not, even though most prefixed verbs are perfective.

In some instances, imperfective is the longer version of the verb, like in:

(imperfective – perfective)	
kupovati – kupiti	to buy
počinjati – početi	to start
uzimati – uzeti	to take

In other instances, when prefixes are added, the perfective form is longer:

(imperfective – perfective)	
čitati – pročitati	to read
rasti – odrasti	to grow – to grow up
pjevati – zapjevati = *pevati – zapevati*	to sing – to start singing, to break into song
učiti – naučiti	to study – to master (a subject)
slikati – naslikati	to paint

In some instances they are of the same length, and the only difference is the final vowel before the infinitive ending *-ti*. In this case the *-ATI* infinitive is the imperfective form, while the *-ITI* infinitive is its perfective pair:

(imperfective – perfective)	
spremati – spremiti	to prepare
snimati – snimiti	to film, to record

primati – primiti	to receive
odgovarati – odgovoriti	to reply
odmarati se – odmoriti se	to rest
otvarati – otvoriti	to open

N.B. In some verbs (as in the case with the last three examples, the penultimate vowel before the infinitive *-ti* ending also changes).

How to form perfective-imperfective pairs

Perfective and imperfective verbs are formed in two ways:

1 By adding a prefix to an imperfective verb:

(imperfective – perfective)

piti – popiti	to drink, to drink up
jesti – pojesti	to eat, to eat up
čitati – pročitati	to read, to finish reading
pisati – napisati	to write, to finish writing

N.B. Prefixation sometimes alters the meaning of a verb:

piti – napiti	to drink – to get drunk
jesti – prejesti	to eat – to eat too much
pisati – potpisati	to write – to sign
pisati – upisati	to write – to enrol

2 By internal modification of the perfective verb:

(perfective – imperfective)

početi – počinjati	to start
završiti – završavati	to finish
dati – davati	to give
ustati – ustajati	to get up

Imperfective and perfective verbs may belong to two different conjugations:

spremati – spremam	(imperf A conjugation)
spremiti – spremim	(perf I conjugation)
uzimati – uzimam	(imperf A conjugation)
uzeti – uzmem	(perf E conjugation)

kupovati – kupujem	(imperf E conjugation)
kupiti – kupim	(perf I conjugation)

Bi-aspectual verbs

Some verbs do not have two forms: they serve as bi-aspectual verbs:

ići, čuti, doručkovati, ručati, večerati, vidjeti = *videti, razumjeti* = *razumeti, kazati* (only in the present tense; in the past and future *kazati* is perfective)

and most verbs derived from foreign words:

analizirati, formirati, funkcionirati (bh-hr) = *funkcionisati* (bh-mont-srb), *organizirati* (bh-hr) = *organizovati* (bh-mont-srb), *parkirati, operirati* (bh-hr) = *operisati* (bh-mont-srb), *telefonirati* etc.

Imperfective only verbs

Some verbs have only the imperfective aspect:

biti, imati, držati, morati, stanovati, smjeti = *smeti, izgledati, postojati, važiti, utjecati* = *uticati.*

Some **aspect pairs are made of two completely different verbs**, linked by their meaning:

govoriti (imperfective) to speak – *reći* or *kazati* (perfective) to say/tell.

Usage tips

IMPERFECTIVE

The imperfective aspect expresses an action in general, something that is done habitually, or something that is done at the present time.

It is used **with the following adverbs**, which denote something that is done now or is done usually:

danas – today; *sad(a)* – now; *trenutno* (bh-mont-srb) or *trenutačno* (hr) – currently; *često* – frequently; *uvijek* = *uvek* – always; *stalno* – continuously; *obično* – usually.

Koju knjigu sada čitaš?	Which book are you reading now?
Trenutno čitam "Rat i mir".	I am currently reading *War and Peace*.
Kakve knjige uglavnom čitaš?	What sort of books do you read in general?
Šta – *što* (hr) *obično jedeš za doručak?*	What do you usually have for breakfast?
Uvijek = *uvek jedem jaja za doručak, ali sam danas pojeo sendvič.*	I always have eggs for breakfast, but today I had a sandwich.

Present actions are mostly expressed by imperfective verbs because the present tense denotes something that is not complete.

Danas pišem jednu studiju o zdravoj hrani.	Today I am writing an essay on healthy food.
Gdje = *gde si sada? U samoposluzi sam, kupujem hranu.*	Where are you now? I am at the supermarket, doing my food shopping.

Imperfective verbs are also used **after the verbs *počinjati* – *početi*** (to start, to begin), ***nastavljati* – *nastaviti*** (to continue) and ***prestajati* – *prestati*** (to stop):

Hajdemo kući, počinje padati kiša.	Let's go home, it's beginning to rain.
Počećemo da jedemo kad svi dođu. (mont-srb) – *Počet ćemo jesti kad svi dođu.* (bh-hr)	We shall start eating when everyone arrives.
Nastavljamo učiti francuski u idućem semestru. (bh-hr) *Nastavljamo da učimo francuski u idućem semestru.* (mont-srb)	We are continuing to study French in the next semester.
Kiša je prestala padati. (bh-hr) – *Kiša je prestala da pada.* (mont-srb)	It has stopped raining.

The imperfective aspect can be used **for future or past actions** when referring to continuous, repeated or habitual actions:

Svake večeri ćemo jesti u restoranima na rivi ovog ljeta = *leta.*	We shall eat in restaurants on the waterfront every evening this summer.
Danas je kiša pala samo jednom, a juče je padala cijeli = *celi dan.*	Today it rained only once, but yesterday it was raining all day.

Morao sam sebe stalno podsjećati = podsećati da nisam neznalica. — I had to keep reminding myself that I am not an ignorant person.

Perfective

Perfective verbs are **mostly used in the past and future tenses**, to describe a completed single action, a sudden action or an action describing the beginning of a process.

Consider this sentence in the past in which two perfective verbs and one imperfective are used:

Poletjeli smo iz Londona u 8 sati, letjeli dva sata, i sletjeli u Tivat u 11 po lokalnom vremenu.
= *Poleteli smo iz Londona u 8 sati, leteli dva sata, i sleteli u Tivat u 11 po lokalnom vremenu.* — We took off from London at 8, flew for two hours and landed in Tivat at 11 local time.

The same sentence can be used in the future tense, with the same distribution of perfective/imperfective verbs:

Poletjećemo iz Londona u 8 sati, letjećemo dva sata, i sletjećemo u Tivat u 11 po lokalnom vremenu. (bh-mont & Iyekavian srb)
Poletjet ćemo iz Londona u 8 sati, letjet ćemo dva sata, i sletjet ćemo u Tivat u 11 po lokalnom vremenu. (bh-hr)
= *Poletećemo iz Londona u 8 sati, letećemo dva sata, i sletećemo u Tivat u 11 po lokalnom vremenu.* (Ekavian srb) — We will take off from London at 8, fly for two hours and land in Tivat at 11 local time.

The first verb – *poletjeti* – is a perfective verb denoting the start of an action – "to start flying" = "to take off ". The second verb – *letjeti* – is imperfective; it describes the action of flying in general that lasts for a time; and the last verb – *sletjeti* – is another perfective verb that denotes a single completed action – "to land".

Perfective verbs can also be used **in the present tense** in the following ways:

- After *kad(a)* (when):

Javi mi se kad stigneš u hotel. — Call me when you arrive at the hotel.

Idemo vani (bh-hr) - *napolje* (bh-mont-srb) *kada uradimo domaću zadaću* (bh-hr) - *domaći zadatak* (mont-srb).	We will go out when we finish (complete doing) our homework.

- In combination with other verbs, in the construction:

  finite verb + infinitive (hr-bh); or
  finite verb + *da* + present tense (mont-srb):

Želim te pozvati na svoj rođendan. (hr-bh)	
Želim da te pozovem na svoj rođendan. (mont-srb)	I want to invite you to my birthday party.
Možemo li kupiti jagode na lokalnoj tržnici? (hr-bh)	
Možemo li da kupimo jagode na lokalnoj pijaci? (mont-srb)	Can we buy strawberries at the local market?

- They can be used in a subordinate clause introduced by the intentional conjunction *da* (that, in order to), expressing the subject's order or desire for another subject to complete an action in the future:

Želim da mi kupiš ovu knjigu kad odeš u Hrvatsku.	I want you to buy me this book when you go to Croatia.
Voljela = volela bih da dođeš sa mnom na more.	I would like you to come with me to the seaside.

7.3.5 *Verbs of motion*

Verbs of motion in BCMS are *ići* (to go), its derivatives and some other verbs such as *letjeti* = *leteti* (to fly), *putovati* (to travel), *plivati* (to swim), *ploviti* (to float or sail) and *trčati* (to run).

Verbs of motion form their perfective aspect by using the following prefixes, some of which are also prepositions; these prefixes retain the meaning of the preposition and slightly change the meaning of the original verb of motion.

The prefix expresses the idea of:

do	arriving at a location, position
u	entering a location
iz	exiting a location
od	departing from a location
po	start moving, starting an action
pro	moving through, moving past
pre	moving across or over
pri	approaching a location/position
s	moving downwards
raz	dispersing from a place, scattering

(see 9.3 "Prepositions with Verbs of Motion")

Ići verbs of motion

These prefixes are added to the verb ***ići***, thus making it a perfective verb with a more specific meaning.

do + ići	*doći*	to come, to arrive
u + ići	*ući*	to enter, to come in
iz + ići	*izaći* or *izići*	to exit, to go out
od + ići	*otići*	to leave, to depart
po + ići	*poći*	to set off, to depart
pro + ići	*proći*	to pass by, to pass through
pre + ići	*preći*	to cross
pri + ići	*prići*	to approach
s + ići	*sići*	to come down, to get off
raz + ići	*razići*	to scatter, to disband

Imperfective verbs formed with *-laziti* ending

To create imperfective verbs from these perfective verbs of motion, the whole stem has to be changed. The imperfective stem for *ići* is ***-laziti.*** The prefixes are the same and have the same meaning:

doći	*dolaziti*
ući	*ulaziti*
izaći	*izlaziti*
otići	*odlaziti*
poći	*polaziti*
proći	*prolaziti*

preći	*prelaziti*
prići	*prilaziti*
sići	*silaziti*
razići	*razilaziti*

Other verbs denoting motion

There are other verbs denoting motion that form their perfective aspect by using the same prefixes with the same spectrum of spatial meaning. Here is a list of those that are used most frequently, with examples of usage:

letjeti* = *leteti

(in all the following examples, *letjeti* in Iyekavian is *leteti* in Ekavian)

doletjeti — *Doletjeli smo u Dubrovnik iz Zagreba.*
We arrived in Dubrovnik on a flight from Zagreb.

odletjeti — *Sve ptice selice su odletjele na jug.*
All migratory birds have flown away to the south.

uletjeti — *Uletio je u sobu sav ljutit.*
He burst into (flew into) the room very angry.

izletjeti — *Izletjela je iz kafea i počela trčati.*
She flew out of the café and started running.

poletjeti — *Poletjeli smo na vrijeme.*
We took off on time.

proletjeti — *Vrijeme = vreme je proletjelo.*
The time has flown (literally: flown by).

preletjeti — *Na letu od Beograda do Dubrovnika preletjet ćemo Sarajevo.*
On our flight from Belgrade to Dubrovnik we will fly over Sarajevo.

sletjeti — *Sletjeli smo sa 30 minuta zakašnjenja.*
We landed with a 30-minute delay.

razletjeti — *Razletjeli su se na sve strane da nađu provalnika.*
They have dispersed in all directions in search of the robber.

putovati

doputovati — *Doputovali smo u Mostar vozom = vlakom* (hr) *iz Sarajeva.*
We arrived in Mostar by train from Sarajevo.

otputovati — *Završili su posao i otputovali na more.*
They finished work and left for the seaside.

proputovati — *Ona je stalno na avionu, proputovala je cijeli svijet = celi svet.*
She is always on a plane, she has travelled all over the world.

plivati

doplivati	*Dugo smo plivali i doplivali do prekrasne uvale.* We swam for a long while and reached (swam up to) a beautiful cove.
isplivati	*Isplivajte iz uvale i plivajte po otvorenom moru.* Swim out of the cove and go swimming in the open sea. *Skandalozna tajna je isplivala na vidjelo = videlo.* A scandalous truth has surfaced. (This verb means "to swim out of" and "to surface".)
otplivati	*Otplivali smo od obale ka otvorenom moru.* We swam away from the shore towards the open sea.
preplivati	*Naša plivačica je preplivala La Manš tri puta.* Our female swimmer has swum across the English Channel three times.

ploviti

doploviti	*Jutros smo doplovili trajektom na Šoltu.* We arrived in Šolta by ferry this morning.
uploviti	*Brod je uplovio u luku.* The boat has sailed into port.
isploviti	*Krstarica će isploviti iz Kotora sutra - sjutra* (mont) *ujutro.* The cruise ship will sail out of Kotor tomorrow morning.
preploviti	*Svojom jahtom su preplovili cijeli svijet = celi svet.* They sailed (across) the world in their yacht.

trčati

dotrčati	*Dotrčala je do kuće da se pozdravi s vama.* She ran up to the house to say hello to you.
utrčati	*Utrčao je u zgradu i sakrio se.* He ran into the building and hid.
istrčati	*Istrčali su iz kuće na ulicu.* They ran out of the house onto the street.
potrčati	*Potrčao sam ka parku da tražim svog psa.* I started running towards the park to look for my dog.
protrčati	*Na putu do stadiona protrčali su kroz park.* On their way to the stadium they ran through the park.
pretrčati	*Pretrčala je preko ulice.* She ran across the street.
pritrčati	*Dijete = dete je pritrčalo majci i počelo je grliti.* The child ran up to his mother and started hugging her.

rastrčati	*Demonstranti su se rastrčali na sve strane.* Protesters have scattered all over the place.

7.3.6 *Modal verbs*

Modal verbs are verbs that cannot stand on their own – they need another verb (a complement). They express a possibility, need, demand, permission or prohibition. In English they are: can/could, may/might, must, shall/should, will/would. In BCMS, most of them have full conjugations (some of them are regular verbs). Like in English, they cannot stand alone.

*Contrast Croatian/Serbian

There is a difference in how Croatian and Serbian use modal verbs: they are followed by an infinitive in Croatian and by *DA* + the present tense of a verb in Serbian in most instances, but not absolutely. Bosnian tends to use the Croatian version, while Montenegrin uses the Serbian one.

Note that this contrast in usage is not absolute; it varies regionally and sometimes depends even on the individual speaker's personal preference. Therefore the (srb) markings in the following examples should not be taken as exclusive.

moći	can, to be able to, may
Mama, mogu li ići u park?	
Mama, mogu li da idem u park? (srb)	Mum, can I go to the park?
Oprosti, nisam mogao doći.	
Izvini, nisam mogao da dođem. (srb)	I am sorry, I was not able to come.
Možemo li vam nešto kupiti?	
Možemo li da vam nešto kupimo? (srb)	Can we buy you something?

morati	must, to have to
Morate često prati ruke.	
Morate često da perete ruke. (srb)	You have to wash your hands regularly.
Moraš poštovati pravila.	
Moraš da poštuješ pravila. (srb)	You must respect the rules.

The negative of *morati* is *ne morati*, and it means "not to have to" rather than "must not".

Ne morate doći ako ne želite.	You do not have to come if you don't want to.
Ne morate da dođete ako ne želite. (srb)	

N.B. "Must not" is not translated as *ne morati*, but as *ne smjeti* = *ne smeti*.

Ne smiješ = smeš kasniti na posao.	You mustn't be late for work.
smjeti = smeti	may, dare, to be allowed to
Smijem li ovdje plivati? *Smem li ovde da plivam?* (srb)	May I swim here?
Smije li se ovdje pušiti? *Sme li ovde da se puši?* (srb)	Is smoking allowed here?
Ne smijete to ovdje raditi. *Ne smete to ovde da radite.* (srb)	You must not do that here.

N.B. *Ne smjeti = smeti* means "must not" rather than "may not".

umjeti = umeti	to know how to, to be able to
Umije li vaš sin čitati? *Ume li vaš sin da čita?* (srb)	Can your son read?
trebati	ought to, should, to need

This verb can be used as a modal verb or an ordinary verb that takes a direct object.

As a modal verb it means "should", "ought to".

The usage of this verb is different in Croatian and Serbian.

As a modal verb:

*Contrast Croatian/Serbian

In Serbian, it is used as an impersonal verb in the 3p sing + *DA* + the present tense (similar to the French *Il faut*).

In Croatian, it is used as a fully conjugated verb + infinitive.

Bosnian uses both versions, whereas Montenegrin uses the Serbian one.

Trebaš kupiti nove skije, ove stare su ti loše. *Treba da kupiš nove skije, ove stare su ti loše.* (srb)	You should buy new skis, your old ones are no good.
Trebaš čitati malo više. *Treba da čitaš malo više.* (srb)	You ought to read a bit more.
Gužva je na cestama, trebali smo ići vlakom. *Gužva je na putevima, trebalo je da idemo vozom.* (srb)	The roads are busy, we should have gone by train.

In Serbian, this verb has only the following forms - *treba* in the present tense, *trebalo je* in the past, *trebaće* in the future, *bude trebalo* in the future exact and *trebalo bi* in the potential mood. To use it in any other person is incorrect, but speakers do.

As a transitive verb:

When *trebati* is not used as a modal verb, that is, when it means "to need something", it takes a direct object, for example – "I am thirsty, I need a glass of water". The usage is again different in Croatian vs Serbian. In Croatian *trebati* is just an ordinary regular verb that is fully conjugated.

Žedan sam, trebam čašu vode.	I am thirsty, I need a glass of water.
Trebate mnogo jagoda za ovaj kolač.	For this cake, you need a lot of strawberries.
Marko treba mnogo novca.	Marko needs a lot of money.

In Serbian, it is again used as an impersonal verb, and the person needing an object is expressed with the dative of a personal pronoun or of a noun:

Žedan sam, treba mi časa vode.	I am thirsty, I need a glass of water.
Mnogo šećera vam treba za ovaj kolač.	For this cake, you need a lot of sugar.
Marku treba mnogo para.	Marko needs a lot of money.

In this usage in Serbian, *treba* can also have the 3p pl form – *trebaju* – if the object that one needs is in the plural:

Trebaju mi nove cipele.	I need new shoes.

Bosnian uses both versions, whereas Montenegrin predominantly uses the Serbian one.

7.3.7 Reflexive verbs

The reflexive pronoun *se* is used with some verbs to form reflexive verbs; *se* is used for all persons, it is always written separately from a verb and it is an enclitic – as such it follows strict word order (see 11.2 "Enclitics").

Many verbs that are not reflexive in English have the reflexive form in BCMS, for example, *nadati se* (to hope), *radovati se* (to rejoice, to look forward to). Not all verbs that have the reflexive form have reflexive meaning (see the following).

Reflexive verbs can be grouped into these categories:

a) Verbs with reflexive meaning

These verbs describe an action that the subject of a sentence performs on themselves.

Povrijedio = povredio sam se na poslu.	I got hurt (hurt myself) at work.
Nemoj tako vikati, kontrološi se (bh-mont-srb) - *kontroliraj se* (bh-hr)!	Don't shout like that, control yourself!

These verbs can also be transitive, when used without *se*:

Mora da sam te povrijedio = povredio tom izjavom.	I must have hurt you by saying that.
Kontrolišite - kotrolirajte svoje emocije.	Control your emotions.

N.B. If a verb has true reflexive meaning, the full reflexive pronoun *sebe* can be used instead of its short form *se*:

Povrijedio = povredio sam sebe na poslu.
Moraš sebe kontrolisati - kontrolirati.

b) Transitive and reflexive form

Some other verbs can also be transitive and reflexive, depending on the context and meaning. However, these are not verbs with reflexive meaning, as the subject of the sentence does not perform the action on themselves (and *se* cannot be replaced by *sebe*):

vratiti (se)

Vrati mi sva pisma koja sam ti poslala! (trans)	Give me back all the letters that I sent you!
Vratio sam se sa odmora juče(r). (reflex)	I came back from holiday yesterday.

sakriti (se)

Sakrila je tu tajnu od mene. (trans)	She hid that secret from me.
Sakrila se pod stol kada je počeo zemoljotres. (reflex)	She hid under the table when the earthquake started.

izgubiti (se)

Izgubili su mnogo novca u ekonomskoj krizi. (trans)	They lost a lot of money in the economic crisis.
Izgubili su se u šumi. (reflex)	They got lost in the woods.

c) Only reflexive form without reflexive meaning

These verbs do not exist without the particle *se*. For example, *nadati se* (to hope) does not exist as the verb *nadati*. However, they do not have reflexive meaning.

These verbs serve to:

- Express feelings or an internal process (when the action takes place inside the subject of the sentence), as in:

  bojati se (to be afraid), *diviti* se (to admire), *kajati* se (to be remorseful), *nadati* se (to hope), *ponositi* se (to be proud), *sjećati* se = *sećati* se (to remember), *stidjeti se* = *stideti* se (to be ashamed), *zaljubiti* se (to fall in love).

Nadamo se da ste dobro.	We hope that you are OK.
Roditelji se ponose svojim sinom.	The parents are proud of their son.
Ne stidite se svoje zemlje.	Don't be ashamed of your country.
Zaljubila se čim ga je srela.	She fell in love as soon as she met him.

- Describe behaviour, as in:

  smijati se = *smejati* se (to laugh), *smješiti* se = *smešiti* se (to smile), *mrštiti* se (to frown), *truditi* se (to try hard, to do one's best).

Smijali = smejali su se klovnu.	They were laughing at the clown.
Trudimo se da vam ugodimo.	We are doing our best to please you.

Some other frequently used verbs like *događati se*, *dešavati se, zbivati se* (to happen), *dopadati se* or *sviđati se* (to appeal to someone) also belong to this group:

Što se ovdje = ovde događa?	What is happening here?
Sviđa mi se biti na moru.	I like to be by the sea.

d) Verbs denoting reciprocal action

In English, reciprocity is expressed by a verb plus "each other" or "one another". In BCMS, the particle *se* is added to a verb to denote reciprocity:

Oni se vole.	They love each other.
Marko i Snežana su se zagrlili.	Marko and Snežana hugged each other.
Nisu se vidjeli = videli na festivalu.	They did not see each other at the festival.

There is another way of expressing reciprocity in BCMS – with the phrase *jedan drugog(a)* (each other, one another); both elements change endings for gender, number and case.

Vladimir i Boris su poslali božićne karte jedan drugome. (nom masc sing – dat masc sing)	Vladimir and Boris sent Christmas cards to each other.
Mara i Janja su razgovarale jedna s drugom. (nom fem sing – inst fem sing)	Mara and Janja chatted with each other.
Moramo poštovati jedni druge. (nom masc pl – acc masc pl)	We have to respect one another.

* * *

The reflexive particle *se* can also be added to verbs as a **structural part of a sentence or part of an idiom** (without reflexive or reciprocal meaning) in the following cases:

- *se* is used to form **present passive** (see 7.8.1 "Present Passive"):

Ovaj stan se *prodaje.*	This flat is for sale (literally: This flat is being sold).
Buka se čuje kroz zid.	Noise can be heard through the wall (literally: Noise is heard through the wall).

- *se* is used in **impersonal sentences** (see 11.4.1 "Impersonal Predicate-Only Sentences"):

Mora se više učiti, a manje pričati.	One needs to study more and talk less.

- *se* is added to verbs to express **desire or intention** to do something (see 11.4.2 "Personalised Predicate-Only Sentences"):

Spava mi se.	I feel like sleeping.

7.4 Tenses

There are seven tenses in BCMS. Simple tenses are the present tense, aorist and imperfect. Compound tenses (which are formed with auxiliary verbs) are perfect, past perfect, future and future exact. Aorist, imperfect and past perfect are not used much in the modern spoken language, and therefore they are not described in this book.

7.4.1 *Present tense*

There is only one present tense in BCMS. It is worth noting here that English has four tenses that describe a present action – present simple (a habitual action), present continuous (current action), present perfect and present perfect continuous (both denoting an action that started in the past and is still in progress or that interests us now).

Thus the following sentences in English are all expressed in BCMS with the present tense:

I read every day.	*Čitam svaki dan.* (a habitual action)
I am reading a good book.	*Čitam jednu dobru knjigu.* (current action)
I have been reading for five hours.	*Čitam već pet sati.* (an action that started in the past and is still in progress)
I have been in London for ten years.	*U Londonu sam već deset godina.*

N.B. English speakers, be careful not to translate the English present continuous tense word for word into BCMS by using the auxiliary verb "to be":

I am working in Soho today.
(incorrect) *Danas sam radim u Sohou.*
(correct) *Danas radim u Sohou.*

Formation – affirmative

The present tense is formed by adding the following endings to the present tense stem of a verb (see "Present Tense Stem" 7.2.1):

sing		plural	
ja	***-m***	mi	***-mo***
ti	***-š***	vi	***-te***
on	-	oni	***-ju, -e, -u***

A conjugation:

imati	
imam	*imamo*
imaš	*imate*
ima	*imaju*

I conjugation

raditi	
radim	*radimo*
radiš	*radite*
radi	*rade*

E conjugation

ići	
idem	*idemo*
ideš	*idete*
ide	*idu*

3p pl

The only difficulty are the 3p pl endings, which depend on the conjugation. In the A conjugation *-ju* is added to the present tense stem. In the I and E conjugations the last vowel of the stem is replaced by *-e* or *-u* respectively:

A conjugation adds *-ju*

imati – ima/m – imaju
čitati – čita/m – čitaju
gledati – gleda/m – gledaju

I conjugation adds -e

raditi – radi/m – rade
voljeti – voli/m – vole
trčati – trči/m – trče
brojati – broji/m – broje

E conjugation adds *-u*

ići – ide/m – idu
jesti – jede/m – jedu
pisati – piše/m – pišu

Negative forms

The negative form of the present tense is created by using the negative particle *NE* directly in front of the verb.

Radiš li danas? Danas ne radim or *Ne radim danas.*	Are you working today? I am not working today.

With reflexive verbs *ne* is always placed immediately in front of the verb, irrespective of the place of the reflexive particle *se*:

Ti se ne kupaš često.	You do not bathe frequently.
Ne kupam se često.	I do not bathe frequently.

Only three verbs create negative present tense by glueing the negative prefix *ne-* to the verb itself: *biti, htjeti = hteti* and *imati:*

jesam – nisam (see 7.3.2.a)
hoću – neću (see 7.3.2.b)
imam – nemam (regular A conjugation)

Question forms

Questions in the present tense are formed:

1 By **subject/verb inversion plus *li*** immediately after the verb:

Mara radi danas u Sohou.	
Radi li Mara danas u Sohou?	Does Mara work in Soho today?
Mi idemo na more ove godine.	
Idemo li mi na more ove godine?	Are we going to the seaside this year?

N.B. If personal pronouns are omitted (which is most frequently the case), questions are formed by simply placing the particle *li* after the verb:

Idemo sutra na more. Idemo li sutra na more?	We are going to the seaside tomorrow. Are we going to the seaside tomorrow?

2 With the question phrase ***da li*** at the start of a sentence (*da li* does not mean anything; it just signals that the sentence being introduced is a question):

Radiš danas u Sohou.
Da li radiš danas u Sohou?

Idemo na more ove godine.
Da li idemo na more ove godine?

N.B. Croatian grammarians say that this is not standard Croatian; however, people use it in the spoken language.

3 In the spoken language – by just changing the intonation.

4 In the modern spoken language, *da li* is sometimes replaced by ***je li*** or ***je l'***

Je li radiš danas u Sohou?	Do you work in Soho today?
Je l' idemo na more ove godine?	Are we going to the seaside this year?

This is an emphatically colloquial way of asking questions.

5 By starting a sentence with one of the following **question words**: *šta – što* (hr), *ko – tko* (hr), *gdje = gde, kuda – kamo* (hr), *odakle, kad(a), kako, koliko, zašto.*

Kada radiš u Sohou?	When do you work in Soho? or When are you working in Soho?
Gdje = gde radiš danas?	Where are you working today?

7.4.2 Past tense (perfect tense)

Even though there are four past tenses in BCMS – the perfect tense, the past perfect, aorist and imperfect – only the perfect tense is used in everyday communication to describe actions that took place in the past. A beginner or an intermediate learner does not need to know the other three tenses. Therefore, the perfect tense is the only one described here, and that is the reason why the perfect is called the past tense in this book.

There are five past tenses in English – past simple, present perfect, past continuous, past perfect and past perfect continuous. Thus the following sentences in English are all expressed in BCMS with the one past tense:

Pročitao si tu knjigu prošle godine.	You read that book last year.
Da li si pročitao tu knjigu?	Have you read that book?
Čitao si tu knjigu kad sam te sreo.	You were reading that book when I met you.
Pročitao si tu knjigu prije = pre nego što je objavljena.	You had read that book before it was published.

Čitao je tu knjigu pet sati prije = pre nego što je ona stigla.	He had been reading that book for five hours before she arrived.

Formation – affirmative

The past tense is a compound tense – it is formed with the **present tense of the auxiliary verb *biti*** (see 7.3.2.a) and the **L-participle** of a verb (see 7.6.1).

The present tense of the verb *biti* (*sam, si, je, smo, ste, su*) agrees with the person or persons performing the action (the subject of a sentence); the L-participle is the main verb that agrees with the gender and the number of the subject.

***Studirala** sam engleski.*	I studied English. (female)
***Studirao** sam engleski.*	I studied English. (male)
*Marko je **studirao** engleski.*	Marko studied English.
*Dijete = dete je **studiralo** engleski.*	The child studied English.
*Marko i Stefan su **studirali** engleski.*	Marko and Stefan studied English.
*Silvana i Mira su **studirale** engleski.*	Silvana and Mira studied English.
*Djeca = deca su **studirala** engleski.*	Children studied English.

Short forms of the auxiliary verb *biti* are enclitics (see 11.2), and as such they have to take the position of a second unit in a sentence:

Ja sam bio u Livnu prije = pre 20 godina or *Bio sam u Livnu prije = pre 20 godina.*	I was in Livno 20 years ago.
U osnovnoj školi si učio francuski.	You studied French at the primary school.

Past tense of the verb *biti*:

ja sam bio	*mi smo bili*
ti si bio	*vi ste bili*
on je bio	*oni su bili* (masc)
ona je bila	*one su bile* (fem)
ono je bilo	*ona su bila* (neut)

Past tense of the verb *imati*:

ja sam imao	*mi smo imali*
ti si imao	*vi ste imali*

on je imao	*oni su imali*
ona je imala	*one su imale*
ono je imalo	*ona su imala*

Reflexive verbs: attention should be paid to the position of the reflexive particle *se* (which is an enclitic) – it always has to be placed after the auxiliary verb *biti* (or any other enclitic) as the second unit in a sentence:

Ja sam se šetao, or *Šetao sam se.*	I went for a walk.
Ti si se šetao, or *Šetao si se.*	You went for a walk.
Ona se šetala, or *Šetala se.**	She went for a walk.
Mi smo se šetali, or *Šetali smo se.*	We went for a walk.
Ti si se mnogo puta šetao rivom u Splitu. or *Mnogo puta si se šetao rivom u Splitu.*	You walked many times on the Split waterfront.
Mi smo ga se sjetili = setili gledajući taj film.	We remembered him while watching that movie.

* A quirky detail about reflexive verbs in the past tense is that the 3p sing of the auxiliary verb *biti* is omitted:

Ona se šetala – correct
Ona se je šetala – incorrect.

Negative forms

Negative forms of the past tense are created with the negative present tense of the auxiliary verb *biti (nisam, nisi, nije, nismo, niste, nisu)* and the L-participle of a verb.

Marko nije studirao latinski.	Marko did not study Latin.
Nismo studirali u Tuzli.	We did not study in Tuzla.

N.B. *Nijesam, nijesi, nije, nijesmo, nijeste, nijesu* forms are used in the Montenegrin variant.

As the negative form of the verb *biti* is not an enclitic, a sentence can start with it:

Nisam nikada bio u Crnoj Gori. Or in Montenegrin: *Nijesam nikada bio u Crnoj Gori.*	I have never been to Montenegro.

Negative past tense of the verb *biti*:

ja nisam bio	*mi nismo bili*
ti nisi bio	*vi niste bili*
on nije bio	*oni nisu bili*
ona nije bila	*one nisu bile*
ono nije bilo	*ona nisu bila*

Negative past tense of the verb *imati* (the negative form *nemati* is not used in the past):

ja nisam imao	*mi nismo imali*
ti nisi imao	*vi niste imali*
on nije imao	*oni nisu imali*
ona nije imala	*one nisu imale*
ono nije imalo	*ona nisu imala*

Negative past tense of reflexive verbs – note the position of the reflexive particle *se*, as it needs to be the second unit in a sentence:

Ja se nisam šetao juče(r).	I did not go for a walk yesterday.
Nisam se šetao juče(r).	I did not go for a walk yesterday.
Nikad se nisam šetao tako dugo.	I have never had such a long walk.
Ja se nikad nisam šetao po centru ovoga grada.	I have never walked in the centre of this city.

Question forms

These are the ways of asking questions in the past tense:

1 By using the emphasised forms of *biti* – ***jesam, jesi, je, jesmo, jeste, jesu*** + ***li***:

Jesi li gledao ovaj film?	Have you seen this movie?
Jeste li završili predjelo?	Have you finished your starter?
Je li stigla naša pošta?	Has our post arrived?

2 By using the question phrase ***da li*** at the start of a sentence:

Da li si gledao ovaj film?	Have you seen this movie?
Da li ste završili predjelo?	Have you finished your starter?
Da li je stigla naša pošta?	Has our post arrived?

N.B.1 Note the position of enclitics (*sam, si, je, smo, ste, su*) – they have to be placed immediately after *da li*.

N.B.2 Croatian grammarians say that this way of asking questions is not standard Croatian; however, people use it in the spoken language.

3 In the spoken language, *da li* is sometimes replaced by ***je li*** or ***je l'***. This is an emphatically colloquial way of asking questions.

The previous examples would read as follows:

Je l' ste završili predjelo?
Je l' si gledao taj film?

4 By starting a sentence with one of the following **question words** – *šta* – *što* (hr), *ko* – *tko* (hr), *gdje* = *gde, kuda* – *kamo* (hr), *odakle, kad(a), kako, koliko, zašto* – followed immediately by the enclitic forms *sam, si, je, smo, ste, su*:

Kada si gledao ovaj film?	When did you see this movie?
Ko – tko (hr) *je završio predjelo?*	Who has finished the starter?
Odakle je stigla ova pošta?	Where has this post arrived from?

Using *vi* in the past tense

The personal pronoun *vi* may be used to refer to groups of people or formally to address one person, both male and female. When addressing one person formally in the past tense, the L-participle is always in the masculine plural form, irrespective of the gender of the subject:

Gospodine, jeste li se dobro odmorili?	Sir, did you have a good rest?
Gospođo Andrić, jeste li se dobro odmorili (NOT *odmorila*)*?*	Mrs Andrić, did you have a good rest?

7.4.3 Future tense

As in English, the future tense is used to describe future actions.

To form the future tense, it is necessary to know short forms of the verb *htjeti* = *hteti*. These auxiliary forms are arrived at by dropping the *ho-* element of its present tense:

ja hoću	**ĆU**	*mi hoćemo*	**ĆEMO**
ti hoćeš	**ĆEŠ**	*vi hoćete*	**ĆETE**
on hoće	**ĆE**	*oni hoće*	**ĆE**

N.B. The short forms are enclitics and as such cannot be placed at the start of a sentence; they have to occupy the position of a second unit in a sentence.

The future tense can be formed in the following three ways:

1 ***Ć**U* **+ infinitive (Croatian, Bosnian)**

ja ću pisati	*mi ćemo pisati*
ti ćeš pisati	*vi ćete pisati*
ona će pisati	*oni će pisati*

2 ***ĆU* + *DA* + present tense (Serbian, Montenegrin)**

In Serbian and Montenegrin there is a preference to replace the infinitive part of the future tense by *da* + the present tense:

ja ću da pišem	*mi ćemo da pišemo*
ti ćeš da pišeš	*vi ćete da pišete*
ona će da piše	*oni će da pišu*

When forming the future tense in this way, personal pronouns have to be used because a sentence cannot start with an enclitic. As verb forms themselves have the markings of the person performing the action, there is a preference not to use personal pronouns; therefore, the form of the future tense listed next is more frequent.

3 **Modified infinitive + *ĆU*** *Contrast Croatian/Serbian

The formation of the future tense in Croatian on the one hand and in Serbian and Montenegrin on the other differs slightly. The Croatian version is used in some parts of Bosnia, while the Serbian-Montenegrin version is used in other parts. The spoken forms sound almost identical.

Croatian (also used in parts of Bosnia):

The final *-i* of the infinitive is dropped and the auxiliary ***ĆU*** element placed after it as a separate word:

pisat ću	*pisat ćemo*
pisat ćeš	*pisat ćete*
pisat će	*pisat će*

For verbs whose infinitive ends in *-ći* (*ići* and its derivatives, plus *moći, reći* etc), the whole unmodified infinitive is used:

ići ću	*ići ćemo*
ići ćeš	*ići ćete*
ići će	*ići će*

Serbian, Montenegrin (also used in parts of Bosnia):

The full infinitive ending *-ti* is dropped and the ***ĆU*** element added to form a single word:

pisaću	*pisaćemo*
pisaćeš	*pisaćete*
pisaće	*pisaće*

The formation of the future tense for verbs whose infinitives end in *-ći* is the same as in Croatian, described previously.

For the verbs whose infinitives end in *-sti*, the infinitive ending *-ti* is dropped and the consonant *-s-* undergoes consonant alternation when the ***ĆU*** element is added to form a single word:

jes/ti	*ješću, ješćeš, ješće, ješćemo, ješćete*
sres/ti	*srešću, srešćeš, srešće, srešćemo, srešćete*
preves/ti	*prevešću, prevešćeš, prevešće . . .*

Future tense of the verb *biti*:

ja ću biti	*mi ćemo biti*
ti ćeš biti	*vi ćete biti*
on će biti	*oni će biti*

Future tense of the verb *imati*:

ja ću imati	*mi ćemo imati*
ti ćeš imati	*vi ćete imati*
on će imati	*oni će imati*

N.B If personal pronouns are omitted the future tense of *biti* is the same as for all other verbs:

Croatian (and parts of Bosnia)

bit ću	*bit ćemo*
bit ćeš	*bit ćete*
bit će	*bit će*

Serbian, Montenegrin (and parts of Bosnia)

biću	*bićemo*
bićeš	*bićete*
biće	*biće*

Reflexive verbs: it is important to note the position of the reflexive particle *se* (which is an enclitic) – it always has to be placed after the auxiliary verb *ću, ćes, će, ćemo, ćete, će* (or any other enclitic) as the second unit in a sentence:

Ja ću se šetati, or *Šetaću* se or *Šetat ću* se (hr).	I will go for a walk.
Ti ćes se šetati, or *Šetaćeš* se or *Šetat ćeš* se (hr).	You will go for a walk.
Ona će se šetati, or *Šetaće* se or *Šetat će* se (hr).	She will go for a walk.
Mi ćemo se šetati, or *Šetaćemo* se or *Šetat ćemo* se (hr).	We will go for a walk.
Ti ćeš se mnogo puta šetati splitskom rivom.	You will go for many walks on the Split waterfront.
Šetaćeš se mnogo puta rivom u Splitu, or *Šetat ćeš se mnogo puta rivom u Splitu* (hr).	You will go for many walks on the Split waterfront.

Negative forms

Negative forms of the future tense are created with the negative present tense forms of the auxiliary verb *htjeti* = *hteti (neću, nećeš, neće, nećemo, nećete, neće)* and the infinitive of the main verb:

ja neću pisati	*mi nećemo pisati*
ti nećeš pisati	*vi nećete pisati*
ona neće pisati	*oni neće pisati*

As the negative forms (*neću, nećeš, neće . . .*) are not enclitics, they can be placed at the beginning of a sentence when the personal pronoun is not used:

Neću nikome ništa reći o tome. I will not tell anyone anything about it.

Negative future tense of the verb *biti*:

ja neću biti	*mi nećemo biti*
ti nećeš biti	*vi nećete biti*
on neće biti	*oni neće biti*

Negative future tense of the verb *imati* (the negative form *nemati* is not used in the future tense):

ja neću imati	*mi nećemo imati*
ti nećeš imati	*vi nećete imati*
on neće imati	*oni neće imati*

Reflexive verbs: attention should be paid to word order because the reflexive particle *se* is an enclitic, and as such it needs to be in the position of a second unit in a sentence:

Ja se neću šetati.	I will not go for a walk.
Neću se šetati.	I will not go for a walk.
Nikad se više neću šetati tako dugo.	I will never go for such a long walk again.
Ja se nikad više neću šetati po centru.	I will never again go for a walk in the centre.

Question forms

These are the ways of asking questions in the future tense:

1.a Croatian/Bosnian version

Full forms of the verb *htjeti* = *hteti* in the present tense (***hoću, hoćeš, hoće*** . . .) + ***li*** + **infinitive**:

Hoćemo li ići na more?	Shall we go to the seaside?
Hoćeš li doći s njom k meni?	Will you come with her to my house?

1.b Serbian/Montenegrin version

Full forms of the verb *htjeti* = *hteti* in the present tense (***hoću, hoćeš, hoće*** . . .) + ***li*** + ***da*** + **the present tense**:

Hoćemo li da idemo na more?	Shall we go to the seaside?
Hoćeš li da dođeš sa njom kod mene?	Will you come with her to my house?

2 By using the question phrase ***da li*** at the start of a sentence:

Da li ćete pisati mami o svom odmoru?	Will you write to mother about your holiday?
Da li ćemo ići na more?	Shall we go to the seaside?
Da li ćeš doći s njom?	Will you come with her?

N.B.1 When using *da li* to ask questions about the future, the *ću* element is always placed right after *da li* as it is an enclitic.

N.B.2 Croatian grammarians say that this way of asking questions is not standard Croatian, however people use it in the spoken language.

3 In the spoken language, *da li* is sometimes replaced by ***je li*** or ***je l'***. This is an emphatically colloquial way of asking questions:

Je l' ćemo ići na more?	Shall we go to the seaside?
Je l' ćeš doći s njom?	Will you come with her?

4 By starting a sentence with one of the following **question words** – *šta – što* (hr), *ko – tko* (hr), *gdje = gde, kuda – kamo* (hr), *odakle, kad(a), kako, koliko, zašto* – followed immediately by the enclitic forms *ću, ćeš, će, ćemo, ćete, će*:

Kada ćete pisati mami o svom odmoru?	When will you write to mother about your holiday?
Ko – tko (hr) *će ići na more s nama?*	Who will go to the seaside with us?
Zašto ćeš doći s njom?	Why will you come with her?

7.4.4 Future exact

This tense is used to describe an action at a specific – exact – time in the future, either simultaneously with another future action or before it.

Dobićeš (bh-mont-srb) or *dobit ćeš* (bh-hr) *posao kad budeš završio studije.*	You will get a job when you finish your studies.
Kada budeš došao u London možeš me posjetiti = posetiti.	When you come to London you can visit me.
Javite nam se čim budete stigli.	Call us as soon as you arrive.
Ako sutra bude padala kiša, nećemo ići na plažu.	If it rains tomorrow, we will not go to the beach.

This tense is usually introduced by the following conjunctions: *kad(a), ako, dok, čim, pošto, nakon što*. It is also used in If-clauses (see 7.7 "Conditional Clauses").

In many instances, future exact can be replaced by the present tense of a perfective verb, with the same meaning.

Dobićeš (bh-mont-srb) or *dobit ćeš* (bh-hr) *posao kad završiš studije.*	You will get a job when you finish your studies.
Javite nam se čim stignete.	Call us as soon as you arrive.

This tense is formed by using the *budem* forms of the verb *biti* + the L-participle (7.6.1):

ja ***budem*** *pisao*	*mi* ***budemo*** *pisali*
ti ***budeš*** *pisao*	*vi* ***budete*** *pisali*
ona ***bude*** *pisala*	*one* ***budu*** *pisale*

The *budem* form agrees with the person or persons performing the action (the subject of a sentence); the L-participle is the main verb that agrees with gender and number of the subject.

As the *budem* forms are not enclitics, they can be used at the beginning of a sentence:

Bude li dobro vrijeme = vreme, ići ćemo na plažu.	If the weather is good, we will go to the beach.

Grammatically speaking, *budem* forms are perfective forms of *biti* in the present tense.

Negative forms of future exact are created by placing the negative particle *ne* immediately before *budem, budeš, bude, budemo, budete, budu*:

Ako ne budeš dobar, nećeš dobiti sladoled.	If you are not good, you will not get an ice cream.
Sutra - sjutra (mont) *ćemo ići na plažu ako ne bude padala kiša.*	We will go to the beach tomorrow if it does not rain.

7.5 Moods

7.5.1 *Imperative*

The imperative is used to give instructions, orders and advice, to issue invitations or to prohibit action. As such, it is mostly used in the 2p sing and the 2p pl, depending on whether an order is given to one person (2p sing), to a group of people (2p pl), or is given in a formal and polite way to one person (2p pl – the *vi* form).

It can also serve to give orders or encouragement to our group (*mi* – 1p pl) – that is the equivalent to English "let's do this", "let's go there" etc. The imperative can also be indirect, when orders are given to a person that we are not directly addressing – to him, her or them (3p sing or pl).

The imperative is created from the **imperative stem,** which is derived by dropping the final vowel of the 3p pl present tense form of a verb:

gledati-gledam	***gledaj*** */u*
putovati – putujem	***putuj*** */u*
brojati-brojim	***broj*** */e*
raditi-radim	***rad*** */e*
držati-držim	***drž*** */e*
ići-idem	***id*** */u*
jesti-jedem	***jed*** */u*

The stem that ends in ***-J*** is the imperative for the 2p sing.
For the 2p plural add ***-TE***
For the 1p plural add ***-MO***

For all other verbs add ***-I*** for the 2p sing.
For the 2p plural add ***-ITE***
For the 1p plural add ***-IMO***

-J

čitati-čitam	*čitaj/u*	
	čitaj, čitajte, čitajmo	read
pitati-pitam	*pitaj/u*	
	pitaj, pitajte, pitajmo	ask
dati-dam	*daj/u*	
	daj, dajte, dajmo	give
čekati-čekam	*čekaj/u*	
	čekaj, čekajte, čekajmo	wait
piti – pijem	*pij/u*	
	pij, pijte, pijmo	drink
putovati – putujem	*putuj/u*	
	putuj, putujte, putujmo	travel
brojati-brojim	*broj/e*	
	broj, brojte, brojmo	count
stajati-stojim	*stoj/e*	
	stoj, stojte, stojmo	stand, stop

-I

raditi-radim	*rad/e*	
	radi, radite, radimo	work
učiti-učim	*uč/e*	
	uči, učite, učimo	study
trčati-trčim	*trč/e*	
	trči, trčite, trčimo	run
držati-držim	*drž/e*	
	drži, držite, držimo	hold
bježati-bježim	*bjež/e*	
	bježi, bježite, bježimo	run away, escape
= *bežati-bežim*	*bež/e*	
	beži, bežite, bežimo	
ići-idem	*id/u*	
	idi, idite, idimo	go
doći-dođem	*dođ/u*	
	dođi, dođite, dođimo	come
jesti-jedem	*jed/u*	
	jedi, jedite, jedimo	eat

Third person singular and plural "Let them eat cake"

To form the indirect imperative, ***NEK(A)*** is used before the present tense form of a verb in either the 3p sing or the 3p pl:

neka gleda	let him/her look
neka gledaju	let them look
neka pročita	have him/her read
"*Neka jedu kolače*"	

A few frequently used (complicated) imperatives

There are a few very frequently used imperatives, some of which undergo consonant alterations in their stems. At this level of study it is sufficient to memorise them:

infinitive	**imperatives**	
reći	*reci, recite*	say, tell
kazati	*kaži, kažite*	tell
pomoći	*pomozi, pomozite*	help
biti	*budi, budite*	be

There are three useful words in the spoken language that native speakers use to make a proposal or announce departure – ***hajde*** (2p sing), ***hajdete*** (2p pl) and ***hajdemo*** (1p pl):

Hajdemo na more.	Let's go to the seaside.
Hajde sa mnom u kino (bh-hr) or *bioskop* (mont-srb).	Come with me to the cinema.

Negative imperative

The negative imperative is used to tell somebody not to do something. There are a few ways of creating the negative imperative:

1 The most straightforward one is just to place the negative particle ***ne*** in front of the imperative form:

   ne gledaj, ne čitajte, ne idite, ne radimo

   This form sounds a bit abrupt and mostly cannot be used with perfective verbs: it is not possible to say *ne dođite* or *ne pročitajte*.

2 The best way is to place the negative words ***nemoj*** (2p sing), ***nemojte*** (2p pl) or ***nemojmo*** (1p pl) in front of an infinitive (Bosnian and Croatian):

   nemoj gledati, nemojte čitati, nemojmo raditi

3 The negative words *nemoj, nemojte, nemojmo* + *da* + the present tense (Serbian and Montenegrin):

   nemoj da gledaš, nemojte da čitate, nemojmo da radimo.

7.5.2 Potential mode

The potential mode is used:

1 To express one's intention or desire politely or to ask a polite question:

Želio = želeo bih popiti čašu crnog vina.	I would like to have a glass of red wine.
Biste li mi mogli posuditi (bh-hr) - *pozajmiti* (bh-mont-srb) *malo novca?*	Would you be able to lend me some money?
Mi bismo došli sutra – sjutra (mont) *oko pet popodne.*	We would like to come at around 5 p.m. tomorrow.

2 In conditional clauses (see 7.7).

To form the potential mode it is necessary to know the auxiliary ***BIH*** forms of *biti:*

ja	***bih***	*mi*	***bismo***
ti	***bi***	*vi*	***biste***
on	***bi***	*oni*	***bi***

The *bih* form is the aorist tense of the verb *biti.*

N.B. Colloquially, only the *bi* form is used for all persons singular and plural.

The potential is formed by combining the *bih* forms with the L-participle (see 7.6.1).

ja bih čitao	*mi bismo čitali*
ti bi čitao	*vi biste čitali*
on bi čitao	*oni bi čitali*
ona bi čitala	*one bi čitale*
ono bi čitalo	*ona bi čitala*

The *bih* form agrees with the person or persons performing the action (the subject of a sentence); the L-participle is the main verb that agrees with gender and number of the subject.

Negative potential is formed by placing the negative particle *ne* right in front of the auxiliary verb:

ne bih čitao
ne bi čitala
On traži pare od mene.
Ne bih mu ih nikad dao, or
Nikad mu ih ne bih dao, or
Ja mu ih nikad ne bih dao. — He has asked me for money. I would never give it to him.

Questions in potential are formed in two ways:

1 By inserting the question particle ***li*** after the auxiliary verb:

Biste li čitali ovu knjigu? — Would you read this book?

N.B. This sounds quite formal.

2 With the question phrase ***da li:***

Da li biste čitali ovu knjigu?	Would you read this book?

3 By starting a sentence with one of the following **question words** – *šta – što* (hr), *ko – tko* (hr), *gdje = gde, kuda – kamo* (hr), *odakle, kad(a), kako, koliko, zašto* – followed immediately by the enclitic forms *bih, bi, bismo, biste:*

Kada biste željeli = želeli popiti čašu crnog vina?	When would you like to have a glass of red wine?
Kuda – kamo (hr) *bismo mogli ići na ljetovanje = letovanje ove godine?*	Where could we go on summer holiday this year?
Šta – što (hr) *biste htjeli = hteli popiti?*	What would you like to drink?

7.6 Participles

7.6.1 L-participle

The L-participle is a verbal form used to create two compound tenses and one mode: the past tense (7.4.2), the future exact tense (7.4.4) and the potential mode (7.5.2). It is marked for masculine, feminine and neuter gender, singular and plural, but it does not have the markings of a person. The L-participle agrees with the subject of a sentence in number and gender.

The L-participle is formed by adding the following endings to the infinitive stem of a verb:

singular		plural	
-o	masculine gender	**-*li***	masculine and mixed groups
-***la***	feminine gender	**-*le***	feminine groups only
-***lo***	neuter gender	**-*la***	neuter plural

Marko je studirao latinski.	Marko studied Latin.
Jasna, ti si studirala u Beču?	Jasna, did you study in Vienna?
Mi smo studirali u Tuzli.	We studied in Tuzla.

The formation of L-participles depends on the infinitive type:

1 Infinitives ending in *-TI*

Drop this ending and add the L-participle endings:

čita/ti	*čitao, čitala, čitalo, čitali . . .*
krenu/ti	*krenuo, krenula, krenulo, krenuli . . .*
uze/ti	*uzeo, uzela, uzelo, uzeli . . .*
pi/ti	*pio, pila, pilo, pili . . .*
bi/ti	*bio, bila, bilo, bili . . .*
ima/ti	*imao, imala, imalo, imali . . .*

2 Infinitives ending in *-STI*

For the most frequently used verbs in this group drop this ending and add the L-participle endings:

je/sti	*jeo, jela, jelo, jeli . . .*
sje/sti	*sjeo, sjela, sjelo, sjeli.*
= se/sti	*= seo, sela, selo, seli . . .*
pa/sti	*pao, pala, palo, pali . . .*

N.B. There is a small subgroup of these verbs that form the L-participle in a different way (see point 6 in this list).

3 Verbs of motion derived from *IĆI*

Drop the *-ći* ending and add the following L-participle endings:

-šao	*-šli*
-šla	*-šle*
-šlo	*-šla*
i/ći	*išao, išla, išlo, išli . . .*
do/ći	*došao, došla, došlo, došli . . .*
pro/ći	*prošao, prošli . . .*

The verb *naći* (to find) and its derivatives (*pronaći, snaći se*) also add these endings, although they are not verbs of motion.

4 Other infinitives ending in *-ĆI*

Other verbs whose infinitive ends in *-ći* which are not verbs of motion (and the verb of motion *stići*) drop the *-ći* suffix and add either:

-gao	*-gli*
-gla	*-gle*
-glo	*-gla*
mo/ći	*mogao, mogla, moglo, mogli . . .*
pomo/ći	*pomogao, pomogla, pomoglo, pomogli . . .*
sti/ći	*stigao, stigla, stiglo, stigli . . .*

or

-kao	*-kli*
-kla	*-kle*
-klo	*-kla*
re/ći	*rekao, rekla, reklo, rekli . . .*
pe/ći	*pekao, pekla, peklo, pekli . . .*
vu/ći	*vukao, vukla, vuklo, vukli . . .*

5 L-participles for *-JETI* infinitives (Iyekavian)

There is a small subgroup of very frequently used verbs whose infinitive ends in ***-JETI*** (*voljeti, vidjeti, živjeti, željeti, letjeti, htjeti, razumjeti, donijeti*, and Montenegrin *sjedjeti*); their masculine singular L-participle is irregular:

volio, vidio, živio, želio, htio, razumio, letio, donio, sjedio

In all other forms the infinitive ending *-TI* is dropped and the regular L-participle endings are added.

volje/ti	*volio, voljela, voljeli*
vidje/ti	*vidio, vidjela, vidjeli*
živje/ti	*živio, živjela, živjeli*
želje/ti	*želio, željela, željeli*
letje/ti	*letio, letjela, letjeli*
htje/ti	*htio, htjela, htjeli*
razumje/ti	*razumio, razumjela, razumjeli*
donije/ti	*donio, donijela, donijeli*
sjedje/ti	*sjedio, sjedjela, sjedjeli* (mont)

N.B. In Ekavian, this L-participle is regular: *voleti – voleo, volela, voleli* etc.

6 **Subgroups of -*STI* infinitives**

For a small subgroup of -*STI* verbs whose pattern is -*STI* -*ZEM* (verbs like *dovesti-dovezem, izvesti-izvezem, odvesti-odvezem, prevesti-prevezem, uvesti-uvezem* and *gristi-grizem*; see 14.4.10.c) the L-participle is formed by dropping the -*STI* ending and adding:

-zao	*-zli*
-zla	*-zle*
-zlo	*-zla*
dove/sti	*dovezao, dovezla, dovezli . . .*
preve/sti	*prevezao, prevezla, prevezli . . .*
uve/sti	*uvezao, uvezla, uvezli . . .*

For a few verbs of the -*STI* -*STEM* pattern (*rasti-rastem* and with prefixes: *izrasti, odrasti*; see 14.4.10.d) the L-participle is formed by dropping the -*STI* ending and adding:

-stao	*-sli*
-sla	*-sle*
-slo	*-sla*
ra/sti	*rastao, rasla, rasli . . .*
odra/sti	*odrastao, odrasla, odrasli . . .*

7.6.2 Passive participle

Passive participles are adjectives created from transitive verbs. Being adjectives, they have the markings of gender, number and case and must agree with the noun which they describe. All of them can be used as adjectives to describe a noun, for example, *mljevena kafa* or *kava* (hr) = *mlevena kafa* (ground coffee), *obrano mlijeko* = *obrano mleko* (skimmed milk), *oženjeni muškarac* (married man). They are also used to create past and future passive sentences (7.8.2).

The passive participle is created in the following ways:

1 **Infinitives ending in -*ATI*** drop the -*ti* ending and add **-*N***:

potpisa/ti	*potpisan*
izabra/ti	*izabran*
izbroja/ti	*izbrojan*
poštova/ti	*poštovan*
sačuva/ti	*sačuvan*

2 **All regular I conjugation verbs in *-ITI*** drop the whole ending and add ***-JEN***, which causes *J*-changes (they occur where the initial *-j* of the ending blends with the last consonant of the verb root – see 2.3.3 "*J*-changes")

urad/iti	*urađen*
izgrad/iti	*izgrađen*
posjet/iti	*posjećen*
= *poset/iti*	*posećen*
korist/iti	*korišćen*
začud/iti	*začuđen*
iznenad/iti	*iznenađen*

N.B If the last letter of the root is a soft consonant or *r* (in the examples here – *č, ž, š, r*), the initial *-J-* of the ending is dropped:

označ/iti	*označen*	to mark – marked
nauč/iti	*naučen*	to learn – learnt
posluž/iti	*poslužen*	to serve – served
potroš/iti	*potrošen*	to spend – spent
stvor/iti	*stvoren*	to make – made

3 **I conjugation infinitives that end in *-ETI*** (*-eti -im* pattern) drop the whole ending and add ***-JEN:***

željeti = *želeti*	*željen*
voljeti = *voleti*	*voljen*
vidjeti = *videti*	*viđen*

4 **Infinitives ending in *-NUTI*** drop the final *-i:*

pokrenuti	*pokrenut*
skinuti	*skinut*
taknuti	*taknut*
zabrinuti	*zabrinut*
pomenuti	*pomenut*

In the formation of past participles for other verb groups, there are many exceptions and additional rules that govern some spelling changes. For this level it is sufficient to remember these three endings and learn some irregular past participles by heart, as one would learn new adjectives.

As adjectives, passive participles agree with the noun to which they refer in gender, number and case.

Versajski mirovni sporazum je potpisan 1918. (masc nom sing)	The Versailles peace treaty was signed in 1918.

Potpisano pismo je na stolu. (neuter nom sing)	The signed letter is on the table.
Vidio = video sam netaknutu prirodu Plitvičkih jezera. (fem acc sing)	I saw the untouched beauty of the Plitvice Lakes.
Divili su se netaknutoj prirodi Plitvičkih jezera. (fem dat sing)	They admired the untouched beauty of the Plitvice Lakes.
Demonstracije su planirane za sutra – sjutra (mont). (fem nom pl)	Demonstrations have been planned for tomorrow.

7.7 Conditional clauses

If-clauses express three degrees of conditionality/probability:

realistic	(usually referring to future or present events),
currently possible	(present) and
unrealistic	(referring to past events that did not happen or present events that cannot happen).

In English all three levels of conditionality are introduced by one conjunction – **if**; in BCMS, each level has its own conjunction: ***AKO, KAD(A) and DA.***

7.7.1 *Realistic* – ako

These conditional clauses express something that is likely to happen; therefore, they mostly refer to future events and sometimes to present ones.

The conjunctions *ako* and sometimes *ukoliko* are used.

Distribution of tenses

If-clause:	Present tense or future exact
Main clause:	Future tense, present tense or imperative

All these combinations of tenses produce the same meaning.

Ako imam para, ići ću na Hvar.	
Ako budem imao para, ići ću na Hvar.	
Ako budem imao para, idem na Hvar.	If I have money, I will go to Hvar.
Ako imaš para, idi na Hvar.	
Ako budeš imao para, idi na Hvar.	If you have money, go to Hvar.
Ukoliko je sutra – sjutra (mont) *toplo, idemo na plažu.*	

Ukoliko sutra – sjutra (mont) *bude toplo, ići ćemo na plažu.*	If it's warm tomorrow, we will go to the beach.

7.7.2 *Currently possible* – kad(a)

These conditional clauses express something that may happen in the present time, although it is not very likely – or the speaker does not expect it to be possible.

They are introduced by the conjunction *kad(a)*.

Distribution of tenses

If-clause: Potential mode
Main clause: Potential mode

Kad bih imao para, išao bih na Hvar.	If I had money, I would go to Hvar. (The speaker most likely does not have the money.)
Kad bi bilo toplo, išli bismo na plažu.	If it was warm, we would go to the beach. (The speaker is saying this on a cold day.)

7.7.3 *Unrealistic* – da

These conditional clauses can refer either to an unrealistic situation in the present or a situation that did not happen. They are introduced by the conjunction *da*.

Present unrealistic

These clauses describe a situation in the present which is impossible.

Distribution of tenses

If-clause: Present tense
Main clause: Potential mode

Da sam mlađi 20 godina, ponovo bih išao na Triglav.	If I were 20 years younger, I would again go to Mt Triglav.

Past unrealistic

These clauses describe an imaginary situation that did not happen.

Distribution of tenses

If-clause: Past tense
Main clause: Potential mode

Da sam imao para, otišao bih na Hvar.	If I had had money, I would have gone to Hvar.
Da je juče bilo toplo, otišli bismo na plažu.	If it had been warm yesterday, we would have gone to the beach.

7.8 Passive voice

The passive voice is used when a doer of the action is unknown or is not important to mention, and thus the object of a sentence becomes the subject.

Active: Somebody broke the glass door.
Passive: The glass door has been broken.

If it is still necessary to mention the doer, they are introduced by the phrase *od strane* (plus the genitive), meaning "by":

Ova bolnica je otvorena od strane ministra zdravlja.	This hospital was opened by the minister of health.

7.8.1 Present passive

This passive tense is formed by adding the reflexive particle *se* to the third person singular or plural of the main verb in the present tense:

Piletina se lako vari.	Chicken is easily digested.
Kuće u Londonu se brzo prodaju.	Houses in London sell fast (literally: are sold fast).
Takve stari se teško zaborave.	Such things are hard to forget (literally: are forgotten with difficulty).

7.8.2 Past and future passive

These two passive tenses are formed with the appropriate form of the auxiliary verb *biti* and the passive participle (7.6.2) of the main verb. The past participle has to agree with the subject of a sentence in gender and number.

Past passive:

Both the present and past tense of the verb *biti* are used to form the past passive without any difference in meaning:

Naša škola je otvorena 1991 godine.

or

Naša škola je bila otvorena 1991.	Our school was opened in 1991.
Našu školu koja je otvorena prošle godine je posjetio = posetio ministar prosvjete = prosvete.	Our school which was opened last year was visited by the minister of education.

Future passive:

The future tense of the verb *biti* is used to form future passive (see 14.1.1 "BITI"):

Škola će biti otvorena za tri godine.	The school will be opened in three years.

7.9 Verbal adverbs

The present and past verbal adverbs sound bookish and are not used frequently in the spoken language, but they are used in the media. Therefore, it is useful to know what they mean and to learn how they are formed.

7.9.1 *Present verbal adverb*

The present verbal adverb is broadly equivalent to the English -ing form. It is used to describe two simultaneous actions performed by the same subject:

He was working on his project while watching TV.

This verbal adverb is formed from imperfective verbs when the ending ***-ĆI*** is added to the 3p pl form of the present tense:

oni gledaju	*gledajući*
oni idu	*idući*
oni rade	*radeći*

Radio je na svom projektu gledajući TV.	He was working on his project while watching TV.
Gledao je TV radeći na svom projektu.	He was watching TV while working on his project.
Šetajući parkom ugledao je svoju prijateljicu.	While walking in the park he saw his friend.

7.9.2 Past verbal adverb

This verbal adverb is used to describe that an action happened immediately before another action – both of them performed by the same subject (equivalent to the English phrase "having done", "having arrived" etc):

Uradivši svoj projekt, počeo je gledati TV.	Having done his project, he started watching TV.

This verbal adverb is formed from -L participles of perfective verbs when the *-la* ending is replaced by ***-VŠI*** :

pogleda-la	*pogledaVŠI*
uradi-la	*uradiVŠI*
doš-la	*došAVŠI*
rek-la	*rekaVŠI*

Note that an *-a-* is inserted between the verb stem and the *-vši* ending if the stem ends in a consonant, as in *doš-* or *rek-*.

Chapter 8

Adverbs

Like adjectives, adverbs are words that provide additional information. Unlike adjectives, which define nouns and sometimes pronouns, adverbs provide more information on verbs, adjectives, other adverbs, or even a sentence.

An adverb modifying a verb:

Govorila je glasno.	She spoke loudly.

An adverb modifying an adjective:

Njen – njezin (hr) *glas je bio vrlo glasan.*	Her voice was fairly loud.

An adverb modifying another adverb:

Govorila je jako glasno.	She spoke very loudly.

An adverb modifying a sentence:

Začuđujuće, govorila je jako glasno.	Surprisingly, she spoke very loudly.

8.1 -LY adverbs and equivalents in BCMS

While many adverbs are not created from other words, the most obvious adverbs in English are those that are created by adding the suffix -ly to adjectives. They most frequently express the manner of doing something:

She is very loud. ("loud" is an adjective as it describes the person)
She spoke loudly. ("loudly" is an adverb as it describes the action)

DOI: 10.4324/9781003154525-8

In BCMS, many adverbs are also related to adjectives. Neuter gender forms of adjectives serve as adverbs:

dobar, dobra, dobro	good
Mara govori engleski dobro.	Mara speaks English well.
tih, tiha, tiho	quiet
Mara je tiho govorila.	Mara spoke quietly.

There is a group of adjectives ending in *-ski, -čki* and *-ški* that use masculine gender form, rather than neutral, to act as adverbs:

herojski, herojska, herojsko	heroic
Herojski su se borili.	They fought heroically.
statistički, statistička, statističko	statistical
Statistički govoreći, u krizi smo.	Statistically speaking, we are in a crisis.

8.2 Comparison

Just like adjectives, adverbs described in 8.1 can have comparatives and superlatives. Notice that neuter forms of comparatives and superlatives of adverbs do not end in *-o* (as many neuter adjectives do) but in *-e* because the ending is preceded by a soft consonant:

brz, brza, brzo	fast (adjective)
brži, brža, brže	comparative – the neuter form serves as an adverb
najbrži, najbrža, najbrže	superlative – the neuter form serves as an adverb
Moj sin je trčao brzo.	My son ran fast.
Tvoj sin je trčao brže.	Your son ran faster.
Njegov sin je trčao najbrže.	His son ran fastest.

There are a few irregular comparatives and superlatives, the same as the corresponding adjectives:

dobro	*bolje*	*najbolje*	well, better, best
loše	*gore*	*najgore*	bad, worse, worst
mnogo	*više*	*najviše*	a lot, more, most
malo	*manje*	*najmanje*	a little, less, least

nego što or ***no što*** – **"than"**

If the elements of comparison are verbs or clauses, *nego* or *no* need to be coupled with *što* (thus turning them into compound conjunctions – see 10.2 "Compound Conjunctions").

On govori brže nego što misli.	He speaks faster than he thinks.
Došli smo ranije no što smo obećali.	We arrived earlier than promised.

8.3 Adverbs as stand-alone words

While it would be impractical to list all adverbs here (a dictionary is the right place for it), here are the most frequently used ones, grouped according to their meaning.

Adverbs denoting place

ovdje (Iyekavian) = *ovde* (Ekavian)* – here

tu – here; *tamo* – there; *ondje* = *onde* – there; *blizu* – near; *daleko* – far; *gore* – up there; *dolje* = *dole* – down there; *lijevo* = *levo* – left; *desno* – right; *pravo* (bh-mont-srb) or *ravno* (hr) – straight.

*This difference (Iyekavian = Ekavian) will be marked by = in the rest of the chapter (see "How to Use This Book").

Adverbs denoting time

sad(a) – now; *juče* or *jučer* (hr) – yesterday; *sutra* (bh-hr-srb) or *sjutra* (mont) – tomorrow; *danas* – today; *jutros* – this morning; *večeras* – this evening; *noćas* – tonight; *ujutro* – in the morning; *prije podne* = *pre podne* – before noon; *poslije podne* = *posle podne*, or *popodne* – in the afternoon; *uveče* or *naveče* – in the evening; *danju* – at daytime; *noću* – at night; *zimi* – in wintertime; *ljeti* = *leti* – in summertime; *često* – frequently; *rijetko* = *retko* – seldom; *odmah* – immediately; *povremeno* – from time to time; *uskoro* – soon; *davno* or *odavno* – a long time ago; *uvijek* = *uvek* – always; *stalno* – continuously; *nekada* – sometimes; *nikada* – never; *obično* – usually.

Adverbs denoting quantity (quantifiers)

malo – a little, a bit, a few; *mnogo* or *puno* – many, a lot; *dosta* – enough; *suviše* or *previše* – too much, too many; *premalo* – too little, too few; *ovoliko* – this much; *toliko* – that much; *onoliko* – that much; *nekoliko* – a few.

Adverbs denoting manner

Most adverbs of manner are the adverbs related to adjectives (neuter forms of adjectives, as described in 8.1), such as *brzo* – quickly; *sporo* – slowly; *loše* – badly; *dobro* – well; *odlično* – superbly etc. There are other adverbs denoting manner that are not related to adjectives, such as: *ovako* – this way; *tako* – that way; *onako* – that way.

8.4 Learning tip: adverb families

To form adverbs meaning "today", "this morning", "this evening", "tonight", the ending ***-S*** or ***-AS*** is added to the relevant noun:

dan	*danas*	day	today
jutro	*jutros*	morning	this morning
večer	*večeras*	evening	this evening
noć	*noćas*	night	tonight

8.4.1 ne-, ni-, i- *adverbs*

There is a quick and easy way to learn a number of adverbs which are formed from question words ***gdje*** = ***gde, kuda*** – ***kamo*** (hr), ***kad(a)*** and ***kako*** (see Table 8.1).

The prefix ***NE-***

adds the meaning of an indefinite place, time etc, as in "somewhere", "sometimes" etc.

The prefix ***NI-***

adds the negative meaning of no place, no time etc, as in "nowhere", "never" etc.

The prefix ***I-***

adds the meaning of an emphasised indefinite place, time etc, as in "any place at all", "any time at all" etc.

Learning tip: adverb families

Table 8.1

gdje = gde Where	kuda – kamo (hr) Where to	kad(a) When	kako How
negdje = *negde* somewhere	*nekuda* – *nekamo* (hr) to somewhere	*nekad(a)* sometimes	*nekako* somehow
nigdje = *nigde* nowhere	*nikuda* – *nikamo* (hr) to nowhere	*nikad(a)* never	*nikako* no way
igdje = *igde* anywhere at all	*ikuda* – *ikamo* (hr) to anywhere at all	*ikada(a)* any time at all	*ikako* any way at all

8.4.2 ov-, t-, on- *adverbs*

The root triad of the demonstrative pronouns ***ovaj***, ***taj***, ***onaj*** is used to form some adverbs (whereby the root ***OV-*** denotes something close to the speaker, ***T-*** something close to the listener and ***ON-*** something far from both the speaker and the listener) (for illustrative examples of these roots used in demonstrative pronouns, see 5.3). These prefixes are added to the question words ***gdje = gde, kuda – kamo*** (hr), ***kako, koliko*** and ***kad(a)*** (Table 8.2).

Table 8.2

gdje = gde Where	kuda – kamo (hr) Where to	kako How	koliko How much How many	kada When
ovdje = *ovde* here	*ovuda* this way	*ovako* in this manner	*ovoliko* this much this many	*sada* now
tamo there	*tuda* that way	*tako* in that manner	*toliko* that much that many	*tada* then
ondje = *onde* there	*onuda* that way	*onako* in that manner	*onoliko* that much that many	*onda* then

8.4.3 Emphasised indefinite adverbs (wherever, whenever)

The particles ***BILO, MA*** and ***GOD***, used to create emphasised indefinite pronouns (see 5.6.1), can also be added to the question words ***gdje = gde, kuda – kamo*** (hr), ***kad(a)*** , ***kako*** and ***koliko*** to create emphasised indefinite adverbs. *Bilo* and *ma* are placed in front of the them, *god* is added after.

All three particles are synonymous – meaning: "wherever", "no matter where to", "however", "whenever" and "however much/however many".

Table 8.3

gdje = gde Where	*kuda – kamo* (hr) Where to	*kako* How	*kada* When	*koliko* How much How many
bilo gdje = bilo gde	*bilo kuda – bilo kamo*	*bilo kako*	*bilo kada*	*bilo koliko*
ma gdje = ma gde	*ma kuda – ma kamo*	*ma kako*	*ma kada*	*ma koliko*
gdje god = gde god	*kuda god – kamo god*	*kako god*	*kada god*	*koliko god*
wherever	no matter where to	however	whenever	however much however many

Chapter 9

Prepositions

A preposition is a word that stands in front of nouns, adjectives, pronouns and numerals and expresses relationships that they form with each other and with the rest of the sentence, mostly in terms of space and time.

A particular difficulty in BCMS is the choice of the case that is used with a particular preposition. Sometimes the same preposition can be followed by more than one case, depending on the meaning in a particular phrase.

Two basic rules to remember initially:

1 No preposition is followed by the nominative case.*
2 Most prepositions are followed by the genitive case.

* Exception: preposition *po* may be used in the nominative case in a distributive meaning.

9.1 Prepositions used with only one case

9.1.1 Only with the genitive

For space:

blizu – near, *do* – next to, up to, to, *duž* – along, *iz* – from, *iza* – behind, *izvan* – outside, *između* – between, *iznad* – above, *ispred* – in front of, *ispod* – below, *kod* – at, near, at someone's place, *kraj* – next to, *mimo* – past, *nasred* – in the middle of, *nasuprot* – opposite, *od* – from, *oko* – around, about, *pokraj* – next to, *poput* – like, *pored* – next to, *poslije* – (Iyekavian) = *posle* (Ekavian)* after, *prije* = *pre* – before, *preko* – across, *van* – outside.

*This difference (Iyekavian = Ekavian) will be marked by = in the rest of the chapter (see "How to Use This Book").

For time:

od – from, *do* – up to, to, *prije* = *pre* – before, *poslije* = *posle* after, *nakon* – after, *oko* – around, *uoči* – on the eve of.

DOI: 10.4324/9781003154525-9

Other:

bez – without, *zbog* – due to, *mjesto* = *mesto* – instead of, *umjesto* = *umesto*– instead of, *osim* – apart from, *poput* – like, *protiv* – against, *radi* – with the view to.

For the examples of usage, see 3.3.4 "Genitive".

KOD

The preposition *kod* needs further explanation because it does not have a direct equivalent in English (in French its direct equivalent is *chez*). It means "at somebody's place", "in somebody's house", "at", "near" or "on" (as in "I have no money on me" – *Nemam para kod sebe*).

Sutra uveče je zabava kod Jelene.	The party is at Jelena's tomorrow evening.
Jesi li kod kuće kasnije?	Are you at home later?
Vidimo se kod Starog mosta.	See you at (or near) the Old Bridge.

***contrast Croatian-Serbian**

In Bosnian, Montenegrin and Serbian *kod* can be used for a location (as described previously) and for the direction of movement. In Croatian, it is only used for the location, whereas the preposition ***k(a)*** (plus dative) is used for the direction of movement.

Dođite u subotu kod nas na večeru. (bh-mont-srb)
Dođite u subotu k nama na večeru. (hr) Come to our place for dinner on Saturday.

9.1.2 Only with the dative

k(a)	towards
prema	towards
pri	at, on, near to

For the examples of usage, see 3.3.5 "Dative".

9.1.3 Only with the accusative

uz	alongside
niz	alongside
kroz	through

For the examples of usage see 3.3.6 "Accusative".

9.2 Prepositions used with two cases

The frequently-used prepositions ***u, na, po, za, nad, pod, pred*** can be used with different cases, depending on the meaning.

The general rule is:

- when they denote **movement** towards a location they are followed by the accusative;
- when they denote something **stationary** they are followed either by:

  1 The locative (*u, na, po*) or
  2 The instrumental (*za, nad, pod, pred*).

9.2.1 *Used with the locative or accusative*

U

location (loc)

Ja sam u Bosni.	I am in Bosnia.
Moja kuća je u Podgorici.	My house is in Podgorica.

movement towards a location (acc)

Idem u Bosnu.	I am going to Bosnia.
Sretan (bh-hr) – *srećan* (mont-srb) *put u Bosnu.*	Have a good trip to Bosnia.
Putujem u Podgoricu sutra – sjutra (mont).	I am travelling to Podgorica tomorrow.

NA

location (loc)

Na fakultetu sam.	I am at college.
Večeras smo na koncertu.	We are at a concert this evening.

movement towards a location (acc)

Idem na fakultet.	I am going to college.
Večeras idemo na koncert.	We are going to a concert this evening.

PO

location (loc)

Otišao je u šetnju po šumi.	He went for a walk in (around) the woods.
Od jutros trčim po gradu.	I've been rushing around town since this morning.

movement – idiomatic (acc)

Otišla je po vodu.	She went to fetch some water.
Otići ću po kruh (hr) or *hljeb* = *hleb kasnije.*	I will go to get some bread later.

9.2.2 *Used with the instrumental or accusative*

ZA

location (instr)

Sjedili (bh-hr) or *sjedjeli* (mont) = *sedeli su za solom.*	They were sitting at the table.

movement, destination (acc)

Ovo je let za Pulu.	This is a flight for Pula.

NAD

location (instr)

Nad Tuzlom je oluja.	There is a storm over Tuzla.

movement, destination (acc)

Nagnuli su se nad provaliju.	They leant over the cliff edge.

POD

location (instr)

Pod suncobranom nije vruće.	It is not hot under the sun umbrella.

movement, destination (acc)

Stavila je novac pod jastuk.	She put the money under the pillow.

PRED

location (instr)

Pred kućom stoji neki neznanac.	A stranger is standing in front of the house.

movement, destination (acc)

Svatovi su stigli pred kuću.	The wedding party came up to the house.

* * *

S(A) can mean "with" or "from":

The preposition *s* is used in its long form *sa* in front of the words that start with *s, z, š* and *ž* and in *sa mnom* (with me).

"With" – in this meaning it is followed by the **instrumental**:

Idem s mamom u Sisak.	I am going to Sisak with my mum.
Obično pijem čaj s limunom.	I usually drink tea with lemon.

"From" – in this meaning it is followed by the **genitive**:

Vratio se s mora prošlog vikenda.	He returned from the seaside last weekend.
Ona je rodom s Brača.	She is originally from Brač.

9.2.3 *Learning tip: when to use* U, *when* NA

Both prepositions *u* and *na* mean "in", "on" or "at" when they indicate a location (used with the locative case) or "to" when they indicate a destination (used with the accusative case).

The preposition *NA* is used to refer to islands, peninsulas, mountains, planets and when something is on top of something else, for example:

na Balkanu	in the Balkans
na Korčuli	on (the island of) Korčula
na planini	on the mountain

na Alpima	in the Alps
na Marsu	on Mars
na stolu	on the table
na polici	on the shelf
na glavi	on the head
na otoku (bh-hr) – *ostrvu* (mont-srb)	on the island

In all other instances ***U*** is used:

u Beogradu	in Belgrade
u Italiji	in Italy
u školi	at school

Also, broadly speaking, *u* is used when one speaks of a physical, real location/destination; *na* is mostly used in an abstract sense.

physical location

u gradu	in the city
u šumi	in the woods
u boci	in the bottle
u ormaru	in the wardrobe
u Hercegovini	in Herzegovina

abstract sense

na predavanju	at the lecture
na operi	at the opera
na koncertu	at the concert
na ispitu	at the exam
na poslu	at work
na pauzi	on a break
na odmoru	on holiday
na zapadu	in the west
na nebu	in the sky
na engleskom	in English (language)

There are a few exceptions to this rule, when ***NA*** is used for a physical location:

na trgu	in the square, at the square
na fakultetu	at the college

na aerodromu	at the airport
na pošti	at the post office
na rivi	at the waterfront
na ulici	in the street, on the street
na stadionu	at the stadium
na groblju	at the cemetery
na cesti (bh-hr), or *na putu* (mont-srb)	on the road
na univerzitetu, or *na sveučilištu* (hr)	at university
na stanici, or *na kolodvoru* (hr)	at the bus or railway station

9.2.4 *Correlation between* U – IZ *and* NA – SA

There is a strict correlation between these two pairs of prepositions.

- If *u* is used to denote a location or destination, then *iz* must be used to describe departure from that location, or origin from that location.
- The same applies to the *NA – SA* pair:

u – iz

Živim u Londonu.	I live in London.
Ja sam iz Londona.	I am from London.
Večeras idem u London.	I am going to London this evening.
Eurostar je krenuo iz Londona.	Eurostar has departed from London.
Rođena sam u Australiji.	I was born in Australia.
Iz Australije sam.	I am from Australia.
Večeras putujem u Australiju.	I am travelling to Australia this evening.
Avion je poletio = poleteo iz Australije.	The plane has taken off from Australia.

na – s(a)

Ona je na Visu.	She is on (the island of) Vis.
Ona je s Visa.	She is from Vis.
Otišla je na Vis prošlog petka.	She went to Vis last Friday.
Ona se vratila s Visa.	She has returned from Vis.
Na trgu ima mnogo ljudi.	There are a lot of people in the square.
S trga se vidi crkva.	A church can be seen from the square.

Idemo na trg da popijemo aperitiv.	We are going to the square to have an aperitif.
Otišli su s trga na Kalemegdan.	They went to Kalemegdan from the square.

9.3 Prepositions with verbs of motion

When using verbs of motion in a sentence, prepositions used as prefixes to create them (see 7.3.5 "Verbs of Motion") – *do, uz, iz, od, s, pre* – have to be repeated after the verb:

doći, dolaziti – do

Došli su do mosta i zaplesali (bh-hr) or *zaigrali* (bh-mont-srb) *kolo.*	They came up to the bridge and started dancing kolo.

ući, ulaziti – u

Svi koji ulaze u Republiku Srbiju moraju imati važeći pasoš.	All those entering the Republic of Serbia must have a valid passport.

izaći, izlaziti – iz

Crno nikad neće izaći iz mode.	Black will never go out of fashion.

otići, odlaziti – od

Kad netko hoće otići od tebe, pusti ga da ode. (hr)	
Kad neko hoće da ode od tebe, pusti ga da ode. (bh-mont-srb)	When somebody wants to leave you (go away from you), let them go.

sići, silaziti – s(a)

Siđite s tramvaja na glavnom trgu i tu me sačekajte.	Get off the tram at the main square and wait for me there.

preći, prelaziti – preko

Upravo smo prešli preko čuvenog mosta u Višegradu.	We have just crossed the famous bridge in Višegrad.

Chapter 10

Conjunctions and particles

Conjunctions are small words that connect words, phrases, clauses and sentences.

Here is a list of the most common conjunctions that may pose difficulties in usage due to their multiple meanings, which change depending on the context.

In BCMS, there are simple conjunctions (consisting of one word, which mostly connect words or sentences) and compound conjunctions (consisting of two or more words, which connect clauses).

10.1 Simple conjunctions

***I* – and, also, too**

***i* and**

This conjunction is used to connect words or sentences.

Ana i Slavko idu u Split.	Ana and Slavko are going to Split.
Džem i mlijeko (Iyekavian) = *mleko* (Ekavian)* *su na stolu.*	Jam and milk are on the table.
Izašao je iz kuće i zaključao vrata.	He came out of the house and locked the door.

*This difference (Iyekavian = Ekavian) will be marked by = in the rest of the chapter (see "How to Use This Book").

***i . . . i* both . . . and**

I Ana i Slavko idu u Split.	Both Ana and Slavko are going to Split.
I Kotor i Budva su u Crnoj Gori.	Both Kotor and Budva are in Montenegro.

***i* also, too** (here it acts as a particle)

DOI: 10.4324/9781003154525-10

When meaning "also" it has to be placed next to the noun/pronoun to which it refers.

Ana hoće čaj. I ja hoću čaj.	Ana wants some tea. Me too.
Ana hoće čaj. Dajte i meni.	Ana wants some tea. Please, give it to me too.

A **– and, but**

This conjunction connects two statements in which a speaker emphasises that the second statement is in contrast to the first. It does not have a direct equivalent in English; its usage should be noted, as it is used very frequently:

Ana hoće čašu vina, a ja hoću jedno pivo.	Ana wants a glass of wine, and I want a beer. (While Ana wants a glass of wine, I want a beer).
Najavili su kišu, a sad je sunčano.	The forecast was for rain, but now it's sunny.
Mi idemo u Beograd, a vi u Bor.	We are going to Belgrade and you are going to Bor.

AL(I) **– but**

This conjunction is used in the same way as the conjunction "but" in English:

Nisam umoran, ali sam gladan.	I am not tired, but I am hungry.
Uzeo je ključ, al nije zaključao vrata.	He took the key but did not lock the door.

ILI **– or**

This conjunction is used in the same way as the conjunction "or" in English:

Želite li čaj ili kafu – kavu (hr)*?*	Do you want tea or coffee?

ili . . . ili **either . . . or**

Idemo ili u Pariz ili u London.	We are going either to Paris or to London.

NI(TI) . . . NI(TI) **– neither . . . nor**

Ni vi ni ja ne znamo ruski.	Neither you nor I know Russian.
Niti vi niti ja ne znamo ruski.	Neither you nor I know Russian.

Both forms are equal, with the *niti* form having a slightly stronger emphasis.

If two verbs need to be connected, only *niti . . . niti* can be used:

On voli zdrav život. Niti pije, niti puši.	He likes to live healthily. He neither drinks nor smokes.

***BILO . . . BILO* – either . . . or**

(synonymous with *ili . . . ili*)

Idite bilo kod njega, bilo kod nje. (bh-mont-srb) – *Idite bilo k njemu, bilo k njoj.* (hr)	Go either to his place or to hers.

***KAO* – as, like**

KAO (I)

Radi kao učitelj.	He works as a teacher.
Živi kao carica kod roditelja.	She lives like a princess at her parents'.
Ona je iz Hrvatske, kao i ja.	She is from Croatia, like me.

***NEGO* – than, but (rather)**

Nego is used to compare two nouns or pronouns (see 4.6.3 "How to Say 'Than'"):

Bolja je nego njena sestra.	She is better than her sister.

It can also be used to connect two sentences with the meaning "but rather":

Nije studirala francuski, nego je studirala lingvistiku.	She did not study French but linguistics.

***VEĆ* – but (rather)**

Već is used synonymously with *nego* in the latter's second meaning:

Nije studirala francuski, već je studirala lingvistiku.	She did not study French but linguistics.
Nisam gladan, već sam žedan.	I am not hungry, but rather I am thirsty.

DA and ***ŠTO*** are the most widely used conjunctions. They are sometimes interchangeable, but not always.

DA

Da can also act as a **particle**, in which case it means **"yes"**.

As a conjunction, it has the following meanings:

- It is used to connect two statements or sentences meaning **"that"**:

Rekao mi je da će doći.	He told me that he will come.
Bili su sigurni da su u pravu.	They were sure that they were right.

- **(In order) to**

In this meaning it is used in sentences that express a wish, desire, intention or encouragement (after *hajde*) to do (or not to do) something:

Došli smo da vas vidimo.	We have come (in order, wishing) to see you.
Idemo na more da se kupamo.	We are going to the seaside (with the intention) to swim.
Željela = želela bih da mi se javiš češće.	I wish you called me more often (literally: I would like that you call me more often).
Volio = voleo bih da te ne volim.	I wish I didn't love you (literally: I wish that I don't love you).
Hajde da ludujemo ove noći!	Let's go crazy tonight.
Hajde da se ne svađamo!	Let's not argue!

- **If-clauses** – to express an unrealistic condition (see 7.7.3 "Unrealistic – *da*"):

Da sam mlađi išao bih na Triglav.	If I was younger, I would go to Mt Triglav.

- **Let's** – to express proposal, wish or order:

Da počnemo sa radom.	Let's start working.

- **After question words** to express uncertainty:

Koliko da platimo?	How much shall we pay?
Kada da idemo?	When shall we go?
Gdje = gde da parkiramo auto?	Where shall we (or can we) park the car?

- In the construction **finite verb + *da* + present tense** (in Serbian and Montenegrin):

Želim da popijem kafu.	I want to have a coffee.

In this case Croatian and Bosnian use the **verb + infinitive construction**:

Želim popiti kavu.

ŠTO

When meaning **"that"**, it is used to connect two clauses:

Žao mi je što se nećemo vidjeti = videti.	I am sorry that we will not see each other.

In many instances *što* can be replaced by *da*. In this example, the conjunction *da* can also be used:

Žao mi je da se nećemo vidjeti = videti.

Difference between DA *and* ŠTO

The general rule is:

Da introduces a statement of fact, expresses an intention to do something, or replaces an infinitive in Serbian and Montenegrin.

Što introduces a clause expressing the reason for what is described in the main sentence.

***Što* cannot be used in the following examples:**

When a statement of fact is introduced:

Čuli smo da ste se vratili.	We have heard that you are back.
Rekao je da je jako umoran.	He said that he was very tired.

When an intention is expressed:

Idemo u park da se prošetamo.	We are going to the park for a walk.

***Da* cannot be used in the following examples:**

When *što* essentially means "because" and thus can be replaced with *zato što* – also in English when "that" can be replaced with "because".

Zabrinuta je što joj se sin nije javio već deset dana.	She is worried that (or because) her son has not called her for ten days.

Radovala se što je položila ispit.	She was happy that (or because) she had passed the exam.

PA

Pa can act as a conjunction or a particle.

As a conjunction, it can be used for:

Listing a sequence of things or actions:

Kad stignete u Split uzmite autobus do luke, pa trajekt do Hvara.	Once (you arrive) in Split, take a bus to the port and then a ferry to Hvar.

Expressing the result of an action:

Kupio sam puno povrća, pa sam skuhao (bh-hr) – *skuvao* (mont-srb) *veliki paprikaš.*	I bought a lot of vegetables and prepared a big stew.

In the following examples, *pa* acts **as a particle;** it is used to express:

Surprise, disapproval:

Pa zašto se tako ponašaš?	Why on earth are you behaving like that?
Pa super što si došao.	Wow, great that you came.

Emphatic affirmative reply:

Možeš li mi pomoći? Pa naravno.	Can you help me? But of course.

Agreement:

Pa dobro, možemo onda tako uraditi.	Ok then, we can do it that way.

Uncertainty or confusion:

Kada želiš ići na more? Pa ne znam, možda neću imati para.	When do you want to go to the seaside? Well, I don't know; maybe I won't have any money.

AKO, KAD, DA – **IF** conjunctions

(see 7.7 "Conditional Clauses")

KAKO

Kako can be a question word or a conjunction; as a question word it means "**how**".

As a conjunction, *kako* means "**as**":

Kako smo već rekli, jako nam se sviđa vaš novi stan.	As we have already said, we really like your new flat.

It also plays a specific role as a conjunction after the **verbs of perception** such as *vidjeti* = *videti* (to see), *primjetiti* = *primetiti* (to notice), *gledati* (to watch), *spaziti* (to notice), *čuti* (to hear) etc to form the following construction:

Vidio = *video sam kako plivaju u bazenu.*	I saw them swimming in the pool.

(Literal translation: "I saw as they are swimming in the pool").

Čujem kako ulazi u sobu.	I can hear him (or her) walking into the room.
Vidimo vas svaki dan kako šetate po rivi.	We see you every day taking a walk on the waterfront.

N.B. In BCMS this phrase is formed with the construction: **a verb of perception + *KAKO* + a verb in the present tense**, not a verbal noun or the present verbal adverb, which English speakers would instinctively try to use to translate the English -ing form (swimming, walking etc) into BCMS.

10.2 Compound conjunctions

When two sentences or clauses need to be connected, prepositions in English also act as conjunctions:

Let's go for an ice-cream <u>after work</u>. (a preposition preceding a noun)
Let's go for an ice-cream <u>after we finish work</u>. (a conjunction introducing a clause)

BCMS is more precise. It cannot use prepositions (such as *prije* = *pre, poslije* = *posle, zbog* etc) to connect two clauses. It needs to transform them into conjunctions. It does so by creating compound conjunctions: by adding the conjunctions *što* or *da* to the required preposition, adverb or another conjunction.

Thus, the same two sentences would read:

Idemo na sladoled nakon posla.	(the preposition *nakon* requires a noun or a pronoun that follows to be in the genitive case).
Idemo na sladoled nakon što završimo posao.	(the conjunction *što* is added to the preposition *nakon* to be able to introduce a clause).

NAKON ŠTO – after

or

POŠTO – after

Pošto is the blended version of the compound conjunction ***poslije toga što*** = ***posle toga što*** – after. It is widely used in the spoken language.

Pošto su završili posao otišli su na sladoled.	
Poslije = posle toga što su završili posao, otišli su na sladoled.	After they had finished working, they went for an ice cream.

PRIJE NEGO (or ***NO) ŠTO*** = *pre nego što* – before

Javite nam se prije nego što = pre nego što odete na odmor, or *Javite nam se prije no što = pre no što odete na odmor.*	Call us before you go on holiday.

NEGO ŠTO, NO ŠTO – than

These compound conjunctions are used to compare two verbs or two clauses:

On govori brže nego što misli.	He speaks faster than he thinks.
Bolje je nego što smo se nadali, or *Bolje je no što smo se nadali.*	It's better than we thought.

KAO ŠTO – as

Bilo je kao što sam ti rekao.	It was as I had told you.
Kao što smo se dogovorili, krećemo na put rano ujutro.	As we agreed, we are setting off early in the morning.

KAO DA – **as if**

Troši pare kao da je milioner – milijunaš (hr).	He is spending money as if he were a millionaire.

ZATO, ZATO ŠTO, JER, ZBOG, ZBOG TOGA ŠTO

These words are used to answer "why" questions. They mean "therefore", "because", "because of".

ZATO – therefore, hence

Zato is an adverb, but it is practical to list it in this section together with other ways of saying "because".

Bio sam gladan, zato sam otišao u restoran.	I was hungry; therefore, I went to a restaurant.

ZATO ŠTO – because

Zato forms the most frequent way of saying "because", with the addition of the conjunction *što*.

Zašto je tužna? Zato što nije dobila posao.	Why is she sad? Because she didn't get the job.

JER – because

Jer is used synonymously with *zato što*.

Zašto je tužna? Jer nije dobila posao.	Why is she sad? Because she didn't get the job.

ZBOG TOGA ŠTO – because

This conjunction is synonymous with *zato što* and *jer*:

Zašto je ljuta? Zbog toga što nije dobila posao.	Why is she angry? Because she didn't get the job.

ZBOG – because of, due to

Zbog is a preposition, but it is practical to list it here together with other ways of saying "because".

It is used in front of a noun or a pronoun which need to be in the genitive case.

Letovi su otkazani zbog lošeg vremena.	Flights have been cancelled due to bad weather.
Zbog virusa su uvedene nove preventivne mjere = mere.	Because of the virus, new prevention measures have been introduced.

10.3 Particles

EVO, ETO, ENO

These particles are used for attracting attention or pointing at something. They are followed by a noun or a pronoun in the genitive case. *Evo* is used to point at someone or something close to the speaker, *eto* for someone or something close to the listener, and *eno* for someone or something far from both the speaker and the listener:

Evo me.	Here I am.
Eto našeg dobrog prijatelja, ulazi u sobu.	There is our good friend, entering the room.
Eno našeg tramvaja, na kraju ulice.	There is our tram, at the end of the street.

NEKA

This particle is used to create imperative for the third person singular or plural (indirect imperative) (see 7.5.1 "Imperative")

Neka se igra ako hoće.	Let him play if he wants.

ZAR **– negative questions**

This particle is used to ask questions when the opposite answer is expected.

In negative questions to which an affirmative reply is expected:

Zar se nismo dogovorili o ovoj cijeni = ceni? Naravno da smo se dogovorili.	Did we not agree on this price? Of course we did.

In questions to which a negative answer is expected:

Zar želiš potrošiti (bh-hr) – *da potrošiš* (bh-mont-srb) *toliko novca? Ma ne, samo fantaziram.*	Do you really want to spend that much money? Of course not, I am only daydreaming.

It is also used to express a surprise:

Zar si toliko platio za novu kuću?!	Wow, you paid that much for your new house?!

N.B. This question particle is immediately followed by enclitics, if there are any in a sentence.

ZAR NE

This particle is used in question tags:

Sviđa ti se u Mostaru, zar ne?	You like it here in Mostar, don't you?
Došla je avionom, zar ne?	She arrived by plane, didn't she?
Vi ste Englez, zar ne?	You are English, aren't you?

Question tags are more difficult in English. In BCMS, irrespective of the tense used in the question, it is only necessary to add *zar ne* at the end, like *n'est-ce pas* in French.

Chapter 11

Sentence structure

11.1 Free word order

Word order in BCMS is fairly free. This is thanks to many case markings – case endings for nouns, some pronouns, adjectives and some numbers and different case forms for some pronouns – which define their precise role in a sentence. This is in contrast to English, whose sentence structure is fairly rigid because the role that a word plays in a sentence depends on its place in it; for example, a subject always comes before a verb, which is then followed by the object.

"Marko loves Maja" is the only way in English that this sentence can be formulated to mean this.

In BCMS, it can be formulated as:

Marko voli Maju.

but also as:

Maju voli Marko.

This is because both Marko and Maja can be modified with the object case ending (in this example it is the feminine accusative *-u*), and wherever these nouns are placed in a sentence, they will thus be marked as the object of somebody's love (in this instance it's the lucky Maja).

Flexibility of word order in BCMS is best illustrated by the many ways in which the following sentence in English can be translated (in this example 17 variations):

I will say one thing to him.

Ja ću mu reći jednu stvar.
Ja ću mu jednu stvar reći.
Ja ću reći jednu stvar njemu.
Ja ću reći njemu jednu stvar.
Ja ću njemu reći jednu stvar.

DOI: 10.4324/9781003154525-11

Ja ću njemu jednu stvar reći.
Ja ću jednu stvar njemu reći.
Ja ću jednu stvar reći njemu.
Reći ću mu jednu stvar.
Reći ću njemu jednu stvar.
Reći ću jednu stvar njemu.
Njemu ću jednu stvar reći.
Njemu ću reći jednu stvar.
Jednu stvar ću mu reći.
Jednu stvar ću reći njemu.
Jednu ću mu stvar reći.
Jednu ću stvar njemu reći.

It is evident from these examples that the same elements are used; they can be tumbled around according to one's preference and according to what one wants to emphasise.

11.2 Enclitics

However, one element of the sentence is rigid and requires careful consideration – these are unemphasised (mostly) single syllable words that are called enclitics. In the previous example the enclitics are *ću* and *mu*.

They follow strict word order – they are always placed as the second unit in a sentence (not necessarily the second word). It is evident that, however, these 17 sentences are shuffled, these short words are always in the same place.

Not all short words are enclitics.

Enclitics are:

1 **Question particle *li***
2 **Verbal enclitics**

a) short present tense forms of *biti*: *sam, si, je, smo ste su.*
b) auxiliary verb for the future tense: *ću, ćeš, će, ćemo, ćete, će.*
c) *bih* (potential) forms of *biti:* *bih, bi, bi, bismo, biste, bi*

(These are short auxiliary verbs used to form the past tense, future tense and the potential mode.)

3 **Personal pronoun enclitics**

Dative *mi, ti, mu, joj, nam, vam, im*
Genitive/accusative *me, te, ga, je* (or *ju*), *nas, vas, ih*

4 **Reflexive particle *se***

Ten golden rules that govern enclitic order

1 They can never be placed at the start of a sentence or a subordinate clause.
2 They are positioned as close as possible to the beginning of a sentence – as the second unit in it (not necessarily as the second word).
3 If a few of them appear in a sentence, they have to be grouped together.
4 When a sentence contains more than one enclitic, there is a **strict order** that they must adhere to:

a) First comes the interrogative particle *li*, followed by
b) verbal enclitics,
c) personal pronoun enclitics,
d) the reflexive particle *se*,
e) *je* – 3p sing of *biti* to form the past tense.

*Da **li si im se** javio?* (four enclitics together)	Have you called them?
*Ne znamo jesmo **li im se** svidjeli* (Iyekavian) = *svideli* (Ekavian)* (three enclitics together)	We do not know if they liked us.

*This difference (Iyekavian = Ekavian) will be marked by = in the rest of the chapter (see "How to Use This Book").

5 If more than one personal pronoun enclitic is used in a sentence, then the order is **dat + gen/acc**:

*Dali su **joj ga**.*	They have given it to her.
*Jeste li **im ga** prijavili?*	Have you reported him to them?
*Donio = doneo **mu ih** je.*	He has brought them to him.

6 The **auxiliary verb form *je*** (3p sing of the verb *biti* used to form the past tense) is always placed as the final enclitic.

*Da **li joj ih je** prijavio?*	Has he reported them to her?
*Kupila **mu ga je.***	She has bought it for him.

7 They are always placed immediately **after the interrogatives** *gdje = gde, kuda – kamo* (hr), *odakle, kad(a), ko – tko* (hr), *šta – što* (hr), *čiji, zašto, zar*:

*Gdje = gde **smo se** upoznali?*	Where did we meet?
*Ne znam odakle **ste** vi.*	I do not know where you are from.
*Kada **ćeš mu** reći ovu vijest = vest?*	When will you tell him this news?

8 Enclitics are always placed immediately **after the conjunctions *da, što, ako, jer, ali, pa*** that introduce another statement (clause):

Rekao je da ***će*** *doći.*	He said that he would come.
Idemo u Niš zato što ***je*** *tamo naša tetka.*	We are going to Niš because our aunt is there.
Ljutit je jer ***si mu se*** *javila prekasno.*	He is angry because you called him too late.
Drago mi je ako ***sam vam*** *pomogao.*	I am glad if I have helped you.

9 **Conjunctions *a*, *i*** and ***ni*** are never followed by an enclitic but by an emphasised form of either an auxiliary verb or an emphasised form of a personal pronoun:

Dajte mu jedan sok, a meni dajte jedno pivo (NOT *Dajte mu sok, a mi dajte jedno pivo*)	Please give him a juice, and give me a beer.
Meni se dopao film, a tebi?	I liked the movie, and you?
I njoj i njemu se sviđa Korčula. (NOT *I joj i mu se sviđa Korčula*)	Both she and he like Korčula.

10 The **negative particle *ne*** is not an enclitic and therefore can be placed at the beginning of a sentence. This particle always immediately precedes the verb:

Ne želiš mu ga dati. or *Ti mu ga ne želiš dati.*	You do not want to give it to him.

N.B.1 Negative forms of auxiliary verbs (*nisam, nisi, nije, nismo, niste, nisu* and *neću, nećeš, neće, nećemo, nećete, neće*) are not enclitics and therefore can be used at the beginning of a sentence:

Past: *Niste mu se nikad javili*, or *Nikad mu se niste javili.* or *Vi mu se nikad niste javili.*	You have never called him.
Future: *Neću im se nikad više javiti*, or *Nikad više im se neću javiti*, or *Ja im se nikad više neću javiti.*	I will never call them again.

N.B.2 The negative particle *ne* is always placed right in front of the auxiliary forms for the potential mode: *bih, bi, bismo, biste*. This continues to apply when enclitics are involved:

Tražio je pare od mene. ***Ne bih*** *mu ih nikad dao*, or *Nikad mu ih* ***ne bih*** *dao*, or *Ja mu ih nikad* ***ne bih*** *dao.*	He has asked me for money. I would never give it to him.

11.3 Direct and indirect speech

In BCMS, indirect (reported) speech is guided by simpler rules than in English. When reporting what somebody said, the same tense is used in the reported speech as in the original statement:

Idemo *sutra* = *sjutra* (mont) *na more.*	We are going to the seaside tomorrow.
Oni su rekli da ***idu*** *sutra na more.*	They said they were going to the seaside the following day.

Which conjunctions are used to connect the main sentence with the reported speech depends on whether the original sentence is a statement or a question.

11.3.1 Reporting statements

Statement – conjunction *DA*

If reporting a statement the conjunction *da* is used. Note the location of enclitics as they need to be placed immediately after the conjunction *da*.

Idemo sutra – sjutra (mont) *na more.*	We are going to the seaside tomorrow.
Oni su rekli ***da*** *idu sutra – sjutra* (mont) *na more.*	They said they were going to the seaside the following day.
Stigli smo.	We have arrived.
Kažu ***da*** *su stigli.*	They say that they have arrived.
Doći ću kod vas – k vama (hr) *u subotu.*	I will come to your place on Saturday.
Kazao je ***da*** *će doći kod nas – k nama* (hr) *u subotu.*	He said that he would come to our place on Saturday.

11.3.2 Reporting questions

Questions using question words

If reporting a question asked by the question words *gdje = gde, kad(a), koliko, ko – tko* (hr)*, kuda – kamo* (hr), word order remains the same.

Kada idemo na more?	When are we going to the seaside?
Pitali su me kada idemo na more.	They asked me when we were going to the seaside.

Questions using *li*

If reporting a question asked by *li*, word order also remains the same.

Jeste li vi naš novi profesor?	Are you our new teacher?
Pitaju me jesam li ja njihov novi profesor.	They are asking me if I am their new teacher.
Da li idete na odmor sutra – sjutra (mont)?	Are you going on holiday tomorrow?
Pitali su nas da li idemo na odmor sutra – sjutra (mont).	They asked us if we were going on holiday tomorrow.

Learning tip – the conjunction *ako* cannot be used to translate the "if" conjunction from English in reported speech (as in the last two examples). In BCMS, *ako* is only used in conditional clauses.

11.4 Predicate-only sentences

All sentences in English have a subject and a predicate (verb plus its complements). If a subject is not a person or a named thing, the subject is still expressed by "it", as in: "It is very cold today".

In BCMS there are sentences which only have the predicate; hence their name, predicate-only sentences. In these sentences the verb is in the third person singular or, in compound tenses, the L-participle is in neuter gender, and there is no noun or pronoun in the nominative case that would be perceived as the grammatical subject. Some of them have a logical subject.

Predicate-only sentences can be impersonal and personalised (those with a logical subject).

11.4.1 Impersonal predicate-only sentences

Describing a state or weather conditions

These sentences are usually translated into English as "It is", "It was".

The English speaker will be tempted to start this type of sentence with *Ovo je* or *To je*, literally translating "it" with the demonstrative pronouns *ovo* or *to*. This is wrong. Just use the verb in the third person singular, the adjective in neuter gender or the L-participle in neuter gender in a compound tense.

Note word order with the enclitic *je*, which needs to be in the second place in a sentence. *Nije* is not an enclitic and can be placed at the start of a sentence.

Zimi je hladno u centralnoj Bosni.	It is cold in central Bosnia in winter time.
Bilo je hladno na Kopaoniku.	It was cold on Mt Kopaonik.
Bilo je vruće u toj sobi.	It was hot in that room.
Kako je na fakuletu? Teško je.	How is it at the university? It is hard.
Dobro je. Nije dobro.	It's fine. It's not fine.
Nije loše.	It's not bad.
Grmi i sijeva = seva.	There is thunder and lightning.
Jutros se brzo naoblačilo.	It became overcast quickly this morning.

Impersonal sentences with se

These sentences are equivalent to English phrases such as "it seems", "it is believed", "one should", "one can", "it is possible/impossible", "it is to do with" etc. In BCMS they are created by adding the reflexive particle *se* to the 3p sing of a verb (in compound tenses, the L-participle is in neuter gender).

Mora se više učiti, a manje pričati.	One needs to study more and talk less.
Ne može se živjeti = živeti bez sunca.	One cannot live without sunshine.
Nije se moglo prijeći = preći preko Alpa zbog velikoga snijega = snega.	It was impossible to cross the Alps because of a heavy snow.
Ovdje = ovde se ne smije = sme pušiti.	Smoking is forbidden here.
Očekuje se da ćemo pobijediti = pobediti.	We are expected to win (literally: It is expected that we will win).
Vjeruje se = veruje se da ...	It is believed that ...
Činilo se da su sasvim obična obitelj (bh-hr) – *porodica* (mont-srb).	It seemed that they were a completely ordinary family.
U ovom romanu se radi o ljubavi između dvoje tinejdžera.	This novel is about love between two teenagers (literally: In this novel, it is to do about ...).

Telling the time

Predicate-only sentences are used to say "It is . . . o'clock". "It" is omitted, the verb *biti* is in the 3p sing (*je*) and in compound tenses, the L-participle is in neuter gender (*je bilo*).

Šest je sati.	It is six o'clock.
Vratila se sa posla. Bilo je šest sati.	She returned from work. It was six o'clock.

N.B. English speakers should be careful not to say *Ovo je šest sati* or *To je šest sati*, literally translating "It is six o'clock" (see 6.9 "How to Tell the Time").

Existentials *ima/nema*

In this usage, these two forms no longer have the meaning of possession but of existence; therefore, they are called existentials.

Ima is the 3p sing present tense of the verb *imati* (to have). Used in predicate-only sentences, it means "there is" or "there are" (identical to the French – *il y a*).

Nema is the 3p sing present tense of the verb *nemati* (not to have). Used in predicate-only sentences it means "there isn't" or "there aren't" (identical to the French *Il n'y a pas*).

Ima finih zgrada na trgu.	There are nice buildings in the square.
Danas nema vode.	There is no water today.
Nema problema.	No problem.

N.B. English speakers should be careful not to say *Tamo su fine zgrade na trgu*, literally translating "There are nice buildings in the square".

Cases used with existentials *ima/nema*:

When *ima* is followed by a countable noun denoting one item or person, it is followed by the **nominative singular** (the number one – *jedan, jedna, jedno* – is frequently added):

Ima jedno divno jezero blizu Subotice.	There is a beautiful lake near Subotica.
Ima jedan dobar doktor koji radi u ovoj bolnici.	There is a good doctor working in this hospital.

In all other instances *ima* is followed by the **genitive**:

When *ima* is followed by a **noun denoting a substance** (something that cannot be counted – like sugar, butter etc), it is followed by the genitive singular:

Ima li šećera u tegli?	Is there any sugar in the jar?

When *ima* is followed by **countable nouns** they are in the genitive plural:

Ima li studenata u vašem gradu?	Are there students in your town?

Nema is always followed by the **genitive, singular or plural**:

Danas nema vode.	There is no water today.
Na trgu nema ljudi.	There are no people in the square.

Existentials in the past, future and future exact tenses and the potential mode

Ima/nema indicate existence/presence or a lack of presence in the present tense; in all other tenses (and the potential mode) the verb *biti* is used to denote existence or a lack of existence:

Future:	*biće* or *bit će* (hr)	*neće biti*
Past:	*bilo je*	*nije bilo*
Future exact:	*bude bilo*	*ne bude bilo*
Potential:	*bilo bi*	*ne bi bilo*

Danas ***ima*** *puno posla.*	There is a lot of work today.
Sutra ***će biti*** *puno posla.* or ***Biće*** or *bit će* (hr) *puno posla sutra* = *sjutra* (mont).	There will be a lot of work tomorrow.
Nije bilo *posla juče(r).*	There was not work yesterday.
Danas ***nema*** *struje.*	There is no electricity today.
Večeras ***neće biti*** *struje.*	There will be no electricity this evening.
Danas ***ima*** *divnih filmova na festivalu.*	There are great movies at the festival today.
Bilo je *divnih filmova na festivalu ove godine.*	There were great movies at the festival this year.
Danas ***nema*** *vode, pa se ne možemo istuširati.*	There is no water today, so we cannot take a shower.
Prošle subote ***nije bilo*** *vode, pa se nismo mogli istuširati.*	Last Saturday there was no water, and we could not take a shower.

11.4.2 Personalised predicate-only sentences

These sentences do not have a subject in the nominative case. However, a person is mentioned, either in the dative or the accusative case, and that is the logical subject of the sentence.

Describing how a state affects a human being

A noun or a pronoun referring to a person can be inserted into impersonal predicate-only sentences expressing a state (11.4.1) to describe how that particular state affects the person. The noun or the pronoun are in the dative case.

Hladno mi je u Londonu.	I am cold in London.
Bilo joj je hladno u Londonu.	She was cold in London.
Mariji je bilo vruće u kafeu.	Marija was hot in the café.

Note that the person feeling the cold is expressed by the dative case – *Hladno mi je* – literally translated into English as "It is cold to me".

Expressing a subjective feeling

Identical to these sentences are predicate-only sentences that describe a person's subjective feeling. A noun or a pronoun describing a person are also in the dative case:

Lijepo = lepo mi je ovdje = ovde u Zagrebu.	I like it here in Zagreb.
Nije vam dobro, imate li temperaturu?	You are not feeling well; do you have a temperature?
Marku je bilo teško na fakultetu.	Marko found it difficult at college.
Žao mi je.	I am sorry.
Drago mi je.	Pleased to meet you.
Bilo bi mi lakše da si ovdje = ovde sa mnom.	I would find it easier if you were here with me.
Neprijatno mi je u ovoj situaciji.	I feel awkward in this situation.

Expressing a desire

This idiom is equivalent to the English phrase – "I feel like doing" and is formed by:

a) adding the reflexive particle *se* to a verb,
b) using the verb in the impersonal 3p sing (in compound tenses the L-participle is in neuter gender), and
c) adding a personal pronoun or a noun in the dative case.

The logical subject is a noun or a personal pronoun in the dative case (the person desiring to do something), while the desired action is expressed by adding *se* to a verb:

Spava mi se.	I feel like sleeping.
Ne spava mi se.	I don't feel like sleeping.
Spavalo mi se.	I felt like sleeping.
Nije mi se spavalo.	I did not feel like sleeping.
Jede mi se sladoled.	I feel like eating an ice cream.
Ne jede mi se ništa.	I don't feel like eating anything.
Nije nam se išlo na posao.	We did not feel like going to work.
Ide li ti se u šetnju?	Do you feel like going for a walk?
Njima se nije išlo na posao.	They did not feel like going to work.
Mladenu se nije putovalo brodom.	Mladen did not feel like travelling by boat.
Ani se neće ići tako kasno na piće.	Ana will not feel like going out for drinks that late.

Note the position of enclitics *mi, ti, mu, joj, nam, vam, im* – as they have to be placed as the second unit in a sentence, grouped with other enclitics (see 11.2 "Enclitics").

Expressing shame, fear or indifference

Personalised predicate-only sentences are used in idioms expressing shame, fear or indifference. The logical subject is in the accusative case, while the nouns denoting shame (*stid* or *sramota*), fear (*strah*) or indifference (*briga*) are in the nominative case. The verb *biti* is in 3p sing (*je*) (in compound tenses the L-participle is in neuter gender – *bilo je, biće – bit će* (hr), *bilo bi*). In English, the person feeling shame, fear or indifference is the subject of the sentence:

Strah me je.	I am afraid.
Biće – bit će (hr) *me strah.*	I will be afraid.
Bilo me je strah.	I was afraid.
Stid (or *sramota*) *me je što sam se tako ponašao prema tebi.*	I am ashamed that I behaved towards you in that way.
Bilo ih je strah od jakog nevremena na otvorenom moru.	They were afraid of a severe storm in the open sea.
On je otišao na odmor, nije ga bilo briga što si ti u bolnici.	He went on holiday; he did not care that you were in hospital.
Baš me briga!	I do not care!

11.5 Negative sentences – multiple negatives

To negate a verb in the present tense, BCMS uses the particle *ne* placed right in front of a verb as a separate word; for example:

Danas radim. Danas ne radim.	I am working today. I am not working today.
Ručamo zajedno svaki dan. Ne ručamo zajedno svaki dan.	We have our lunch together every day. We don't have our lunch together every day.

This rule does not apply to three verbs which are written together with the negative particle in the present tense:

biti	*nisam, nisi nije, nismo, niste, nisu*
htjeti = hteti	*neću, nećeš, neće, nećemo, nećete, neće*
imati – nemati	*nemam, nemaš, nema, nemamo, nemate, nemaju*

For the negative forms in the past, future and future exact tenses, and for the negative forms of the imperative and potential moods – see the relevant sections in Chapter 7, "Verbs".

Forming negative sentences in BCMS is different from English. Whereas only one negative is tolerated in an English sentence, with double negatives being considered ungrammatical, a negative sentence in BCMS has to contain as many negative markings as possible – the best way to characterise them is multiple negatives. This is how negative sentences are formed:

One negative – whereby the verb is negated:

Ideš li na more ove godine?	Are you going to the seaside this year?
Ne *idem na more, idem na planinu.*	I am not going to the seaside, I am going to the mountains.

Two negatives – a negated verb plus a negative adverb or a negative pronoun:

Nikada ne *idem na more zimi.*	I never go to the seaside in winter (literally – I don't never go to the seaside in winter).

(N.B. It is impossible to say: *Nikada idem na more zimi*).

Nikoga ne *poznajem u Rijeci.*	I don't know anyone in Rijeka (literally – I do not know nobody in Rijeka).

Three negatives – a negated verb plus negative adverbs and negative pronouns:

Nikada ništa ne *radim zimi.*	I never do anything in winter (literally – I don't never do nothing in winter).

Four negatives – a negated verb plus negative adverbs and negative pronouns:

Nisam nikada nikoga ništa *pitao o tome.*	I have never asked anybody about it (literally – I haven't never asked nobody nothing about it).

Even though the literal translations sound comical in English, this is the standard way of producing negative sentences in BCMS.

As these examples illustrate, one negative is possible only if a negated verb is present in a sentence. As soon as a negative adverb or a pronoun (like nobody, nothing, never, nowhere) needs to be used, the verb has to be negated too.

As the multiple negatives are required to form these sentences, negative pronouns such as "nobody", "nothing" and negative adverbs such as "nowhere", "never" are used much more frequently than in English (see 5.6 "Indefinite Pronouns" and 8.4.1 "*ne-, ni-, i-* Adverbs").

Pronouns

niko – nitko (hr)	nobody
ništa	nothing
nijedan	not a single one
ničiji	no one's
nikakav	no kind of

Adverbs

nigdje = nigde	nowhere
nikuda – nikamo (hr)	to nowhere
nikad(a)	never
nikako	no way

In English, indefinite pronouns and adverbs such as "anybody", "anyone", "anywhere", "ever", "anyhow" etc are used very frequently, as double negatives must be avoided. In BCMS, dictionary equivalents of these indefinite pronouns and adverbs are: *iko – itko* (hr), *išta, igdje = igde, ikada, ikako* (see 5.6 and 8.4.1.). However, they are not used much due to the multiple negatives rule and are mostly used in questions:

Da li si ikada bio na Lovćenu?	Have you ever been on Lovćen?
Nisam – nijesam (mont) *nikada bio na Lovćenu.*	I have never been on Lovćen.
Da li ti se išta sviđa u ovom hotelu?	Do you like anything at all in this hotel?
Ništa mi se ne sviđa u ovom hotelu.	I don't like anything in this hotel.
Bolje išta nego ništa.	Something is better than nothing.

Chapter 12

Word creation

This chapter only lists the most productive prefixes and suffixes that students can use as a tool to learn many new words easily from the vocabulary that they will encounter at the beginner and intermediate levels.

In many instances of word creation in BCMS, logical and relatively consistent rules are followed to create new words, for example, creating negatives of adjectives and nouns, nouns naming professions or ethnicities with masculine and feminine suffixes, adopting foreign words and turning them into verbs and then into verbal nouns, transforming imperfective verbs into perfective verbs etc.

12.1 The power of word creation

To illustrate the power of word creation, here is an example of what can be done with one simple three-letter word root:

RAD **–** work
nouns

The negative prefix ***ne-*** transforms the root into *nerad* (no-work – idleness).

The suffix ***-nik*** denoting a masculine doer transforms the root into *radnik* (male worker).

The suffix ***-nica*** denoting a feminine doer transforms the root into *radnica* (female worker).

The negative prefix ***ne-*** added to these newly created nouns produces – *neradnik* and *neradnica* (male or female idler).

The location suffix ***-onica*** transforms the root into *radionica* (workshop).

DOI: 10.4324/9781003154525-12

adjectives

This root can be transformed into an adjective by adding the suffix ***-ni*** – *radni, radna, radno* – something relating to work, as in *radni dan* (work day).

The negative prefix ***ne-*** added to these adjectives gives – *neradni, neradna, neradno* – as in *neradni dan* (non-working day).

Another adjective suffix ***-čki*** can be added to *radnik* – *radnički* – something relating to workers, as in *radnička prava* (workers' rights).

verbs

This root can also be transformed into a verb by adding ***-iti: raditi*** (to work).

The imperfective verb *raditi* can now be transformed into its perfective pair by adding the prefix ***u-: uraditi*** (to complete a task).

It can also be given a new nuance by turning it into another perfective verb by adding the prefix ***iz-: izraditi*** (to produce).

This newly coined perfective verb *izraditi* can now be transformed into its imperfective pair by having the infix ***-iva-*** added: ***izrađivati***.

Other prefixes can be added to the verb *raditi*, as in *preraditi* (to adapt, to revise, to rework or to work too much), *proraditi* (to start working after repairs), *razraditi* (to elaborate) etc.

In some instances, adding a prefix or a suffix to a word causes changes either in the prefix or suffix or in the word itself. These changes are not explained here – for explanations see 2.3 "Consonant and Vowel Alternations".

12.2 Nouns

12.2.1 Suffixes for professions, doers, athletes

Many nouns naming professions, doers and athletes are created from other nouns or verbs with the addition of suffixes. Most of these suffixes are masculine. A further addition of feminine suffixes creates nouns naming female professions, doers and athletes. There are slight differences – highlighted here – in how the same set of suffixes to form these nouns is used in Bosnian, Croatian, Montenegrin and Serbian.

Masculine suffixes

The most commonly used masculine suffixes are ***-ar, -telj, -ač, -nik, -ac, -lac, -ist(a), -aš*** and ***-er***:

-*AR*

This is the most frequently used suffix to create masculine names of professions, **mostly from nouns**:

zub	tooth	*zubar* – dentist
meso	meat	*mesar* – butcher
stol	table	*stolar* – carpenter
banka	bank	*bankar* – banker
apoteka	pharmacy	*apotekar* – pharmacist (bh-mont-srb)
lijek = *lek**	medication	*ljekar* = *lekar* – physician
politika	politics	*političar* – politician
zid	wall	*zidar* – builder
biblioteka	library	*bibliotekar* – librarian
konoba	tavern	*konobar* – waiter
peći	to bake	*pekar* – baker
kuhati	to cook	*kuhar* (bh-hr) – cook
or *kuvati*		or *kuvar* (mont-srb)

*This difference (Iyekavian = Ekavian) will be marked by = in the rest of the chapter (see "How to Use This Book").

-*TELJ*

This is a very frequently used suffix to form masculine names of professions/doers **from verbs**:

učiti	to teach	*učitelj* – teacher
snimati	to shoot	*snimatelj* – cameraman
ljubiti	to kiss, love	*ljubitelj* – fan
prevoditi	to translate	*prevoditelj* – translator (hr)
čitati	to read	*čitatelj* – reader (hr)
gledati	to watch	*gledatelj* – viewer (hr)
slušati	to listen	*slušatelj* – listener (hr)

-*AČ*

This is another widely-used suffix to form masculine names of professions/doers/athletes **from verbs**:

voziti	to drive	*vozač* – driver
pjevati	to sing	*pjevač* – singer
= *pevati*		= *pevač*
navijati	to support	*navijač* – (sport team) supporter

kovati	to forge	*kovač* – blacksmith
birati	to elect	*birač* – voter
prodavati	to sell	*prodavač* (bh-hr) – shop assistant or *prodavac* (mont-srb)
plivati	to swim	*plivač* – swimmer
plesati	to dance	*plesač* – dancer
čistiti	to clean	*čistač* – cleaner
krojiti	to tailor	*krojač* – tailor

-NIK

This is another frequently used suffix to form masculine names of professions/doers **from nouns and verbs**:

raditi	to work	*radnik* – worker
carina	customs	*carinik* – customs officer
liječiti	to heal	*liječnik* (hr) – physician
lijek	medicine	*ljekarnik* (hr) – pharmacist
predsjedati = *predsedati*	to preside	*predsjednik* – president = *predsednik*
savjetovati = *savetovati*	to advise	*savjetnik* – advisor = *savetnik*

-AC

This is another frequently used suffix to form masculine names for professions/doers **from verbs**:

pisati	to write	*pisac* – writer
kupiti	to buy	*kupac* – buyer
trgovati	to trade	*trgovac* – trader, shop-owner
prodavati	to sell	*prodavac* (mont-srb) or *prodavač* (bh-hr)

-LAC

This is a frequently used suffix to form masculine names for professions/doers, mostly in Bosnian-Montenegrin-Serbian. The suffix *-telj* is preferred in Croatian (see previous examples):

prevoditi	to translate	*prevodilac* – translator
čitati	to read	*čitalac* – reader

gledati	to watch	*gledalac* – viewer
slušati	to listen	*slušalac* – listener

N.B. *-AC, -LAC* forms do not have feminine gender.

Ona je prevodilac.	She is a translator. (bh-mont-srb)
On je prevodilac.	He is a translator. (bh-mont-srb)

A different noun for this profession is used in Croatian: *prevoditelj* (masc) and *prevoditeljica* (fem).

-IST or *-ISTA*

This suffix is used to create names of professions/doers/athletes **from foreign roots**. The Croatian version is *-ist;* Bosnian, Montenegrin and Serbian is *-ista*. It does not have a female version. In Bosnian, Montenegrin and Serbian these nouns are not of feminine gender, even though they end in *-a*.

pijanist(a)	pianist
violinist(a)	violinist
ekonomist(a)	economist
karatist(a)	karate player
taksist(a)	taxi driver
optimist(a)	optimist
pesimist(a)	pessimist
gitarist(a)	guitar player
vaterpolist(a)	water polo player
biciklist(a)	cyclist

-AŠ

This suffix is used to create names of some athletes:

košarka	basketball	*košarkaš* – basketball player
nogomet	football	*nogometaš* (hr) – football player
skijanje	skiing	*skijaš* – skier
rukomet	handball	*rukometaš* – handball player
odbojka	volleyball	*odbojkaš* – volleyball player

-ER

This suffix is used to create names of some athletes/professions in Bosnian, Montenegrin and Serbian:

fudbal	football	*fudbaler* (bh-mont-srb) – football player
tenis	tennis	*teniser* (bh-mont-srb) or *tenisač* (hr) – tennis player
frizura	hairstyle	*frizer* – hairdresser

Feminine suffixes

The most commonly used feminine suffix is ***-ica.*** Another two suffixes – ***-ka*** and ***-inja*** – are used less.

These suffixes are added to the masculine nouns listed earlier denoting professions/doers/athletes:

-ICA

Professions:

konobar – konobarica	waitress
kuhar – kuharica (bh-hr)	
or *kuvar – kuvarica* (mont-srb)	female cook
sobar – sobarica	chambermaid
učitelj – učiteljica	female teacher
prevoditelj – prevoditeljica (hr)	female translator
pjevač – pjevačica	
= *pevač – pevačica*	songstress
prodavač – prodavačica (bh-hr)	
or *prodavac – prodavačica* (mont-srb)	female shop assistant
plesač – plesačica	female dancer
čistač – čistačica	cleaning lady
krojač – krojačica	seamstress

Athletes:

plivač – plivačica	female swimmer
košarkaš – košarkašica	female basketball player
nogometaš – nogometašica (hr)	female football player
skijaš – skijašica	female skier
rukometaš – rukometašica	female handball player
odbojkaš – odbojkašica	female volleyball player

To form feminine nouns from masculine nouns denoting doers/professions ending in *-nik*, the final *-k* is dropped before the suffix ***-ca*** is added:

radnik -radnica	female worker
carinik – carinica	female customs officer
književnik – književnica	female author
predsjednik – predsjednica	
= predsednik – predsednica	female president
savjetnik – savjetnica	
= savetnik – savetnica	female advisor
liječnik – liječnica (hr)	female doctor
ljekarnik – ljekarnica (hr)	female pharmacist

The feminine suffix ***-ica*** is also used to create names for many wild female animals:

lav – lavica	lion – lioness
majmun – majmunica	monkey – female monkey
vuk – vučica	wolf – female wolf
lisac – lisica	fox – vixen
tigar – tigrica	tiger – tigress
zec – zečica	male rabbit (buck) – female rabbit (doe)
slon – slonica	male elephant – female elephant
miš – mišica	mouse – female mouse

The suffix ***-ica*** is also added to the following masculine nouns:

šef – šefica	boss – female boss
kralj – kraljica	king – queen
car – carica	tsar – tsarina
grof – grofica	count – countess
svetac – svetica	saint – female saint
starac – starica	old man – old woman

To form feminine nouns for some professions, ***-ica*** is added in Bosnian/Croatian and ***-ka*** in Montenegrin/Serbian:

bh-hr	mont-srb	
profesorica	*profesorka*	female professor
zubarica	*zubarka*	female dentist
bankarica	*bankarka*	female librarian

apotekarica	*apotekarka*	female pharmacist
tenisačica	*teniserka*	female tennis player
ministrica	*ministarka*	female minister
doktorica	*doktorka*	female doctor

-KA

This suffix is added to a few masculine nouns to transform them into feminine:

bibliotekar – bibliotekarka	female librarian
političar – političarka	female politician
ljekar – ljekarka	
= *lekar – lekarka*	female physician
N.B. *liječnik – liječnica* (hr)	
frizer – frizerka	female hairdresser

-INJA

This frequently used feminine suffix is used to form feminine names of nationalities (see 12.2.2) and a few other feminine nouns, such as:

bog – boginja	god – goddess
crnac – crnkinja	black man – black woman
pjesnik – pjesnikinja	
= *pesnik – pesnikinja*	poet – poetess
rob – robinja	slave – female slave
sudac – sutkinja (hr)	judge – female judge
N.B. *sudija* (bh-mont-srb)	judge (both genders)

12.2.2 *Suffixes for ethnicities, city dwellers, regional populations*

The most common pair of suffixes for the names of ethnicities is ***-(N)AC*** for masculine nouns and ***-(N)KA*** for feminine nouns:

Albanija	*Albanac*	*Albanka*	Albanian man/woman
Amerika	*Amerikanac*	*Amerikanka*	American man/woman
Austrija	*Austrijanac*	*Austrijanka*	Austrian man/woman
Australija	*Australac*	*Australka* (hr)	
	– Australijanac (bh-mont-srb)	*– Australijanka*	Australian man/woman

Argentina	*Argentinac*	*Argentinka*	Argentinian man/woman
Bosna	*Bosanac*	*Bosanka*	Bosnian man/woman
Brazil	*Brazilac*	*Brazilka*	Brazilian man/woman
Belgija	*Belgijanac*	*Belgijanka*	Belgian man/woman
Crna Gora	*Crnogorac*	*Crnogorka*	Montenegrin man/woman
Iran	*Iranac*	*Iranka*	Iranian man/woman
Japan	*Japanac*	*Japanka*	Japanese man/woman
Jermenija	*Jermenac*	*Jermenka*	Armenian man/woman
Nizozemska	*Nizozemac*	*Nizozemka* (hr)	Dutch man/woman
Portugal	*Portugalac*	*Portugalka*	Portuguese man/woman
Slovenija	*Slovenac*	*Slovenka*	Slovene man/woman
Španjolska – *Španija*	*Španjolac* – *Španac*	*Španjolka* (hr) –*Španjolka* (bh-mont-srb)	Spanish man/woman
Švicarska – *Švajcarska*	*Švicarac* – *Švajcarac*	*Švicarka* (hr) – *Švajcarkinja* (mont-srb)	
– *Švajcarska*	– *Švajcarac*	– *Švajcarka* (bh)	Swiss man/woman
Ukrajina	*Ukrajinac*	*Ukrajinka*	Ukrainian man/woman

– And some regional populations:

Hercegovina	*Hercegovac*	*Hercegovka*	Herzegovina man/woman
Slavonija	*Slavonac*	*Slavonka*	Slavonian man/woman
Dalmacija	*Dalmatinac*	*Dalmatinka*	Dalmatian man/woman
Zagorje	*Zagorac*	*Zagorka*	Zagorje man/woman
Šumadija	*Šumadinac*	*Šumadinka*	Šumadija man/woman

There is another pair of suffixes for the names of ethnicities: ***-IN*** or ***-JANIN*** for masculine and ***-KA*** for feminine nouns:

Bugarska	*Bugarin*	*Bugarka*	Bulgarian man/woman
Europa – *Evropa*	*Europljanin* – *Evropljanin*	*Europljanka* (hr) – *Evropljanka* (bh-mont-srb)	European man/woman
Holandija	*Holanđanin*	*Holanđanka*	Dutch man/woman (bh-mont-srb)
Kanada	*Kanađanin*	*Kanađanka*	Canadian man/woman
Norveška	*Norvežanin*	*Norvežanka*	Norwegian man/woman
Švedska	*Šveđanin*	*Šveđanka*	Swedish man/woman
Vels	*Velšanin*	*Velšanka*	Welshman/woman
Škotska	*Škotlanđanin*	*Škotlanđanka*	Scottish man/woman

N.B. Note that *J*-changes occur in some nouns where the initial *-j* of the suffix blends with the previous consonant.

In some pairs, masculine nouns either do not have a suffix or a variety of suffixes are added, while for feminine nouns the suffix ***-KINJA*** is added:

Arabija	*Arapin*	*Arapkinja*	Arabian man/woman
Češka	*Čeh*	*Čehinja*	Czech man/woman
Danska	*Danac*	*Dankinja*	Danish man/woman
Engleska	*Englez*	*Engleskinja*	Englishman/woman
Francuska	*Francuz*	*Francuskinja*	Frenchman/woman
Finska	*Finac*	*Finkinja*	Finnish man/woman
Grčka	*Grk*	*Grkinja*	Greek man/woman
Irska	*Irac*	*Irkinja*	Irish man/woman
Kina	*Kinez*	*Kineskinja*	Chinese man/woman
Poljska	*Poljak*	*Poljakinja*	Polish man/woman
Rusija	*Rus*	*Ruskinja*	Russian man/woman
Srbija	*Srbin*	*Srpkinja*	Serbian man/woman
Turska	*Turčin*	*Turkinja*	Turkish man/woman

For some nationalities masculine nouns either do not have a suffix or a variety of suffixes is added, while for feminine nouns either ***-ICA*** or ***-KA*** is added:

Hrvatska	*Hrvat*	*Hrvatica*	Croatian man/woman
Italija	*Talijan*	*Talijanka* (hr)	
	– *Italijan*	*Italijanka* (bh-mont-srb)	Italian man/woman
Mađarska	*Mađar*	*Mađarica*	Hungarian man/woman
Njemačka	*Nijemac*	*Njemica*	
= *Nemačka*	– *Nemac*	– *Nemica*	German man/woman
Rumunjska	*Rumunj*	*Rumunjka* (hr)	
– *Rumunija*	– *Rumun*	– *Rumunka* (bh-mont-srb)	Romanian man/woman

There is a very useful pair of masculine/feminine suffixes for the names of city dwellers: ***-JANIN*** (masculine) and ***-JANKA*** (feminine):

Beograd	*Beograđanin*	*Beograđanka*	man/woman from Belgrade
Zagreb	*Zagrepčanin*	*Zagrepčanka*	man/woman from Zagreb
Novi Sad	*Novosađanin*	*Novosađanka*	man/woman from Novi Sad
Split	*Splićanin*	*Splićanka*	man/woman from Split
Dubrovnik	*Dubrovčanin*	*Dubrovčanka*	man/woman from Dubrovnik
Kragujevac	*Kragujevčanin*	*Kragujevčanka*	man/woman from Kragujevac
Banja Luka	*Banjalučanin*	*Banjalučanka*	man/woman from Banja Luka

Cetinje	*Cetinjanin*	*Cetinjanka*	man/woman from Cetinje
Osijek	*Osječanin*	*Osječanka*	man/woman from Osijek
Pariz	*Parižanin*	*Parižanka*	man/woman from Paris

N.B.1 Note that *J*-changes occur in some nouns where the initial *-j* of the suffix blends with the previous consonant.

N.B.2 To form the plural of these masculine nouns, the final *-n* is dropped, e.g. *Beograđanin – Beograđani* – inhabitants of Belgrade.

12.2.3 -CIJA *suffix for adopting foreign words*

This suffix is used to adopt foreign words into BCMS – those in English that end in -tion (information, occupation, organisation etc).

organisation	*organizacija*
complication	*komplikacija*
information	*informacija*
combination	*kombinacija*
construction	*konstrukcija*
operation	*operacija*
occupation	*okupacija*
inflation	*inflacija*
radiation	*radijacija*
isolation	*izolacija*

12.2.4 *Diminutives*

Diminutives are nouns used to name cute little things. An interesting fact is that typical family names in BCMS are those that end in *-ić*, such as *Milanović, Jovanović, Petrović*, meaning "the (little one) son of Milan, of Jovan or Petar".

-(Č)IĆ

This is the most productive diminutive suffix for masculine nouns:

muž	husband	*mužić*	hubby
sin	son	*sinčić*	sonny
zec	rabbit	*zečić*	bunny
leptir	butterfly	*leptirić*	little butterfly
papir	piece of paper	*papirić*	little piece of paper

stan	flat	*stančić*	little flat
ručak	lunch	*ručkić*	luncheon, sweet little lunch
prst	finger	*prstić*	tiny little finger

-(Č)ICA

This is the most productive diminutive suffix for feminine nouns:

žena	wife	*ženica*	wifey
baka	grandmother	*bakica*	granny
kćerka	daughter	*kćerkica*	cute little daughter
kuća	house	*kućica*	little house
riba	fish	*ribica*	little fish
žaba	frog	*žabica*	little frog
glava	head	*glavica*	little head
noga	leg	*nožica*	little leg

12.2.5 Augmentatives

Augmentatives are used to name big things, or more frequently beings or things that are described as unappealing, offensive or annoying.

-(Č)INA

This is the most productive augmentative suffix for masculine nouns:

komad	piece	*komadina*	big piece
muškarac	man	*muškarčina*	big he-man
lažov	liar	*lažovčina*	terrible liar
lopov	thief	*lopovčina*	horrible thief
seljak	peasant	*seljačina*	very ignorant person
prostak	simpleton	*prostačina*	ignoramus

-ETINA

This is the most productive augmentative suffix for feminine nouns:

žena	woman	*ženetina*	ugly woman
krava	cow	*kravetina*	horrible woman
baba	old woman	*babetina*	old hag
riba	fish	*ribetina*	big fish

mačka	cat	*mačketina*	big fat cat
gužva	crowd	*gužvetina*	big annoying crowd
budala	fool	*budaletina*	big silly fool
gomila	pile, crowd	*gomiletina*	an annoying pile

-URDA

This is a very useful suffix to describe a big and potentially ugly body part:

glava	head	*glavurda*	big ugly head
nos	nose	*nosurda*	big unattractive nose
noga	leg	*nožurda*	big ugly leg
ruka	hand	*ručerda*	big hand

12.2.6 Location suffixes

-(L)IŠTE

This is a very productive location suffix:

šetati	to walk	*šetalište*	promenade
parkirati	to park	*parkiralište*	parking
igrati	to play	*igralište*	playground
kazati	to say	*kazalište*	theatre (hr)
pozor	attention	*pozorište*	theatre (bh-mont-srb)
stuba	step	*stubište*	stairs (hr)
stepenica	step	*stepenište*	stairs (bh-hr-mont-srb)
dvor	court	*dvorište*	courtyard
klizati se	to skate	*klizalište*	skating rink

-ANA **and *-ARA***

These suffixes are also quite frequent:

teret	weight	*teretana*	gym
kugla	bowl	*kuglana*	bowling alley
šećer	sugar	*šećerana*	sugar refinery
so(l)	salt	*solana*	saltworks
knjiga	book	*knjižara*	book store
pekar	baker	*pekara* (bh-hr-mont-srb) – *pekarnica* (hr)	bakery

pivo	beer	*pivara*	beer brewery
meso	meat	*mesara* (bh-mont-srb)	
		– *mesnica* (hr)	butcher's

12.2.7 Suffix naming types of meat

-(T)INA

pile	chick	*piletina*	chicken meat
pure	turkey	*puretina*	turkey meat (bh-hr)
– *ćurka*		– *ćuretina*	turkey meat (mont-srb)
ovca	sheep	*ovčetina*	mutton
janje	lamb	*janjetina*	lamb meat (bh-hr)
– *jagnje*		– *jagnjetina*	lamb meat (mont-srb)
tele	calf	*teletina*	veal
june	heifer	*junetina*	heifer meat
govedo	cattle	*govedina*	beef
prase	piglet	*prasetina*	suckling pig meat
svinja	pig	*svinjetina*	pork

12.2.8 Suffixes for abstract nouns

Some abstract nouns in BCMS are formed from adjectives or other nouns with the addition of suffixes. The most productive suffixes are:

-OST

This suffix is used to create abstract nouns from adjectives. Nouns ending in *-ost* are of feminine gender even though they end in a consonant – they decline according to the Third Declension (see 3.3.13):

mlad	young	*mladost*	youth
star	old	*starost*	old age
slab	weak	*slabost*	weakness
hrabar	brave	*hrabrost*	bravery
vjeran	loyal	*vjernost*	
= *veran*		= *vernost*	loyalty
vlažan	humid	*vlažnost*	humidity
ženstven	feminine	*ženstvenost*	femininity
stvaran	real	*stvarnost*	reality

This suffix is also added to words of foreign origin to form abstract nouns:

normalan	normal	*normalnost*	normality
lojalan	loyal	*lojalnost*	loyalty
realan	realistic	*realnost*	reality
profesionalan	professional	*profesionalnost*	professionalism

-OĆA

This suffix is also used to create abstract nouns from adjectives:

hladan	cold	*hladnoća*	coldness, cold weather
skup	expensive	*skupoća*	high cost of living, costliness
jeftin	cheap	*jeftinoća*	cheapness
težak	difficult	*teškoća*	difficulty
lak	easy	*lakoća*	ease

-OTA

This suffix is also used to create abstract nouns from adjectives:

dobar	good	*dobrota*	goodness
lijep	beautiful	*ljepota*	
= lep		*= lepota*	beauty
topao	warm	*toplota*	warmth
krasan	gorgeous	*krasota*	gorgeousness

-INA

This suffix is also used to create abstract nouns from adjectives and one adverb (*koliko*) – mostly to do with sizes and measures:

dug	long	*dužina*	length
velik	big	*veličina*	greatness, size
visok	high	*visina*	height
težak	heavy	*težina*	weight
koliko	how much	*količina*	quantity

-STVO

This suffix is used to create abstract nouns from other nouns:

prijatelj	friend	*prijateljstvo*	friendship
neprijatelj	enemy	*neprijateljstvo*	enmity
čitatelj	reader	*čitateljstvo*	readership
slušatelj	listener	*slušateljstvo*	listenership
graditelj	builder	*graditeljstvo*	construction industry
slikar	painter	*slikarstvo*	art of painting

12.2.9 *Verbal nouns* -NJE

This is a very useful and productive suffix used to transform almost all imperfective verbs into neuter nouns. They usually describe a process, and that is why they are formed from imperfective verbs.

Infinitives ending in ***-ATI***

The *-ti* ending is dropped and *-NJE* added:

pliva/ti	*plivanje*	swimming
spava/ti	*spavanje*	sleeping
kupova/ti	*kupovanje*	shopping
planira/ti	*planiranje*	planning
čeka/ti	*čekanje*	waiting
broja/ti	*brojanje*	counting
drža/ti	*držanje*	holding
predava/ti	*predavanje*	lecture
putova/ti	*putovanje*	travelling
očekiva/ti	*očekivanje*	expectation

For regular I conjugation verbs in ***-ITI*** and subgroup ***-(J)ETI***

The whole ending is dropped and – ***JENJE*** is added (*J*-changes occur because the suffix starts with a *-j-*):

izlaz/iti	*izlaženje*	going out
ulaz/iti	*ulaženje*	going in
provod/iti	*provođenje*	spending time
prevod/iti	*prevođenje*	translation

bud/iti	*buđenje*	awakening
korist/iti	*korišćenje*	using, usage
misl/iti	*mišljenje*	thinking – opinion
grad/iti	*građenje*	building, construction
vid/jeti = *vid/eti*	*viđenje*	seeing

N.B.1 Exception: *J*-changes do not occur in some verbs like *sjediti* (bh-hr) or *sedeti* (srb) (to sit) – *sjedenje* or *sedenje*; *rasti* (to grow) – *rastenje; letjeti* = *leteti* (to fly) – *letenje*.

N.B.2 *J*-changes occur in Montenegrin for *sjedjeti* – *sjeđenje* (sitting).

If the last letter of the root is a soft consonant or *r* (in the examples that follow – *č, ž, š, r*), the initial *-j-* of the ending is dropped:

druž/iti se	*druženje*	socialising
znač/iti	*značenje*	meaning
puš/iti	*pušenje*	smoking
uč/iti	*učenje*	learning
ostvar/iti	*ostvarenje*	realization

In terms of usage, verbal nouns are similar to the -ing form in English, but not identical. There is a variety of translations into English, depending on the context. They are very widely used in BCMS:

Plivanje je moj omiljeni sport.	Swimming is my favourite sport.
Idem na spavanje obično oko ponoći.	I usually go to sleep at around midnight.
U formularu morate popuniti dan svoga rođenja.	In the form you have to fill in your date of birth.
Umorio se od napornog studiranja svaki dan.	He got tired of studying strenuously every day.
Najbolja sniženja su nakon novogodišnjih praznika.	The best sales are after New Year's holidays.

Verbal nouns can be created from some perfective verbs, when emphasis on the result of an action is needed. These verbal nouns have become nouns in their own right, as they do not describe a process.

iznenaditi	*iznenađenje*	to surprise – a surprise
sniziti	*sniženje*	to reduce – reduction – sales
osloboditi	*oslobođenje*	to liberate – liberation
obećati	*obećanje*	to promise – a promise

roditi	*rođenje*	to be born – birth
riješiti	*rješenje*	to decide, to resolve – decision, resolution
= *rešiti*	= *rešenje*	
zapaliti	*zapaljenje*	to set on fire – infection
utvrditi	*utvrđenje*	to fortify – fortification

12.2.10 *Negative nouns* NE-

Nouns (and many more adjectives – see 12.3) in BCMS can be created by using this prefix. The translation into English is usually not possible by prefixing an English noun with no- or non- but by finding a word that means the exact opposite to the original noun:

rad	work	*nerad*	non-work, i.e. idleness
radnik	worker	*neradnik*	idler, lazy-bones
prijatelj	friend	*neprijatelj*	non-friend, i.e. enemy
sreća	fortune	*nesreća*	misfortune
red	order	*nered*	chaos, disorder
(pl. *neredi* – riots)			
mir	peace	*nemir*	disquiet, anxiety
znanje	knowledge	*neznanje*	ignorance
dolazak	arrival	*nedolazak*	failure to show up, no-show
vrijeme	weather	*nevrijeme*	bad weather
= *vreme*		= *nevreme*	
čovjek	man/person	*nečovjek*	bad person
= *čovek*		= *nečovek*	
lojalnost	loyalty	*nelojalnost*	disloyalty
profesionalnost	*neprofesionalnost*	unprofessionalism	

12.3 Adjectives

In BCMS, the derivation of adjectives from nouns with suffixes is very important and much more frequent than in English. This is because it is impossible to place one noun in front of another and consider it to be an adjective relating to the noun that it describes, as English does in many instances.

For example, "a school book" or "a school teacher" cannot be translated by two nouns into BCMS as *škola knjiga* or *škola učitelj*. The noun "school" in this instance describes the book or the teacher, which means that it performs the function of an adjective. Therefore, in BCMS it has to be transformed into an adjective with the markings of gender, number and case to agree with the noun that it describes: *školska knjiga* or *školski učitelj*.

By their meaning and form, adjectives can be divided into two large groups: relational and descriptive.

Relational adjectives express a relation to a corresponding noun, such as *planina* – *planinski* (mountain – mountainous), *inflacija* – *inflacioni* (inflation – inflationary), *godina* – *godišnji* (year – yearly). They only have long forms and cannot be compared.

Descriptive adjectives, as their name suggests, describe a characteristic of a noun (*gladan* – hungry, *žut* – yellow, *hrabar* – brave). They can have both long and short forms and can be compared.

12.3.1 Relational adjectives

These are the most productive suffixes for relational adjectives (all forms are given in the masculine nominative singular – for female adjectives replace the final *-i* with *-a*, and for neuter with *-o*):

-SKI

The most productive suffix for this group is *-ski* and its variations *-čki* (after *c, č, k*), *-ški* (after *g, h, š, ž*) and *-ki*, they are used to create:

a) Adjectives relating to **human beings**:

doktor	*doktorski*	doctor, doctor's, doctoral
liječnik	*liječnički* (hr)	physician, physician's
dama	*damski*	lady, ladies', ladylike

b) Adjectives relating to **places and institutions**:

more	*morski*	sea, maritime
planina	*planinski*	mountainous
jezero	*jezerski*	lake
fabrika	*fabrički*	factory
škola	*školski*	school
kancelarija	*kancelarijski*	office
or *ured*	*uredski*	office (hr)

c) Adjectives relating to **geographic names** – they are also used to name languages and some countries:

Hrvat	Croatian man
hrvatski	Croatian language

Hrvatska	Croatia
Francuz	Frenchman
francuski	French language
Francuska	France
Englez	Englishman
engleski	English language
Engleska	England
Srbija	Serbia
srpski	Serbian language
srpska himna	Serbian anthem
Bosna	Bosnia
bosanski	Bosnian language
bosanska književnost	Bosnian literature
Afrika	Africa
afrički, afrička, afričko	
afrička muzika	African music
Amerika	America
američki, američka, američko	
Sjedinjene američke države	*SAD* (United States of America)
Pariz	Paris
pariski or *pariški* (hr) *kafei*	Parisian cafés
pariska or *pariška* (hr) *moda*	Parisian fashion

N.B.1 These adjectives are not capitalised (unless they are used as names of countries).

N.B.2 The names of languages are always masculine adjectives, as they refer to *jezik* (language), while some country names are feminine adjectives as they refer to *zemlja* (country); even though they are used as nouns, they decline as adjectives, for example, *u Engleskoj* – in England; *na engleskom* – in English – see subheading in 3.3.9 "Locative of Country Names".

-NI

This is a very productive suffix. Among other things, it is used to create adjectives for:

a) Parts of body:

ruka	hand	*ručni*
noga	leg	*nožni*
nos	nose	*nosni*

koža	skin	*kožni*	
pluća	lungs	*plućni*	
oko	eye	*očni*	

b) Points of compass:

istok	East	*istočni*	eastern
zapad	West	*zapadni*	western
sjever	North	*sjeverni*	northern
= *sever*		= *severni*	
jug	South	*južni*	southern

c) Time expressions:

dan	day	*dnevni*	daily
noć night	*noćni*	nightly	
tjedan	week	*tjedni* (hr)	weekly
or *sedmica*		*sedmični* (bh-mont)	
or *nedjelja*		*nedjeljni* (bh-mont & srb iyekavian)	
or *nedelja*		*nedeljni* (srb)	
mjesec	month	*mjesečni*	monthly
= *mesec*		= *mesečni*	

or ***-(Š)NJI***

danas	today	*današnji*	today's
jučer	yesterday	*jučerašnji*	yesterday's
sutra	tomorrow	*sutrašnji*	tomorrow's
jutros	this morning	*jutrošnji*	this morning's
večer	evening	*večernji*	evening's
večeras	this evening	*večerašnji*	this evening's
noćas	tonight	*noćašnji*	tonight's

-ONI

This suffix is used to transform nouns adopted from foreign languages ending in *-cija* (12.2.3 "*-CIJA* Suffix for Adopting Foreign Words") into adjectives:

organizacija	*organizacioni*	organisation
operacija	*operacioni*	operation
konstrukcija	*konstrukcioni*	construction
okupacija	*okupacioni*	occupation
inflacija	*inflacioni*	inflation
informacija	*informacioni*	information
radijacija	*radijacioni*	radiation

-EĆI

This suffix is used to transform nouns naming domestic animals into adjectives referring to meat:

pile	*pileći*	*pileći batak*	chicken leg
pure	*pureći*	*pureći odrezak*	turkey steak (bh-hr)
or *ćurka*	– *ćureći*	– *ćureća šnicla*	turkey steak (mont-srb)
tele	*teleći*	*teleći odrezak*	veal cutlet

-ĆI

This suffix is in effect the present verbal adverb suffix (see 7.9.1 "Present Verbal Adverb"). As an adjective it no longer has the meaning of a verbal adverb but has assumed a meaning of its own, closely related to the verb from which it is derived:

leteći tanjir or *leteći tanjur* (hr)	flying saucer (from the verb *letjeti* = *leteti* – to fly)
važeća dokumenta	valid documents (from the verb *važiti* – to be valid)
tekući račun	current account (from the verb *teći* – to flow)
budući	future (from the verb *biti* – to be)
zabrinjavajuće vijesti = *vesti*	worrying news

(from the verb *zabrinjavati* – to worry, to give cause for concern)

-OV and *-IN*

These are suffixes for possessive adjectives – see 4.5 "Possessive Adjectives (*Markov, Vesnin*)".

12.3.2 Descriptive adjectives

This is a large group of adjectives which describe characteristics of nouns. They have both long and short forms and can be compared.

Many of them are not derived from other words, such as *zelen* (green), *mali* (little), *topao* (warm) etc. There are many that are derived from other words, mostly nouns and verbs. There is a large number of suffixes used for their creation, and only the most frequent ones are listed here:

-AN

This is the most frequent suffix to create adjectives from nouns and some verbs. This ending is the short masculine nominative singular form; feminine and neuter endings are *-na*, *-no* respectively, due to the fleeting *-a-* rule (see 4.2 "Gender"): for example, hungry – *gladan, gladna, gladno*. Long form adjectives end in *-ni, -na, -no – gladni, gladna, gladno*.

Created from nouns:

glad	hunger	*gladan, gladna, gladno*	hungry
žeđ	thirst	*žedan, žedna, žedno*	thirsty
umor	fatigue	*umoran, umorna, umorno*	tired
odmor	rest	*odmoran, odmorna, odmorno*	rested
mast	fat	*mastan, masna, masno*	fatty, greasy
korist	use	*koristan, korisna, korisno*	useful
mir	peace	*miran, mirna, mirno*	peaceful
snijeg	snow	*snježan, snježna, snježno*	snowy
= sneg		*= snežan, snežna, snežno*	

Created from verbs:

prolaziti	pass	*prolazan, prolazna, prolazno*	fleeting, temporary, passable
prelaziti	cross	*prelazan, prelazna, prelazno*	transitional

This is a very productive suffix for creating adjectives from words adopted from Latin and ancient Greek:

romantičan, romantična, romantično	romantic
idiličan, idilična, idilično	idyllic
minimalan, minimalna, minimalno	minimal
skandalozan, skandalozna, skandalozno	scandalous
fantastičan, fantastična, fantastično	fantastic
imaginaran, imaginarna, imaginarno	imaginary

-(OV)IT

This productive suffix transforms some nouns into adjectives:

zakon	law	*zakonit, zakonita, zakonito*	lawful
riječ	word	*rječit, rječita, rječito*	eloquent
= reč		*= rečit, rečita, rečito*	
brdo	hill	*brdovit, brdovita, brdovito*	hilly
kiša	rain	*kišovit, kišovita, kišovito*	rainy

vjetar	wind	*vjetrovit, vjetrovita, vjetrovito*	windy
= vetar		*= vetrovit, vetrovita, vetrovito*	
lijek	medication	*ljekovit, ljekovita, ljekovito*	curative, medicinal
= lek		*= lekovit, lekovita, lekovito*	
dar	gift	*darovit, darovita, darovito*	gifted, talented

12.3.3 Adjective prefixes pre-, bez-, ne-

There are three very useful and very productive prefixes for adjectives:

PRE-

This very much used prefix intensifies a characteristic described by an adjective. Its English equivalent would be "super" placed in front of another adjective to intensify its meaning, like "expensive – super expensive", or the Italian "*issimo*" suffix (*bellissimo* – very beautiful).

skup	expensive	*preskup*	super expensive, exorbitant
divan	superb	*predivan*	wonderful, miraculous
krasan	beautiful	*prekrasan*	magnificent
lijep	beautiful	*prelijep*	fabulous
sretan	happy	*presretan* (bh-hr)	
or *srećan*		*presrećan* (mont-srb)	overjoyed

This prefix can also be added to adverbs to intensify their meaning. These adverbs are used extensively.

malo	little	*premalo*	too little
više	more	*previše*	too much
blizu	near	*preblizu*	too close
daleko	far	*predaleko*	too far

BEZ-

This widely used prefix creates adjectives to denote that a characteristic described by a particular adjective is absent, e.g. worthless, useless, carefree, non-alcoholic etc.

opasan	dangerous	*bezopasan*	danger-free, harmless
koristan	useful	*beskoristan*	useless
vrijedan	worthy	*bezvrijedan*	worthless
= vredan		*= bezvredan*	
brižan	caring	*bezbrižan*	carefree
alkoholni	alcoholic	*bezalkoholni*	non-alcoholic

NE-

This prefix is used to produce negatives of some adjectives.

This is a much simpler way of creating negative forms of adjectives than in English. In English, one needs to learn adjectives and their negative pairs, e.g. kind – unkind, responsible – irresponsible, mobile – immobile, legal – illegal, complete – incomplete, satisfied – dissatisfied etc.

For all these negative prefixes in English BCMS has only this one:

kind – unkind	*ljubazan – neljubazan*
stable – unstable	*stabilan – nestabilan*
interesting – uninteresting	*zanimljiv – nezanimljiv*
patient – impatient	*strpljiv – nestrpljiv*
possible – impossible	*moguć – nemoguć*
polite – impolite	*pristojan – nepristojan*
responsible – irresponsible	*odgovoran – neodgovoran*
legal – illegal	*zakonit – nezakonit*
legible – illegible	*čitljiv – nečitljiv*
logical – illogical	*logičan – nelogičan*
formal – informal	*formalan – neformalan*
complete – incomplete	*kompletan – nekompletan*
loyal – disloyal	*lojalan – nelojalan*
honest – dishonest	*pošten – nepošten*
satisfied – dissatisfied	*zadovoljan – nezadovoljan*

12.4 Verbs

A rich array of prefixes, infixes and suffixes is used to create new verbs or to add a nuance to the meaning of the root verb. The selection listed here includes only the most productive suffixes and prefixes that will help the student understand how many verbs are created.

12.4.1 *Suffixes that change foreign words into verbs*

– IRATI

This suffix is used to adopt foreign words into BCMS and to change them into verbs – of the regular A-conjugation (*-IRATI -IRAM)*.

The application of this prefix is consistent in Croatian – all foreign words transformed into Croatian verbs add this ending. For Bosnian, Montenegrin and Serbian, there are another two endings, *-OVATI* and *-ISATI*.

to plan	*planirati – planiram*
to finance	*finansirati*

to study	*studirati*
to analyse	*analizirati*
to forecast	*prognozirati* (from prognosis)
to telephone	*telefonirati*
to graduate	*diplomirati* (from diploma)
to attain a PhD	*doktorirati* (from doctorate)

– *OVATI*

This suffix is used to adopt foreign words in Bosnian, Montenegrin and Serbian and transform them into verbs of the *-OVATI -UJEM* pattern in the E-conjugation:

N.B. Croatian uses *-IRATI* for these verbs.

to discuss	*diskutovati – diskutujem* (hr – *diskutirati – diskutiram*)
to organise	*organizovati – organizujem* (hr – *organizirati – organiziram*)
to politicise	*politizovati – politizujem* (hr – *politizirati – politiziram*)
to broadcast	*emitovati – emitujem* (hr – *emitirati – emitiram*)
to conduct	*dirigovati – dirigujem* (to conduct an orchestra) (hr – *dirigirati – dirigiram*)

– *ISATI*

This suffix is used to adopt foreign words in Bosnian, Montenegrin and Serbian and transform them into verbs of the *-ISATI -IŠEM* pattern in the E-conjugation:

N.B. Croatian uses *-IRATI* for these verbs.

to reserve	*rezervisati – rezervišem* (hr – *rezervirati – rezerviram*)
to function	*funkcionisati – funkcionišem* (hr – *funkcionirati – funkcioniram*)
to concentrate	*koncentrisati – koncentrišem* (hr – *koncentrirati – koncentriram*)
to decorate	*dekorisati – dekorišem* (hr – *dekorirati, dekoriram*)
to construct	*konstruisati – konstruišem* (hr – *konstruirati, konstruiram*)
to be hysterical	*histerisati – histerišem* (hr – *histerizirati – histeriziram*)

12.4.2 Prefixes

A wide array of prefixes is used to create new verbs. Sometimes prefixes change imperfective verbs into perfective, e.g. *raditi – uraditi, pisati – napisati, čitati – pročitati;* or they are used with the verbs of motion to create new sets of verbs, both perfective and imperfective, e.g. *ići – doći – dolaziti, ići – preći – prelaziti* etc.

Many verbal prefixes are prepositions and in their basic spatial usage retain the meaning of the preposition. The following are the most widely used verbal prefixes (for usage in sentences – see 7.3.5 "Verbs of Motion"):

do	arriving at a position close to speaker
od	departing from a location
u	entering a location
iz	exiting a location
po	to start moving, starting an action
pre	moving across or over
pri	approaching a location
pro	moving through, going past
raz	dispersing from a location, scattering
s	moving downwards

DO-

This prefix retains the original meaning of the preposition – arriving at a location/destination/position close to the speaker.

In addition to the verbs of motion (see 7.3.5) such as:

ići doći	*dolaziti*
trčati	*dotrčati*
letjeti	*doletjeti*
= leteti	*= doleteti*
plivati	*doplivati*
putovati	*doputovati*
ploviti	*doploviti*

the following verbs use this prefix with the same meaning:

root verb	imperfective	perfective	
nositi	*donositi*	*donijeti* *= doneti*	to carry – to fetch, to bring to
voditi	*dovoditi*	*dovesti*	to lead – to lead (bring) to the speaker
voziti	*dovoziti*	*dovesti*	to drive – to drive to the speaker

This prefix also has the meaning of adding something, such as:

dati	*dodati*	to give – to add
pisati	*dopisati*	to write – to add in writing
graditi	*dograditi*	to build – to build on, to add a building
platiti	*doplatiti*	to pay – to make an additional payment
kupiti	*dokupiti*	to buy – to make an additional purchase

Adding this prefix to some verbs changes their original meaning:

govoriti	*dogovoriti se*	to speak – to agree
čekati	*dočekati*	to wait – to welcome
kazati	*dokazati*	to tell – to prove
seliti se	*doseliti se*	to move house – to settle, to immigrate
staviti	*dostaviti*	to place – to deliver
živjeti	*doživjeti*	to live – to experience
= živeti	*= doživeti*	

OD-

This prefix retains the original meaning of the preposition – departing from a location/position close to the speaker.

In addition to the verbs of motion (see 7.3.5) such as:

ići	*otići*	*odlaziti*
trčati	*otrčati*	
letjeti	*odletjeti*	
= leteti	*= odleteti*	
plivati	*otplivati*	
ploviti	*otploviti*	

the following verbs use this prefix with the same meaning:

root verb	imperfective	perfective	
nositi	*odnositi*	*odnijeti* *= odneti*	to carry – to carry away from a location
voditi	*odvoditi*	*odvesti*	to lead – to lead away from a location
voziti	*odvoziti*	*odvesti*	to drive – to drive away

Adding this prefix to some verbs changes their original meaning:

govoriti	*odgovoriti*	to speak – to reply
ljubiti	*odljubiti se*	to kiss – to fall out of love
držati	*održati*	to hold – to maintain
kazati	*otkazati*	to say – to cancel
uzeti	*oduzeti*	to take – to confiscate
kriti	*otkriti*	to hide – to discover
seliti se	*odseliti se*	to move house – to move out, to emigrate

With some verbs it is used to turn imperfective forms into their perfective pair:

igrati	*odigrati*	to play
gledati	*odgledati*	to watch
slušati	*odslušati*	to listen
spavati	*odspavati*	to sleep
plakati	*otplakati*	to cry
rasti	*odrasti*	to grow, to grow up
sjeći	*odsjeći*	to cut, to cut off
= seći	*= odseći*	
pjevati	*otpjevati*	to sing
= pevati	*=otpevati*	

U-

This prefix retains the original meaning of the preposition – the idea of entering a location.

In addition to the verbs of motion (see 7.3.5) such as:

ići	*ući*	*ulaziti*
trčati	*utrčati*	
letjeti	*uletjeti*	
= leteti	*= uleteti*	
ploviti	*uploviti*	

the following verbs use this prefix with the same meaning:

root verb	imperfective	perfective	
nositi	*unositi*	*unijeti*	to carry – to bring in
		= uneti	
voditi	*uvoditi*	*uvesti*	to lead – to lead in, to bring in
voziti	*uvoziti*	*uvesti*	to drive – to import

Adding this prefix to some verbs changes their original meaning:

dati	*udati se*	to give – to get married (for a woman)
poznati	*upoznati se*	to recognise – to make an acquaintance
govoriti	*ugovoriti*	to speak – to negotiate
stati	*ustati*	to stand – to get up
jesti	*ujesti*	to eat – to bite
pisati	*upisati*	to write – to enrol
graditi	*ugraditi*	to build – to build into, incorporate
platiti	*uplatiti*	to pay – to pay in
seliti se	*useliti se*	to move house – to move in, to immigrate

With some verbs it is used to turn imperfective forms into their perfective pair:

pitati	*upitati*	to ask
gledati	*ugledati*	to look, to spot
raditi	*uraditi*	to work, to do

IZ-

This prefix retains the original meaning of the preposition – exiting a location.

In addition to the verbs of motion (see 7.3.5) such as:

ići	*izići* or *izaći*	*izlaziti*
trčati	*istrčati*	
letjeti	*izletjeti*	
= *leteti*	= *izleteti*	
ploviti	*isploviti*	

the following verbs use this prefix with the same meaning:

root verb	imperfective	perfective	
nositi	*iznositi*	*iznijeti* = *izneti*	to carry – to bring out
voditi	*izvoditi*	*izvesti*	to lead – to lead out, to take out
voziti	*izvoziti*	*izvesti*	to drive – to export

Adding this prefix to some verbs changes their original meaning:

dati	*izdati*	to give – to rent out, to betray, to publish
gledati	*izgledati*	to watch – to look like, to appear
pitati	*ispitati*	to ask – to examine
misliti	*izmisliti*	to think – to invent

govoriti	*izgovoriti*	to speak – to pronounce
praviti	*ispraviti*	to make – to correct, to straighten up
držati	*izdržati*	to hold – to hold out, to endure
platiti	*isplatiti*	to pay – to pay out
seliti se	*odseliti se*	to move house – to move out, to emigrate

With some verbs it is used to turn imperfective forms into their perfective pair:

graditi	*izgraditi*	to build
pričati	*ispričati*	to chat, to speak
koristiti	*iskoristiti*	to use
gubiti	*izgubiti*	to lose
planirati	*isplanirati*	to plan
brojati	*izbrojati*	to count
plakati	*isplakati se*	to cry, to cry one's eyes out

PO-

The main meaning of this prefix is to start moving, to begin an action.

In addition to the verbs of motion (see 7.3.5) such as:

ići	*poći*	*polaziti*
trčati,	*potrčati*	
letjeti	*poletjeti*	
= leteti	*= poleteti*	

the following verbs use this prefix with the same meaning:

root verb	no imperf	perfective	
nositi		*ponijeti*	to carry – to take away
		= poneti	
voditi		*povesti*	to lead – to lead away
voziti		*povesti*	to drive – to drive away

With some verbs this prefix adds a nuance in meaning – doing the action described by the original verb briefly:

pričati	*popričati*	to chat – to have a tiny chat
gledati	*pogledati*	to watch – to have a look
slušati	*poslušati*	to listen – to have a quick listen (also – to obey)
sjediti	*posjediti* (bh-hr)	to sit – to sit down for a short while
= sedeti	*posedeti* (srb)	
= sjedjeti	*posjedjeti* (mont)	

Adding this prefix to some verbs changes their original meaning:

krenuti	*pokrenuti*	to move – to start up, to initiate
znati	*poznati*	to know – to recognize
kazati	*pokazati*	to say – to show
držati	*podržati*	to hold – to support
kriti	*pokriti*	to hide – to cover
stati	*postati*	to stand – to become
praviti	*popraviti*	to make – to repair

With some verbs it is used to turn imperfective forms into their perfective pair:

piti	*popiti*	to drink
jesti	*pojesti*	to eat
slati	*poslati*	to send
misliti	*pomisliti*	to think
nadati se	*ponadati se*	to hope
trošiti	*potrošiti*	to spend
željeti	*poželjeti*	to wish
= *želeti*	= *poželeti*	
zvati	*pozvati*	to call, to invite
rasti	*porasti*	to grow
peti se	*popeti se*	to climb
savjetovati	*posavjetovati*	to advise
= *savetovati*	= *posavetovati*	
vjerovati	*povjerovati*	
= *verovati*	= *poverovati*	to believe
ljubiti	*poljubiti*	to kiss

PRE-

The main meaning of this prefix is to move across or over.

In addition to the verbs of motion (see 7.3.5) such as:

ići	*preći*	*prelaziti*
trčati,	*pretrčati*	
letjeti	*preletjeti*	
= *leteti*	= *preleteti*	
ploviti	*preploviti*	
plivati	*preplivati*	

the following verbs use this prefix with the same meaning:

root verb	imperf	perfective	
nositi	*prenositi*	*prenijeti* = *preneti*	to carry – to transfer, to infect
voziti	*prevoziti*	*prevesti*	to drive – to drive across, to transport

Adding this prefix to some verbs changes their original meaning:

voditi	*prevoditi*	to lead – to translate
pisati	*prepisati*	to write – to copy, to prescribe
gledati	*pregledati*	to watch – to examine
davati	*predavati*	to give – to lecture
živjeti = *živeti*	*preživjeti* = *preživeti*	to live – to survive
praviti	*prepraviti*	to make – to rearrange
uzeti	*preuzeti*	to take – to take over, to download
kriti	*prekriti*	to hide – to cover

With some verbs this prefix adds a nuance in meaning – doing the action described by the original verb too much:

raditi	*preraditi se*	to work – to work too much
jesti	*prejesti se*	to eat – to eat too much
piti	*prepiti se*	to drink – to drink too much
spavati	*prespavati*	to sleep – to oversleep

With some verbs it is used to turn imperfective forms into their perfective pair:

seliti se	*preseliti se*	to move house
slušati	*preslušati*	to listen

PRI-

This prefix retains the original meaning of the preposition – being close to a location.

In addition to the verbs of motion (see 7.3.5) such as:

ići	*prići*	*prilaziti*
trčati	*pritrčati*	

the following verb uses this prefix with the same meaning:

root verb	imperf	perfective	
nositi	*prinositi*	*prinijeti* = *prineti*	to carry – to bring closer to the speaker

This prefix can add a nuance in meaning – doing the action described by the original verb for a while:

čekati	*pričekati*	to wait – to wait a bit
leći	*prileći*	to lie down – to lie down for a while
čuvati	*pričuvati*	to guard, to look after – to guard or to look after for a short while

sjećati se = *sećati se*	*prisjećati* se = *prisećati se*	to remember – to remember vaguely

Adding this prefix to some verbs changes their original meaning:

znati	*priznati*	to know – to admit, to recognize
morati	*primorati*	must – to force
govoriti	*prigovoriti*	to speak – to object
družiti se	*pridružiti* se	to socialise – to join
stati	*pristati*	to stop – to agree to

PRO-

The main meaning of this prefix is to move through or to go past.

In addition to the verbs of motion (see 7.3.5) such as:

ići	*proći*	*prolaziti*
trčati	*protrčati*	
letjeti = *leteti*	*proletjeti* = *proleteti*	

it can be added to the verb *voditi* – to lead – changing its meaning to: to spend (time, holiday):

voditi *provoditi* *provesti*

(e.g. *Fino smo se proveli na moru.* We had a lovely time at the seaside.)

With some verbs this prefix adds a nuance in meaning – starting the action described by the original verb:

govoriti	*progovoriti*	to speak – to start speaking
gledati	*progledati*	to watch – to start seeing
hodati	*prohodati*	to walk – to start walking (a toddler)

raditi	*proraditi*	to work – to resume work after repairs
piti	*propiti* se	to drink – to become a drunkard

With some verbs it is used to turn imperfective forms into their perfective pair:

buditi	*probuditi*	to wake up
čitati	*pročitati*	to read
šetati se	*prošetati* se	to go for a walk

RAZ-

The main meaning of this prefix is to move from a centre in different directions, to scatter.

In addition to the verbs of motion (see 7.3.5) such as:

ići	*razići* se	*razilaziti* se
trčati	*rastrčati* se	
letjeti	*razletjeti* se	
= *leteti*	= *razleteti* se	

the following verb uses this prefix with the same meaning:

root verb	imperfective	perfective	
nositi	*raznositi*	*raznijeti* = *razneti*	to carry – to deliver, to blow up

Adding this prefix to some verbs changes their original meaning:

voditi	*razvoditi* se	to lead – to divorce
staviti	*rastaviti (se)*	to place – to disassemble, to take apart, (with se – to separate)
stajati	*rastajati* se	to stand – to part, to separate
biti	*razbiti*	to beat – to break
očarati	*razočarati* (se)	to fascinate – to disappoint
graditi	*razgraditi*	to build – to take apart
gledati	*razgledati*	to watch – to look around, to browse
boljeti	*razboljeti* se	to hurt – to fall ill
= *boleti*	= *razboleti* se	
pasti	*raspasti* se	to fall – to disintegrate
pitati	*raspitati* se	to ask – to ask around, to inquire

With some verbs it is used to turn imperfective forms into their perfective pair:

plakati	*rasplakati* se	to cry
ljutiti se	*razljutiti* se	to be angry
veseliti se	*razveseliti* se	to be happy, rejoice

S(A)-

The main meaning of this prefix is to move downwards.

In addition to the verbs of motion (see 7.3.5) such as:

ići	*sići*	*silaziti*
letjeti	*sletjeti*	
= *leteti*	= *sleteti*	

the following verbs use this prefix with the same meaning:

root verb	imperfective	perfective	
nositi	*snositi*	*snijeti* = *sneti*	to carry – to bring downwards, downstairs

With some verbs it is used to turn imperfective forms into their perfective pair:

misliti	*smisliti*	to think
graditi	*sagraditi*	to build
lagati	*slagati*	to lie
kriti	*sakriti*	to hide

Chapter 13

Croatian-Serbian glossary

Most common vocabulary differences

As we have seen in the preceding 12 chapters, at the level of essential everyday grammar, BCMS is a single system with very few variations in usage despite the great variety of inflectional morphemes (grammatical endings). In very few cases the four variants use the same endings in slightly different ways, with occasional contrasts. The most common difference is to do with the reflexes of the old long Slavonic vowel *yat* in Bosnian, Croatian and Montenegrin on the one hand (Iyekavian pronunciation) and in Serbian on the other (predominantly Ekavian pronunciation) (see 1.1 "Ekavian and Iyekavian Pronunciations").

However, there is a marked contrast between Croatian and Serbian when it comes to some frequently used words. They are mutually understandable to those who have been exposed to the other variant, but initially may be slightly confusing to those who have not. While foreign words are readily adopted in Serbian, in Croatian words made of Slavonic roots are preferred, for example, *apoteka – ljekarna* (pharmacy), *doktor – liječnik* (physician), *univerzitet – sveučilište* (university) etc.

In some instances, a purely Slavonic word is prescribed in the Croatian standard, but in the colloquial language a majority of Croatian speakers use internationally recognisable versions, for example, *aerodrom – zračna luka* (airport), *avion – zrakoplov* (airplane) etc. Thus a taxi driver in Istria may ask you if you want to go to *Aerodrom Pula*, but when you get there the official sign will read: *Zračna luka Pula.*

As for Bosnian, in some parts of Bosnia people opt for the Croatian version of a particular word, in others they may opt for the Serbian version. In very few instances Bosnian has its own version, and those are words usually imported from Turkish or Arabic. Montenegrin shares the Serbian version of the words included in this brief glossary.

Here we list about 200 words, divided into nouns, adjectives and so on, then subdivided into categories of meaning.

DOI: 10.4324/9781003154525-13

Croatian words are listed on the left, the Serbian and Montenegrin version on the right

- Where only one version is used in Bosnian, it is marked as (+bh) in the relevant column; where not thus marked, both versions are used in Bosnian.
- Montenegrin is only indicated as (mont) where it is different from the Serbian Ekavian version, e.g. *beli luk* or *bijeli luk* (mont).
- Where Bosnian and Montenegrin have their own versions, they are marked as (bh) or (mont).

Even words which differ only by one letter are listed, for example, *Njemačka – Nemačka, tanjur – tanjir* etc.

13.1 Nouns

Geography

inozemstvo	*inostranstvo*	abroad
ocean	*okean* (+bh)	ocean
otok (+bh)	*ostrvo*	island
planet	*planeta*	planet
poluotok (+bh)	*poluostrvo*	peninsula
špilja	*pećina*	cave
zaljev	*zaliv*	cove

Countries

Cipar	*Kipar* (+bh)	Cyprus
Europa	*Evropa*	Europe
Nizozemska	*Holandija* (+bh)	The Netherlands
Njemačka (+bh +mont)	*Nemačka*	Germany
Rumunjska	*Rumunija* (+bh)	Romania
Španjolska	*Španija* (+bh)	Spain
Švicarska	*Švajcarska*	Switzerland

Locations

cesta	*put*	road
prodavaonica, or *dućan,* or *trgovina*	*prodavnica, radnja*	shop
kazalište	*pozorište* (+bh)	theatre
kino (+bh)	*bioskop*	cinema
knjižnica	*biblioteka* (+bh)	library
kolodvor	*stanica* (+bh)	railway or bus station

križanje	*raskrisnica* (+bh)	crossroads
ljekarna	*apoteka* (+bh)	pharmacy
mesnica	*mesara*	butcher's
odjel	*odsek* *odsjek* (bh-mont & srb Iyekavian)	department
općina	*opština*	municipality
pekarnica or *pekarna*	*pekara* (+bh)	bakery
policijska postaja	*policijska stanica* (+bh)	police station
pločnik	*trotoar*	pavement
sveučilište	*univerzitet*	university
tržnica	*pijaca*	market
tvornica	*fabrika*	factory
tvrtka	*kompanija*	company, firm
ured	*kancelarija* (+bh)	office
veleposlanstvo	*ambasada*	embassy
zračna luka	*aerodrom* (+bh)	airport
županija	*okrug*	county

House and household items

blagovaonica	*trpezarija*	dining room
deka	*ćebe*	blanket
dizalo	*lift* (+bh)	lift
glačalo (+bh)	*pegla*	iron
kat	*sprat*	floor
kućanstvo	*domaćinstvo*	household
kupaonica (+bh)	*kupatilo*	bathroom
kut	*ugao*	corner
pećnica	*rerna*	oven
plahta	*čaršaf*	sheet
ručnik	*peškir*	towel
sag	*tepih* *ćilim* (bh)	carpet
smeće	*đubre*	refuse, rubbish
spužva	*sunđer*	sponge
strop	*plafon* *tavanica* (bh)	ceiling
stubište	*stepenište* (+bh)	staircase
šalica	*šoljica*	cup
škare or *nožice*	*makaze* (+bh)	scissors

špaga	*konopac*	rope
šparhet or *štednjak*	*šporet*	cooker
tacna	*poslužavnik*	tray
tanjur	*tanjir* (+bh)	plate
tanjurić	*tacna*	saucer
tava	*tiganj*	frying pan
vilica	*viljuška* (+bh)	fork
vrt	*bašta*	garden
zahod (+bh)	*klozet*	WC
zdjela	*činija*	bowl
zrcalo	*ogledalo* (+bh)	mirror
žarulja	*sijalica* (+bh)	light-bulb
žlica	*kašika* (+bh)	spoon

Clothes

gumb	*dugme* (+bh)	button
hlače	*pantalone*	trousers
naočale (+bh)	*naočare*	glasses
remen	*kaiš*	belt
traperice or *farmerice* (+bh)	*farmerke*	jeans
vesta	*džemper* (+bh)	jumper
žniranac	*pertla* (+bh)	shoelace

Food

cikla	*cvekla*	beetroot
češnjak (+bh)	*beli luk* *bijeli luk* (bh-mont & srb lyekavian)	garlic
grah (+bh)	*pasulj*	beans
janjetina (+bh)	*jagnjetina*	lamb
juha (+bh)	*supa*	soup
kruh (+bh)	*hleb* *hljeb* (bh-mont & srb lyekavian)	bread
krumpir	*krompir* (+bh)	potatoes
luk (+bh)	*crni luk*	onion
lješnjak	*lešnik* *lješnik* (bh-mont & srb lyekavian)	hazelnut

mrkva (+bh)	*šargarepa*	carrot
odrezak	*šnicla*	steak
ploška	*parče, komad*	piece
rajčica	*paradajz* (+bh)	tomato
riža	*pirinač* (+bh)	rice
špinat	*spanać*	spinach

Family and family relations

djed (+bh +mont)	*deda*	grandfather
obitelj (+bh)	*porodica* *familija* (+bh)	family
punica (+bh)	*tašta*	mother-in-law
punac (+bh)	*tast*	father-in-law
rodica or *rođakinja* (+bh)	*rođaka*	female relative, cousin

Professions and workplace

redatelj	*režiser*	film director
glazbenik	*muzičar* (+bh)	musician
kuhar (+bh)	*kuvar*	cook
liječnik	*doktor*	physician
ljekarnik	*apotekar*	pharmacist
natječaj	*konkurs*	competition (for work)
odvjetnik	*advokat* (+bh)	attorney, solicitor
prevoditelj	*prevodilac* (+bh)	translator
prodavač (+bh)	*prodavac*	shop assistant
profesorica (+bh)	*profesorka*	female professor
ravnatelj	*direktor, upravnik*	director
studentica (+bh)	*studentkinja*	female student
sudac	*sudija*	judge
svećenik	*sveštenik*	priest
tajnica (+bh)	*sekretarica*	secretary
umirovljenik	*penzioner*	pensioner
veleposlanik	*ambasador*	ambassador
znanstvenik	*naučnik* (+bh)	scientist
dopust	*godišnji odmor*	annual leave
mirovina	*penzija*	pension
plaća	*plata*	salary
suradnik	*saradnik*	associate

Means of transport

vlak	*voz*	train
zrakoplov	*avion* (+bh)	airplane

Time

jučer	*juče*	yesterday
minuta	*minut*	minute
sekunda (+bh)	*sekund*	second
stoljeće	*vek* *vijek* (bh-mont & srb lyekavian)	century
tjedan	*nedelja* *nedjelja* (bh-mont & srb lyekavian) *sedmica* (bh-mont)	week
večer	*veče*	evening

Plus names of months in Croatian (see 6.8.2 "Months of the Year")

Abstract nouns

dojam	*utisak*	impression
glazba	*muzika* (+bh)	music
kakvoća	*kvalitet*	quality
kemija	*hemija* (+bh)	chemistry
konac	*kraj*	end
neovisnost	*nezavisnost*	independence
okoliš	*životna sredina*	environment
osjećaj	*osećanje* *osjećanje* (bh-mont & srb lyekavian)	feeling
polovica	*polovina*	half
posjet	*poseta* *posjeta* (bh-mont & srb lyekavian)	visit
potpora	*podrška*	support
povjest	*istorija* *historija* (bh)	history
pozornost	*pažnja*	attention
promet	*saobraćaj*	traffic
propuh (+bh)	*promaja*	draft

prosvjed	*protest*	protest
razina	*nivo* (+bh)	level
saopćenje	*saopštenje*	statement
skrb	*briga*	care
sprovod	*sahrana* (+bh) *dženaza* (bh)	funeral
stožer	*sedište, štab* *sjedište* (bh-mont & srb lyekavian)	headquarters
stupanj	*stepen*	degree
suradnja	*saradnja*	cooperation
sustav	*sistem* (+bh)	system
tijek	*tok*	course
tisak	*štampa*	press (newspapers)
tisuća	*hiljada* (+bh)	thousand
tlak	*pritisak*	pressure
ubojstvo	*ubistvo*	murder
učinkovitost	*efikasnost*	efficacy
uputa	*uput* (+bh)	instruction
utjecaj	*uticaj*	influence
uvjet	*uslov*	condition
zemljopis	*geografija*	geography
znanost	*nauka*	science
zrak	*vazduh*	air

Sports

natjecanje	*takmičenje*	competition (sports)
nogomet	*fudbal* (+bh)	football
nogometaš	*fudbaler* (+bh)	football player
tenisač	*teniser*	tennis player

Miscellaneous

cjepivo	*vakcina*	vaccine
cijepljenje	*vakcinacija*	vaccination
dupin	*delfin*	dolphin
inozemac	*stranac*	foreigner
kotač	*točak*	*wheel*
kralježnica	*kičma*	spine
ljepilo (+bh)	*lepak* *lijepak* (bh-mont & srb lyekavian)	glue

osobna iskaznica	*lična karta* (+bh)	ID card
prtljaga	*prtljag* (+bh)	baggage
putovnica	*pasoš* (+bh)	passport
sudionik	*učesnik*	participant
stroj	*mašina*	machine
tekućina	*tečnost*	liquid
točka	*tačka* (+bh)	full-stop, point
val (+bh)	*talas*	wave
žgaravica	*gorušica*	heartburn

13.2 Adjectives

izravan	*direktan*	direct
inozeman	*inostran*	foreign
krivi	*pogrešan*	wrong
lijen (+bh-mont)	*lenj*	lazy
narančast	*narandžast*	orange
neovisan	*nezavisan*	independent
obvezatan	*obavezan* (+bh)	obligatory
redovit	*redovan*	regular
smeđ	*braon*	brown
sretan (+bh)	*srećan*	happy
suh (+bh)	*suv*	dry
točan	*tačan* (+bh)	correct
umjetni	*veštački* *vještački* (bh-mont & srb Iyekavian)	artificial
vanjski (+bh)	*spoljni* or *spoljašnji*	external, foreign

13.3 Verbs

glačati (+bh)	*peglati*	to iron
ispričavati se	*izvinjavati se* (+bh)	to aplogize
ovisiti (+bh)	*zavisiti*	to depend
plesati (+bh)	*igrati*	to dance
posuditi	*pozajmiti*	to lend
prihvaćati	*prihvatati*	to accept
produljiti (+bh)	*produžiti*	to extend
puhati (+bh)	*duvati*	to blow
shvaćati	*shvatati*	to comprehend

surađivati	*sarađivati*	to cooperate
uglazbiti	*komponovati* (+bh)	to compose
uhititi	*uhapsiti* (+bh)	to arrest
utjecati	*uticati*	to influence

Plus verbs made from internationalisms (see 12.4.1 "Suffixes That Change Foreign Words into Verbs")

13.4 Adverbs

djelomice	*delomično* *djelomično* (bh-mont & srb lyekavian)	partly
doista	*zaista*	really
dolje	*dole*	down
iznimno	*izuzetno*	exceptionally
općenito	*uopšteno*	in general terms
osobno	*lično* (+bh)	personally
pješice (+bh)	*peške* *pješke* (bh-mont & srb lyekavian)	on foot
polovicom	*polovinom*	in the middle of
ponovno	*ponovo*	again
posebice	*naročito*	especially
ravno	*pravo*	directly
redovito	*redovno*	regularly
uopće	*uopšte*	at all
vani	*napolju*	outside
vjerojatno (+bh)	*verovatno* *vjerovatno* (bh-mont & srb lyekavian)	perhaps, probably
zacijelo or *jamačno*	*sigurno* (+bh)	certainly

13.5 Everyday expressions

dobar tek	*prijatno*	bon apetit
oprostite	*izvinite* (+bh)	excuse me
dobra večer	*dobro veče*	good evening

Chapter 14

Verb conjugation tables

14.1 Irregular verbs

14.1.1 BITI

Present

singular			plural		
1	jesam	sam*	1	jesmo	smo
2	jesi	si	2	jeste	ste
3	jeste	je	3	jesu	su

* For explanation of short and long forms, see 7.3.2.a.

Present negative (Bosnian-Croatian-Serbian)

1	nisam	1	nismo
2	nisi	2	niste
3	nije	3	nisu

Present negative (Montenegrin)

1	nijesam	1	nijesmo
2	nijesi	2	nijeste
3	nije	3	nijesu

Perfective form – present

1	budem	1	budemo
2	budeš	2	budete
3	bude	3	budu

Future

(Croatian-Bosnian)

1	bit ću	1	bit ćemo
2	bit ćeš	2	bit ćete
3	bit će	3	bit će

DOI: 10.4324/9781003154525-14

(Bosnian-Montenegrin-Serbian)

1	biću	1	bićemo
2	bićeš	2	bićete
3	biće	3	biće

Past

1	bio sam	1	bili smo
2	bio si	2	bili ste
3	bio je	3	bili su

Aorist

1	bih	1	bismo
2	bi	2	biste
3	bi	3	bi

Imperative

2p sing	budi
1p pl	budimo
2p pl	budite

L-participle

bio, bila, bilo
bili, bile, bila

Present verbal adverb

budući

Past verbal adverb

bivši

14.1.2 MOĆI

Present

singular		plural	
1	mogu	1	možemo
2	možeš	2	možete
3	može	3	mogu

Future

1	moći ću	1	moći ćemo
2	moći ćeš	2	moći ćete
3	moći će	3	moći će

Past

1	mogao sam	1	mogli smo
2	mogao si	2	mogli ste
3	mogao je	3	mogli su

L-participle

mogao, mogla, moglo
mogli, mogle, mogla

Present verbal adverb

mogući

Past verbal adverb

mogavši

14.1.3 *HTJETI = HTETI**

* This difference (Iyekavian = Ekavian) will be marked by = in the rest of the chapter (see "How to Use This Book").

Present

singular			plural		
1	hoću	ću**	1	hoćemo	ćemo
2	hoćeš	ćeš	2	hoćete	ćete
3	hoće	će	3	hoće	će

** For explanation of short and long forms – see 7.3.2.b.

Present negative

1	neću	1	nećemo
2	nećeš	2	nećete
3	neće	3	neće

Future

(Croatian-Bosnian)

1	htjet ću	1	htjet ćemo
2	htjet ćeš	2	htjet ćete
3	htjet će	3	htjet će

(Bosnian-Montenegrin & Serbian Iyekavian)

1	htjeću	1	htjećemo
2	htjećeš	2	htjećete
3	htjeće	3	htjeće

(Serbian)

1	hteću	1	htećemo
2	htećeš	2	htećete
3	hteće	3	hteće

Past

(Iyekavian)

singular		plural	
1	htio sam	1	htjeli smo
2	htio si	2	htjeli ste
3	htio je	3	htjeli su

(Ekavian)

1	hteo sam	1	hteli smo
2	hteo si	2	hteli ste
3	hteo je	3	hteli su

Imperative

(Iyekavian)

2p sing	htjedni
1p pl	htjednimo
2p pl	htjednite

(Ekavian)

2p sing	htedni
1p pl	htednimo
2p pl	htednite

L-participle

(Iyekavian)

htio, htjela, htjelo
htjeli, htjele, htjela

(Ekavian)

hteo, htela, htelo
hteli, htele, htela

Present verbal adverb

htijući = hoteći

Past verbal adverb

htjevši or hotjevši = htevši

Verbal noun

htjenje or htijenje = htenje

14.1.4 *SLATI*

Present

singular		plural	
1	šaljem	1	šaljemo
2	šalješ	2	šaljete
3	šalje	3	šalju

Future

(Croatian-Bosnian)

1	slat ću	1	slat ćemo
2	slat ćeš	2	slat ćete
3	slat će	3	slat će

Future

(Bosnian-Montenegrin-Serbian)

1	slaću	1	slaćemo
2	slaćeš	2	slaćete
3	slaće	3	slaće

Past

1	slao sam	1	slali smo
2	slao si	2	slali ste
3	slao je	3	slali su

Imperative

2p sing	šalji
1p pl	šaljimo
2p pl	šaljite

L-participle

slao, slala, slalo
slali, slale, slala

Present verbal adverb

šaljući

Past verbal adverb

poslavši (formed from its perfective pair)

Passive participle

slan, slana, slano
slani, slane, slana
or
slat, slata, slato
slati, slate, slata

Verbal noun

slanje

14.2 A conjugation (regular)

All verbs whose infinitive stem and the present tense stem end in *-a* follow this conjugation. For more verbs, see 7.3.3 "A Conjugation".

znati – znam

Present

singular		plural	
1	znam	1	znamo
2	znaš	2	znate
3	zna	3	znaju

Future

(Croatian-Bosnian)

1	znat ću	1	znat ćemo
2	znat ćeš	2	znat ćete
3	znat će	3	znat će

(Bosnian-Montenegrin-Serbian)

1	znaću	1	znaćemo
2	znaćeš	2	znaćete
3	znaće	3	znaće

Past

1	znao sam	1	znali smo
2	znao si	2	znali ste
3	znao je	3	znali su

Imperative

2p sing	znaj
1p pl	znajmo
2p pl	znajte

L-participle

znao, znala, znalo
znali, znale, znala

Present verbal adverb

znajući

Past verbal adverb

saznavši (formed from its perfective pair)

Passive participle

znan, znana, znano
znani, znane, znana

Verbal noun

znanje

14.3 I conjugation (regular)

All verbs whose infinitive stem and the present tense stem end in ***-i*** follow this conjugation. For more verbs, see 7.3.3 "I Conjugation'.

učiti – učim

Present

singular		plural	
1	učim	1	učimo
2	učiš	2	učite
3	uči	3	uče

Future

(Croatian-Bosnian)

1	učit ću	1	učit ćemo
2	učit ćeš	2	učit ćete
3	učit će	3	učit će

(Bosnian-Montenegrin-Serbian)

1	učiću	1	učićemo
2	učićeš	2	učićete
3	učiće	3	učiće

Past

1	učio sam	1	učili smo
2	učio si	2	učili ste
3	učio je	3	učili su

Imperative

2p sing	uči
1p pl	učimo
2p pl	učite

L-participle

učio, učila, učilo
učili, učile, učila

Present verbal adverb

učeći

Past verbal adverb

naučivši (formed from its perfective pair)

Passive participle

učen, učena, učeno
učeni, učene, učena

Verbal noun

učenje

14.3.1 *I conjugation pattern -ETI -IM*

All verbs whose infinitive ends in ***-eti*** and whose first person sing present tense ends in ***-im*** follow this conjugational pattern. For more verbs, see 7.3.3 "I Conjugation".

željeti – želim = želeti – želim

Present

singular		plural	
1	želim	1	želimo
2	želiš	2	želite
3	želi	3	žele

Future

(Croatian-Bosnian)

1	željet ću	1	željet ćemo
2	željet ćeš	2	željet ćete
3	željet će	3	željet će

(Bosnian-Montenegrin & Serbian Iyekavian)

1	željeću	1	željećemo
2	željećeš	2	željećete
3	željeće	3	željeće

(Serbian)

1	želeću	1	želećemo
2	želećeš	2	želećete
3	želeće	3	želeće

Past

(Iyekavian)

1	želio sam	1	željeli smo
2	želio si	2	željeli ste
3	želio je	3	željeli su

(Ekavian)

1	želeo sam	1	želeli smo
2	želeo si	2	želeli ste
3	želeo je	3	želeli su

Imperative

2p sing	želi
1p pl	želimo
2p pl	želite

L-participle

(Iyekavian)

želio, željela, željelo
željeli, željele, željela

(Ekavian)

želeo, želela, želelo
želeli, želele, želela

Present verbal adverb

želeći

Past verbal adverb

poželjevši = poželevši (formed from its perfective pair)

Passive participle

željen, željena, željeno
željeni, željene, željena

Verbal noun

željenje = želenje

boljeti – boli = boleti – boli
(only used in 3rd p singular or plural)

Present

singular		plural	
3	boli	3	bole

Future

(Croatian-Bosnian)

3	boljet će	3	boljet će

(Bosnian-Montenegrin & Serbian Iyekavian)

3	boljeće	3	boljeće

(Serbian)

3	boleće	3	boleće

L-participle

(Iyekavian)

bolio, boljela, boljelo
boljeli, boljele, boljela

(Ekavian)

boleo, bolela, bolelo
boleli, bolele bolela

Present verbal adverb

boleći

Past verbal adverb

preboljevši = prebolevši (made from its perfective pair)

Verbal noun

boljenje = bolenje

14.3.2 I conjugation pattern -ATI -IM

All verbs whose infinitive ends in ***-ati*** and whose first person singular present tense ends in ***-im*** follow this conjugational pattern. For more verbs, see 7.3.3 "I Conjugation".

držati – držim

Present

singular		plural	
1	držim	1	držimo
2	držiš	2	držite
3	drži	3	drže

Future

(Croatian-Bosnian)

1	držat ću	1	držat ćemo
2	držat ćeš	2	držat ćete
3	držat će	3	držat će

(Bosnian-Montenegin-Serbian)

1	držaću	1	držaćemo
2	držaćeš	2	držaćete
3	držaće	3	držaće

Past

1	držao sam	1	držali smo
2	držao si	2	držali ste
3	držao je	3	držali su

Imperative

2p sing	drži
1p pl	držimo
2p pl	držite

L-participle

držao, držala, držalo
držali, držale, držala

Present verbal adverb

držeći

Past verbal adverb

održavši (made from its perfective pair)

Passive participle

držan, držana, držano
držani, držane, držana

Verbal noun

držanje

14.4 E conjugation patterns

14.4.1 *Pattern -ATI -EM*

a) stajati – stajem

For more verbs, see 7.3.3 "E Conjugation".

Present

singular		plural	
1	stajem	1	stajemo
2	staješ	2	stajete
3	staje	3	staju

Future

(Croatian-Bosnian)

1	stajat ću	1	stajat ćemo
2	stajat ćeš	2	stajat ćete
3	stajat će	3	stajat će

(Bosnian-Montenegrin-Serbian)

1	stajaću	1	stajaćemo
2	stajaćeš	2	stajaćete
3	stajaće	3	stajaće

Past

1	stajao sam	1	stajali smo
2	stajao si	2	stajali ste
3	stajao je	3	stajali su

Imperative

2p sing	staj
1p pl	stajmo
2p pl	stajte

L-participle

stajao, stajala, stajalo
stajali, stajale, stajala

Present verbal adverb

stajući

Verbal noun

stajanje

b) pisati – pišem

(verbs with changes in the final consonant of the root – *J* changes)

For more verbs, see 7.3.3 "E Conjugation".

Present

singular		plural	
1	pišem	1	pišemo
2	pišeš	2	pišete
3	piše	3	pišu

Future

(Croatian-Bosnian)

1	pisat ću	1	pisat ćemo
2	pisat ćeš	2	pisat ćete
3	pisat će	3	pisat će

(Bosnian-Montenegrin-Serbian)

1	pisaću	1	pisaćemo
2	pisaćeš	2	pisaćete
3	pisaće	3	pisaće

Past

singular		plural	
1	pisao sam	1	pisali smo
2	pisao si	2	pisali ste
3	pisao je	3	pisali su

Imperative

2p sing	piši
1p pl	pišimo
2p pl	pišite

L-participle

pisao, pisala, pisalo
pisali, pisale, pisala

Present verbal adverb

pišući

Past verbal adverb

napisavši (formed from its perfective pair *napisati*)

Passive participle

pisan, pisana, pisano
pisani, pisane, pisana

Verbal noun

pisanje

c) zvati – zovem

(verbs with a significant vowel change in the present stem)

For more verbs, see 7.3.3 "E Conjugation".

Present

singular		plural	
1	zovem	1	zovemo
2	zoveš	2	zovete
3	zove	3	zovu

Future

(Croatian-Bosnian)

1	zvat ću	1	zvat ćemo
2	zvat ćeš	2	zvat ćete
3	zvat će	3	zvat će

(Bosnian-Montenegrin-Serbian)

1	zvaću	1	zvaćemo
2	zvaćeš	2	zvaćete
3	zvaće	3	zvaće

Past

1	zvao sam	1	zvali smo
2	zvao si	2	zvali ste
3	zvao je	3	zvali su

Imperative

2p sing	zovi
1p pl	zovimo
2p pl	zovite

L-participle

zvao, zvala, zvalo
zvali, zvale, zvala

Present verbal adverb

zovući

Past verbal adverb

pozvavši (formed from its perfective pair *pozvati*)

Passive participle

zvan, zvana, zvano
zvani, zvane, zvana

Verbal noun

zvanje

brati – berem (prati – perem)

Present

singular		plural	
1	berem	1	beremo
2	bereš	2	berete
3	bere	3	beru

Future

(Croatian-Bosnian)

1	brat ću	1	brat ćemo
2	brat ćeš	2	brat ćete
3	brat će	3	brat će

(Bosnian-Montenegrin-Serbian)

1	braću	1	braćemo
2	braćeš	2	braćete
3	braće	3	braće

Past

1	brao sam	1	brali smo
2	brao si	2	brali ste
3	brao je	3	brali su

Imperative

2p sing	beri
1p pl	berimo
2p pl	berite

L-participle

brao, brala, bralo
brali, brale, brala

Present verbal adverb

berući

Past verbal adverb

ubravši (formed from its perfective pair – *ubrati*)

Passive participle

bran, brana, brano
brani, brane, brana

Verbal noun

branje

14.4.2 *Pattern -ATI -ANEM*

stati – stanem
(to stop, to stand up – perf)

(all verbs derived from ***stati*** with prefixes – these are all perfective pairs of group 14.4.1.a verbs)

For more verbs, see 7.3.3 "E Conjugation".

Present

singular		plural	
1	stanem	1	stanemo
2	staneš	2	stanete
3	stane	3	stanu

Future

(Croatian-Bosnian)

1	stat ću	1	stat ćemo
2	stat ćeš	2	stat ćete
3	stat će	3	stat će

(Bosnian-Montenegrin-Serbian)

1	staću	1	staćemo
2	staćeš	2	staćete
3	staće	3	staće

Past

1	stao sam	1	stali smo
2	stao si	2	stali ste
3	stao je	3	stali su

Imperative

2p sing	stani
1p pl	stanimo
2p pl	stanite

L-participle

stao, stala, stalo
stali, stale, stala

Past verbal adverb

stavši

14.4.3 Pattern -AVATI -AJEM

davati – dajem

(and all verbs derived from *davati* with prefixes)

For more verbs, see 7.3.3 "E Conjugation".

Present

singular		plural	
1	dajem	1	dajemo
2	daješ	2	dajete
3	daje	3	daju

Future

(Croatian-Bosnian)

1	davat ću	1	davat ćemo
2	davat ćeš	2	davat ćete
3	davat će	3	davat će

(Bosnian-Montenegrin-Serbian)

1	davaću	1	davaćemo
2	davaćeš	2	davaćete
3	davaće	3	davaće

Past

1	davao sam	1	davali smo
2	davao si	2	davali ste
3	davao je	3	davali su

Imperative

2p sing	daj
1p pl	dajmo
2p pl	dajte

L-participle

davao, davala, davalo
davali, davale, davala

Present verbal adverb

dajući

Passive participle

davan, davana, davano
davani, davane, davana

Verbal noun

davanje

14.4.4 *Pattern -OVATI -UJEM*

kupovati – kupujem

For more verbs, see 7.3.3. "E Conjugation".

Present

singular		plural	
1	kupujem	1	kupujemo
2	kupuješ	2	kupujete
3	kupuje	3	kupuju

Future

(Croatian-Bosnian)

1	kupovat ću	1	kupovat ćemo
2	kupovat ćeš	2	kupovat ćete
3	kupovat će	3	kupovat će

(Bosnian-Montenegrin-Serbian)

1	kupovaću	1	kupovaćemo
2	kupovaćeš	2	kupovaćete
3	kupovaće	3	kupovaće

Past

1	kupovao sam	1	kupovali smo
2	kupovao si	2	kupovali ste
3	kupovao je	3	kupovali su

Imperative

2p sing	kupuj
1p pl	kupujmo
2p pl	kupujte

L-participle

kupovao, kupovala, kupovalo
kupovali, kupovale, kupovala

Present verbal adverb

kupujući

Passive participle

kupovan, kupovana, kupovano
kupovani, kupovane, kupovana

Verbal noun

kupovanje

14.4.5 *Pattern -IVATI -UJEM*

dočekivati – dočekujem

For more verbs, see 7.3.3 "E Conjugation".

Present

singular		plural	
1	dočekujem	1	dočekujemo
2	dočekuješ	2	dočekujete
3	dočekuje	3	dočekuju

Future

(Croatian-Bosnian)

1	dočekivat ću	1	dočekivat ćemo
2	dočekivat ćeš	2	dočekivat ćete
3	dočekivat će	3	dočekivat će

(Bosnian-Montenegrin-Serbian)

1	dočekivaću	1	dočekivaćemo
2	dočekivaćeš	2	dočekivaćete
3	dočekivaće	3	dočekivaće

Past

1	dočekivao sam	1	dočekivali smo
2	dočekivao si	2	dočekivali ste
3	dočekivao je	3	dočekivali su

Imperative

2p sing	dočekuj
1p pl	dočekujmo
2p pl	dočekujte

L-participle

dočekivao, dočekivala, dočekivalo
dočekivali, dočekivale, dočekivala

Present verbal adverb

dočekujući

Passive participle

dočekivan, dočekivana, dočekivano
dočekivani, dočekivane, dočekivana

Verbal noun

dočekivanje

14.4.6 Pattern -ETI -EM

a) umjeti-umijem = umeti-umem

umjeti-umijem
(Iyekavian)

For more verbs, see 7.3.3 "E Conjugation".

Present

singular		plural	
1	umijem	1	umijemo
2	umiješ	2	umijete
3	umije	3	umiju

Future

(Croatian-Bosnian)

1	umjet ću	1	umjet ćemo
2	umjet ćeš	2	umjet ćete
3	umjet će	3	umjet će

(Bosnian-Montenegrin & Serbian Iyekavian)

1	umjeću	1	umjećemo
2	umjećeš	2	umjećete
3	umjeće	3	umjeće

Past

1	umio sam	1	umjeli smo
2	umio si	2	umjeli ste
3	umio je	3	umjeli su

Imperative

2p sing	umij
1p pl	umijmo
2p pl	umijte

L-participle

umio, umjela, umjelo
umjeli, umjele, umjela

Present verbal adverb

umijući

Verbal noun

umijenje

umeti-umem
(Ekavian)

Present

singular		plural	
1	umem	1	umemo
2	umeš	2	umete
3	ume	3	umeju

Future

1	umeću	1	umećemo
2	umećeš	2	umećete
3	umeće	3	umeće

Past

1	umeo sam	1	umeli smo
2	umeo si	2	umeli ste
3	umeo je	3	umeli su

Imperative

2p sing	umej
1p pl	umejmo
2p pl	umejte

L-participle

umeo, umela, umelo
umeli, umele, umela

Present verbal adverb

umejući

umrijeti – umrem = umreti-umrem

Present

singular		plural	
1	umrem	1	umremo
2	umreš	2	umrete
3	umre	3	umru

Future

(Croatian-Bosnian)

1	umrijet ću	1	umrijet ćemo
2	umrijet ćeš	2	umrijet ćete
3	umrijet će	3	umrijet će

(Bosnian-Montenegrin & Serbian Iyekavian)

1	umrijeću	1	umrijećemo
2	umrijećeš	2	umrijećete
3	umrijeće	3	umrijeće

(Serbian)

1	umreću	1	umrećemo
2	umrećeš	2	umrećete
3	umreće	3	umreće

Past

1	umro sam	1	umrli smo
2	umro si	2	umrli ste
3	umro je	3	umrli su

Imperative

2p sing	umri
1p pl	umrimo
2p pl	umrite

L-participle

umro, umrla, umrlo
umrli, umrle, umrla

Past verbal adverb

umrijevši = umrevši

b) donijeti-donesem = doneti-donesem

(inserting *s* to the root)

For more verbs, see 7.3.3 "E Conjugation".

Present

singular		plural	
1	donesem	1	donesemo
2	doneseš	2	donesete
3	donese	3	donesu

Future

(Croatian-Bosnian)

1	donijet ću	1	donijet ćemo
2	donijet ćeš	2	donijet ćete
3	donijet će	3	donijet će

(Bosnian-Montenegrin & Serbian Iyekavian)

1	donijeću	1	donijećemo
2	donijećeš	2	donijećete
3	donijeće	3	donijeće

(Serbian)

1	doneću	1	donećemo
2	donećeš	2	donećete
3	doneće	3	doneće

Past

(Iyekavian)

1	donio sam	1	donijeli smo
2	donio si	2	donijeli ste
3	donio je	3	donijeli su

(Ekavian)

1	doneo sam	1	doneli smo
2	doneo si	2	doneli ste
3	doneo je	3	doneli su

Imperative

2p sing	donesi
1p pl	donesimo
2p pl	donesite

L-participle

(Iyekavian)

donio, donijela, donijelo
donijeli, donijele, donijela

(Ekavian)

doneo, donela, donelo
doneli, donele, donela

Past verbal adverb

donijevši = donevši

Passive participle

donesen, donesena, doneseno
doneseni, donesene, donesena
or

(Iyekavian)

donijet, donijeta, donijeto,
donijeti, donijete, donijeta

(Ekavian)

donet, doneta, doneto
doneti, donete, doneta

c) uzeti-uzmem

(inserting *m, n* or *nj* to the root)

For more verbs, see 7.3.3 "E Conjugation".

Present

singular		plural	
1	uzmem	1	uzmemo
2	uzmeš	2	uzmete
3	uzme	3	uzmu

Future

(Croatian-Bosnian)

1	uzet ću	1	uzet ćemo
2	uzet ćeš	2	uzet ćete
3	uzet će	3	uzet će

(Bosnian-Montenegrin-Serbian)

1	uzeću	1	uzećemo
2	uzećeš	2	uzećete
3	uzeće	3	uzeće

Past

1	uzeo sam	1	uzeli smo
2	uzeo si	2	uzeli ste
3	uzeo je	3	uzeli su

Imperative

2p sing	uzmi
1p pl	uzmimo
2p pl	uzmite

L-participle

uzeo, uzela, uzelo
uzeli, uzele, uzela

Past verbal adverb

uzevši

Passive participle

uzet, uzeta, uzeto
uzeti, uzete, uzeta

početi-počnem

Present

singular		plural	
1	počnem	1	počnemo
2	počneš	2	počnete
3	počne	3	počnu

Future

(Croatian-Bosnian)

1	počet ću	1	počet ćemo
2	počet ćeš	2	počet ćete
3	počet će	3	počet će

(Bosnian-Montenegrin-Serbian)

1	počeću	1	počećemo
2	počećeš	2	počećete
3	počeće	3	počeće

Past

1	počeo sam	1	počeli smo
2	počeo si	2	počeli ste
3	počeo je	3	počeli su

Imperative

2p sing	počni
1p pl	počnimo
2p pl	počnite

L-participle

počeo, počela, počelo
počeli, počele, počela

Past verbal adverb

počevši

Passive participle

počet, početa, početo,
početi, počete, početa

14.4.7 *Pattern -ITI -IJEM*

piti – pijem

For more verbs, see 7.3.3 "E Conjugation".

Present

singular		plural	
1	pijem	1	pijemo
2	piješ	2	pijete
3	pije	3	piju

Future

(Croatian-Bosnian)

1	pit ću	1	pit ćemo
2	pit ćeš	2	pit ćete
3	pit će	3	pit će

(Bosnian-Montenegrin-Serbian)

1	piću	1	pićemo
2	pićeš	2	pićete
3	piće	3	piće

Past

1	pio sam	1	pili smo
2	pio si	2	pili ste
3	pio je	3	pili su

Imperative

2p sing	pij
1p pl	pijmo
2p pl	pijte

L-participle

pio, pila, pilo
pili, pile, pila

Present verbal adverb

pijući

Past verbal adverb

popivši (formed from its perfective pair – *popiti*)

Passive participle

pit, pita, pito
piti, pite, pita
or
pijen, pijena, pijeno
pijeni, pijene, pijena

N.B. otkriti, pokriti, sakriti, umiti, sašiti have alternative passive participles: otkriven, pokriven, sakriven, umiven, sašiven

Verbal noun

pijenje

14.4.8 *Pattern -UTI -UJEM*

čuti – čujem

For more verbs, see 7.3.3 "E Conjugation".

Present

singular		plural	
1	čujem	1	čujemo
2	čuješ	2	čujete
3	čuje	3	čuju

Future

(Croatian-Bosnian)

1	čut ću	1	čut ćemo
2	čut ćeš	2	čut ćete
3	čut će	3	čut će

(Bosnian-Montenegrin-Serbian)

1	čuću	1	čućemo
2	čućeš	2	čućete
3	čuće	3	čuće

Past

1	čuo sam	1	čuli smo
2	čuo si	2	čuli ste
3	čuo je	3	čuli su

Imperative

2p sing	čuj
1p pl	čujmo
2p pl	čujte

L-participle

čuo, čula, čulo
čuli, čule, čula

Present verbal adverb

čujući

Past verbal adverb

čuvši

Verbal noun

čuvenje

Passive participle

čut, čuta, čuto
čuti, čute, čuta
or
čuven, čuvena, čuveno
čuveni, čuvene, čuvena

14.4.9 Pattern -NUTI -NEM

krenuti-krenem

For more verbs, see 7.3.3 "E Conjugation".

Present

singular		plural	
1	krenem	1	krenemo
2	kreneš	2	krenete
3	krene	3	krenu

Future

(Croatian-Bosnian)

1	krenut ću	1	krenut ćemo
2	krenut ćeš	2	krenut ćete
3	krenut će	3	krenut će

(Bosnian-Montenegrin-Serbian)

1	krenuću	1	krenućemo
2	krenućeš	2	krenućete
3	krenuće	3	krenuće

Past

1	krenuo sam	1	krenuli smo
2	krenuo si	2	krenuli ste
3	krenuo je	3	krenuli su

Imperative

2p sing	kreni
1p pl	krenimo
2p pl	krenite

L-participle

krenuo, krenula, krenulo
krenuli, krenule, krenula

Past verbal adverb

krenuvši

14.4.10 *-STI infinitives*

a) Pattern *-STI -DEM*

jesti-jedem

For more verbs, see 7.3.3 "E Conjugation".

Present

singular		plural	
1	jedem	1	jedemo
2	jedeš	2	jedete
3	jede	3	jedu

Future

(Croatian-Bosnian)

1	jest ću	1	jest ćemo
2	jest ćeš	2	jest ćete
3	jest će	3	jest će

(Bosnian-Montenegrin-Serbian)

1	ješću	1	ješćemo
2	ješćeš	2	ješćete
3	ješće	3	ješće

Past

1	jeo sam	1	jeli smo
2	jeo si	2	jeli ste
3	jeo je	3	jeli su

Imperative

2p sing	jedi
1p pl	jedimo
2p pl	jedite

L-participle

jeo, jela, jelo
jeli, jele, jela

Present verbal adverb

jedući

Past verbal adverb

pojevši (formed from its perfective pair *pojesti*)

Passive participle

jeden, jedena, jedeno
jedeni, jedene, jedena

Verbal noun

jedenje

b) Pattern *-STI -DNEM or -TNEM*

sresti-sretnem

For more verbs, see 7.3.3 "E Conjugation".

Present

singular		plural	
1	sretnem	1	sretnemo
2	sretneš	2	sretnete
3	sretne	3	sretnu

Future

(Croatian-Bosnian)

1	srest ću	1	srest ćemo
2	srest ćeš	2	srest ćete
3	srest će	3	srest će

(Bosnian-Montenegrin-Serbian)

1	srešću	1	srešćemo
2	srešćeš	2	srešćete
3	srešće	3	srešće

Past

1	sreo sam	1	sreli smo
2	sreo si	2	sreli ste
3	sreo je	3	sreli su

Imperative

2p sing	sretni
1p pl	sretnimo
2p pl	sretnite

L-participle

sreo, srela, srelo
sreli, srele, srela

Past verbal adverb

srevši

c) Pattern -*STI* -*ZEM*

dovesti-dovezem

For more verbs, see 7.3.3 "E Conjugation".

Present

singular		plural	
1	dovezem	1	dovezemo
2	dovezeš	2	dovezete
3	doveze	3	dovezu

Future

(Croatian-Bosnian)

1	dovest ću	1	dovest ćemo
2	dovest ćeš	2	dovest ćete
3	dovest će	3	dovest će

(Bosnian-Montenegrin-Serbian)

1	dovešću	1	dovešćemo
2	dovešćeš	2	dovešćete
3	dovešće	3	dovešće

Past

1	dovezao sam	1	dovezli smo
2	dovezao si	2	dovezli ste
3	dovezao je	3	dovezli su

Imperative

2p sing	dovezi
1p pl	dovezimo
2p pl	dovezite

L-participle

dovezao, dovezla, dovezlo
dovezli, dovezle, dovezla

Past verbal adverb

dovezavši

Passive participle

dovezen, dovezena, dovezeno
dovezeni, dovezne, dovezena

d) Pattern *-STI -STEM*

rasti-rastem

For more verbs, see 7.3.3 "E Conjugation".

Present

singular		plural	
1	rastem	1	rastemo
2	rasteš	2	rastete
3	raste	3	rastu

Future

(Croatian-Bosnian)

1	rast ću	1	rast ćemo
2	rast ćeš	2	rast ćete
3	rast će	3	rast će

(Bosnian-Montenegrin-Serbian)

1	rašću	1	rašćemo
2	rašćeš	2	rašćete
3	rašće	3	rašće

Past

1	rastao sam	1	rasli smo
2	rastao si	2	rasli ste
3	rastao je	3	rasli su

Imperative

2p sing	rasti
1p pl	rastimo
2p pl	rastite

L-participle

rastao, rasla, raslo
rasli, rasle, rasla

Present verbal adverb

rastući

Past verbal adverb

porastavši (formed from its perfective pair *porasti*)

14.4.11 -ĆI infinitives

a) Pattern *-ĆI -DEM*

ići – idem otići – odem

Present

singular		plural	
1	idem	1	idemo
2	ideš	2	idete
3	ide	3	idu

Future

1	ići ću	1	ići ćemo
2	ići ćeš	2	ići ćete
3	ići će	3	ići će

Past

1	išao sam	1	išli smo
2	išao si	2	išli ste
3	išao je	3	išli su

Imperative

2p sing	idi
1p pl	idimo
2p pl	idite

L-participle

išao, išla, išlo
išli, išle, išla

Present verbal adverb

idući

Past verbal adverb

išavši

b) Pattern *-ĆI -ĐEM*

doći – dođem

For more verbs, see 7.3.3 "E Conjugation".

Present

singular		plural	
1	dođem	1	dođemo
2	dođeš	2	dođete
3	dođe	3	dođu

Future

1	doći ću	1	doći ćemo
2	doći ćeš	2	doći ćete
3	doći će	3	doći će

Past

1	došao sam	1	došli smo
2	došao si	2	došli ste
3	došao je	3	došli su

Imperative

2p sing	dođi
1p pl	dođimo
2p pl	dođite

L-participle

došao, došla, došlo
došli, došle, došla

Past verbal adverb

došavši

c) Pattern *-ĆI, -GNEM* or *-KNEM*

stići – stignem

For more verbs, see 7.3.3 "E Conjugation".

Present

singular		plural	
1	stignem	1	stignemo
2	stigneš	2	stignete
3	stigne	3	stignu

Future

1	stići ću	1	stići ćemo
2	stići ćeš	2	stići ćete
3	stići će	3	stići će

Past

1	stigao sam	1	stigli smo
2	stigao si	2	stigli ste
3	stigao je	3	stigli su

Imperative

2p sing	stigni
1p pl	stignimo
2p pl	stignite

L-participle

stigao, stigla, stiglo
stigli, stigle, stigla

Past verbal adverb

stigavši

Passive participle

stignut, stignuta, stignuto
stignuti, stignute, stignuta

d) Pattern -*ĆI*, - *ČEM*

peći – pečem

For more verbs see 7.3.3. E conjugation.

Present

singular		plural	
1	pečem	1	pečemo
2	pečeš	2	pečete
3	peče	3	peku

Future

1	peći ću	1	peći ćemo
2	peći ćeš	2	peći ćete
3	peći će	3	peći će

Past

1	pekao sam	1	pekli smo
2	pekao si	2	pekli ste
3	pekao je	3	pekli su

Imperative

2p sing	peci
1p pl	pecimo
2p pl	pecite

L-participle

pekao, pekla, peklo
pekli, pekle, pekla

Present verbal adverb

pekući

Past verbal adverb

ispekavši (formed from its perfective pair ispeći)

Passive participle

pečen, pečena, pečeno
pečeni, pečene, pečena

Verbal noun

pečenje

Bibliography

BCMS and Serbo-Croat

Alexander, R., *Bosnian, Croatian, Serbian: A Grammar with Sociolinguistic Commentary*, The University of Wisconsin Press, Madison, 2006.

Brown, W. and Alt, T., *A Handbook of Bosnian, Serbian, and Croatian*, 2004, http://seelrc.org:8080/grammar/pdf/stand_alone_bcs.pdf

Đorđevic, R., *Engleski i srpskohrvatski jezik, Kontrastivna gramatika imeničke grupe*, Naučna knjiga, Belgrade, 1989.

Drvodelić, M., *Englesko – hrvatski ili srpski rječnik*, Školska knjiga, Zagreb, 1981.

Javarek, V. and Sudjić, M., *Serbo-Croat*, Teach Yourself Books, Hodder and Stoughton, London, 1972.

Bosnian

Jahić, Dž., Halilović, S. and Palić, I., *Gramatika bosanskoga jezika*, Dom štampe, Zenica, 2000.

Pravopis.ba mobile application

Croatian

Anić, V., *Rječnik hrvatskoga jezika*, Novi Liber, Zagreb, 1991.

Bujas, Ž., *Veliki hrvatsko-engleski rječnik*, Nakladni zavod Globus, Zagreb, 2001.

Hrvatski jezični portal, http://hjp.znanje.hr

Institut za hrvatski jezik i jezikoslovlje, http://ihjj.hr

Norris, D., *Complete Croatian*, Teach Yourself, London, 2016.

Silić, J. and Pranjković, I., *Gramatika hrvatskoga jezika*, Školska knjiga, Zagreb, 2007.

Montenegrin

Čigrić, A., Pranjković, I. and Silić, J., *Gramatika crnogorskoga jezika*, Ministarstvo prosvjete i nauke Crne gore, Podgorica, 2010.

Serbian

Владимирович, В., *Сербский яазык – Самоучитель*, Живой яазык, Moscow, 2014.

Danilović, M., *Serbian Step by Step*, Kornet, Belgrade, 2016.

Hammond, L., *Serbian: An Essential Grammar*, Routledge, Abingdon, UK, 2005.

Klajn, I., *Gramatika srpskog jezika*, Zavod za udžbenike i nastavna sredstva, Beograd, 2005.

Index

Printed in Great Britain
by Amazon

83843929R00194